THE NEW FAMILY COOKBOOK

THE NEW
FAMILY COOKBOOK
CAROLE EDWARDS

GALLERY BOOKS
An imprint of W.H. Smith Publishers Inc.
112 Madison Avenue
New York, New York 10016

A Bison Book

Published by Gallery Books
A Division of W H Smith Publishers Inc.
112 Madison Avenue
New York, New York 10016

Produced by
Bison Books Corp.
17 Sherwood Place
Greenwich, CT 06830

Copyright © 1985 Bison Books Corp.

ISBN 0-8317-6342-6

Printed in Hong Kong

1 2 3 4 5 6 7 8 9 10

The publisher would like to thank the following for providing
most of the props used in the photographs:

David Mellor
4 Sloane Square
London SW1 8EE

David Mellor
26 James Street
Covent Garden
London WC2E 8PA

David Mellor
66 King Street
Manchester M2 4NP

Harrods
Knightsbridge
London SW1

Covent Garden Kitchen
Supplies
The Market
Covent Garden
London WC2

Microwave utensils from the
Microwave Supreme range by
Anchor Hocking

Mrs. Robert Iggulden

Food Processor from Magimix
UK (ICTC Electrical Ltd.)
Isleworth

Original photography by Roger Charlesson
Designed by Richard Garratt
Editor: Jane Laslett

Paella Valencia.

Contents

Basic cookery notes

Oven temperature guide

Very cool	200°F
	225°F
	250°F
Cool	275°F
	300°F
Warm	325°F
Moderate	350°F
Moderately hot	375°F
	400°F
Hot	425°F
	450°F
Very hot	475°F
	500°F

General notes

All recipes serve four unless otherwise stated.
Spoon measures are level spoons.
Flour is all-purpose flour except where self-rising flour is
   specified.

A-Z of Cookery Terms and Equipment

Subjects in small capitals indicate a glossary entry.

A

Al dente Refers to pasta when it has been cooked but still
retains a certain amount of firmness or 'bite.'
Antipasto A first course or appetizer which consists of
mixed cold ingredients such as sardines or tuna, artichoke
hearts, tomatoes, lettuce, scallions, celery, potato salad,
shrimp in mayonnaise, ham, salami or mortadella.
Aspic This is a savory jelly used to coat attractively
arranged cold food, usually meats, fish or vegetables.
Traditionally it was made by boiling calves feet or similar
gelatinous meat cuts but nowadays gelatin powder, both
flavored and unflavored, is available as a convenient
option.
Au gratin The crisp crust formed by cooking dishes under
the broiler which have been sprinkled with breadcrumbs
or grated cheese.

B

Bain-marie An open baking tin or other vessel which is
half-filled with water and used for cooking custards and
other delicate dishes in the oven to prevent them from
overheating. It is also used for gently simmering cooked
sauces or gravies on the top of the stove.
Baking A method of cooking by dry heat in an oven.
Baking equipment The choice of baking tins very much
depends on the type of baking that you do, but when buying
new tins always buy the best quality available. Avoid
buying steel with a tinned finish as these rust in time;
instead choose heavy-duty aluminum or heat-proof glass.
Tins wih a non-stick coating ensure a good finish but they
must be well greased before use and handled carefully to
avoid scratching and deterioration.
   Cake tins These should always be loose-bottomed or
   have spring-clipped sides. Start off with an 8in diameter
   size and gradually add different sizes and shapes to your
   collection.
   Loaf tins and pie molds Non-stick loaf tins are
   recommended; these are available in different sizes and
   patterns but bear in mind that the fancy finishes are often
   more difficult to clean. Two 1lb plain loaf tins are a
   useful buy.
   Flan tins and rings Flan or sandwich tins are among the

most versatile pieces of baking equipment – buy a pair of 7in or 8in tins plus a larger flan tin or a fluted ring. Use the ring on an inverted baking tray so that it can be slid off easily. Ovenproof porcelain flan dishes make very attractive serving dishes.

Bun or patty tins These are usually available in trays of 6 or 12, either decorated or plain, ranging from 4in tins to tiny PETIT FOURS trays. You can also choose from a wide range of individual pastry molds and tartlet cases in different sizes.

Other equipment Specialized molds for cakes and pastries are also obtainable – often patterned or with raised or funnelled centers for adding fillings after baking. Make sure that you buy a wire cake rack for cooling baked items and a good-quality rolling pin – this can be wooden, ceramic or even glass (often hollow so that it can be filled with cold water).

Baking blind A method of baking an empty pastry case by either pricking the base with a fork or weighting down the base with beans.

Baking soda A commercial compound used as a raising agent in baking. It contains bicarbonate of soda which gives off carbon dioxide when in contact with water.

Ball scoop Item of equipment, commonly double-ended, used for scooping out ball or pea shapes from foods such as melon and cucumber.

Bard, to To cover lean meat with thin slices of pork fat or bacon during roasting to help prevent the meat from drying out.

Barquette Boat-shaped pastry cases, usually filled with fruit or sometimes a savory mixture.

Baskets Wire baskets which can be hung up are useful for storing eggs or vegetables such as onions. They are also useful for washing salads and are essential for BLANCHING when freezing, and for deep-frying.

Baste, to A method of moistening foods during broiling or roasting by spooning over the pan juices and fats.

Baster, bulb A syringe-like implement with a rubber bulb used for sucking up juices and fats from the pan to BASTE foods during broiling or roasting.

Batter A mixture of eggs, flour, milk or water used for puddings, pancakes and coating for fried foods. The consistency of the mixture varies according to how it is being used. Batter also refers to thicker cake and biscuit mixtures.

Béarnaise A sauce made in the same way as HOLLANDAISE from an emulsion of melted butter and egg yolks flavored with wine vinegar and tarragon.

Beat A method of mixing ingredients rapidly in order to incorporate air for lightness.

Béchamel A classic white sauce made by mixing milk infused with various flavorings into a blonde (white) ROUX of butter and flour.

Beurre manié A method of thickening sauces and stews, slowly and gently, by using equal quantities of flour and butter kneaded together. Add in small amounts towards the end of cooking.

Bigarade A classic sauce based on an ESPAGNOLE sauce and flavored with orange rind and juice, redcurrant jelly and, frequently, red wine or port. The original recipe for this sauce used the bitter Seville oranges.

Bind, to A method of holding dry ingredients together by adding eggs, fats or liquids.

Bisque A rich creamy soup based on seafood ingredients such as lobster, shrimp or crab.

Blanch A technique of treating fresh foods with boiling water for short periods for a number of purposes: to whiten food such as veal or sweetbreads before cooking; to remove excess saltiness in cured foods; to loosen the skins of fruit and vegetables to facilitate peeling, for example peaches and tomatoes; to prepare foods for freezing by killing any bacteria present which might cause the frozen food to deteriorate.

Blanquette A rich stew, usually made with veal or poultry, and thickened with egg yolks and heavy cream.

Blender or liquidizer Used to PURÉE soft or semi-liquid ingredients or to grind or chop dry ingredients such as nuts. *See also* FOOD PROCESSOR.

Bouillon Well-flavored, seasoned stock made from beef, chicken or fish and vegetables and herbs. Often refers to the concentrated stock cubes commercially available.

Bouquet garni A bunch of herbs, which usually includes parsley, thyme, bay and a few peppercorns, tied together with string or in some porous material such as cheesecloth. Bouquets garni are used to flavor soups and stews and can be easily removed before serving.

Bowls, mixing A good selection of bowls is essential in any kitchen. They should range from tiny containers for food storage up to large mixing bowls. It is a good idea to have a range of sizes in heat-proof glass or china for making puddings and sauces such as HOLLANDAISE. A 2-3 pint bowl with a pouring lip is useful when stock-making. Mixing bowls should always be made of glass or china as it is often necessary to keep the ingredients cool, as in pastry making. Copper bowls are said to give the best results when whisking egg whites.

Braise, to A cooking method which combines slow-roasting and steaming; used for poultry, game or meat cuts. Very little liquid is used and, frequently, the meat is placed on a bed of root vegetables (see also MIREPOIX) for added flavor and moisture.

Brine A strong solution of salt and water in which foods are immersed before preserving.

Brochette A skewer, usually steel, on which meat is threaded for broiling.

Broiler A roasting chicken approximately 3-6 months old.

Broth A basic stock made by boiling vegetables, meats or poultry.

Brown, to Browning serves two purposes: either to sear the surfaces of raw meats and poultry cuts to seal in the juices and give a good color to a stew or casserole; or to give an appetizing finish to cooked dishes by placing them under a hot broiler.

Butter cream A filling for pastries and cakes made by beating softened butter with confectioners' sugar until fluffy. It can be flavored with chocolate, coffee, orange or lemon.

C

Cake tins see *Baking equipment.*

Canapés Tiny appetizers, designed to accompany aperitifs, consisting of delicate savory morsels on bases of toast or crackers.

Caramel Sugar syrup which has been heated at fairly high temperature until it is dark brown in color. Its used for flavoring cakes and puddings or can be used to color gravies.

Carbonnade A rich stew based on beef, onions and beer.

Casserole A container used for cooking meat and poultry cuts slowly in the oven which also combines as a serving dish. Casseroles may be made of earthenware, cast iron or heatproof glass. Flameproof cast iron casseroles are a good buy for they are long-lasting and can be used to brown meat on top of the stove or for simmering. Many people consider that, for very long, very slow cooking, earthenware casseroles are best as they do not overheat the food.

Cassoulet A hearty dish of haricot beans, pork, sausage and poultry which originated in southern France. It requires very long, slow cooking in the oven, traditionally in a tall, half-glazed pot.

Chafing dish A large shallow dish which is heated, often over a spirit burner, and used for serving entrées.

Chantilly Heavy cream which is whipped until thick and fluffy then sweetened with superfine sugar and flavored with a little vanilla.

Chasseur French term meaning 'huntsman' applied to casseroles of poultry, game and meat containing white wine, mushrooms and shallots or onions.

Châteaubriand A thick cut of beef taken from the center of a fillet or tenderloin and usually grilled. It is served in thick slices with MAÎTRE D'HÔTEL butter (butter flavored with chopped parsley, lemon juice and seasoning) or with a sauce such as BÉARNAISE.

Chaudfroid A jellied sauce used to mask cold cuts of meat and poultry which can be white (based on a BECHAMEL) or brown (based on ESPAGNOLE). Powdered gelatin is dissolved and stirred into the hot sauce; when the cooling sauce becomes thick and syrupy it is poured over the meat and garnished attractively.

Chine, to A term used by butchers when the backbone is sawn away from the ribs.

Chopper see *Cleaver*.

Chopping Chopping is best done on a heavy wooden or man-made board which can be scrubbed after use in hot water. KNIVES used for chopping should be very sharp, ideally stainless steel with a heavy triangular blade. When chopping finely, hold down the tip of the knife with one hand and chop with a rapid action.

Choux paste A paste made by making a PANADA with fat, boiling water and flour, and then vigorously beating eggs into the mixture. It is used for making éclairs, profiteroles, cream buns and savory gougère.

Chowder A thick, soupy stew originating in the USA made from white fish and/or shellfish, milk, potatoes, and whole kernel corn. It may be made simply of vegetables.

Chutney A savory preserve, originating in India, usually based on fruit and vegetables with a spicy sweet-sour taste and used as an accompaniment to curries and cold meat dishes.

Clarify, to The process of making fats or liquid clear. Butter can be clarified for frying to avoid the sediment browning and discoloring the dish. Heat the required amount of butter in a pan until it ceases to foam; then remove from the heat and allow it to stand for a few minutes to allow the sediment to settle. Carefully pour off the fat, leaving the sediment behind, or strain it through cheesecloth. To clarify meat fats or dripping, place it in a pan with the same quantity of water and bring to the boil. Strain the liquid into a bowl and allow it to get cold. You will then find that a cake of clean fat has formed on the top which you can lift off, scraping away any sediment which has formed on the under side.

To clarify greaseless stock, bring it to the boil and whisk in an egg white together with the crushed shells and simmer it for about 15 minutes. A crust of albumen will form on the top, trapping the impurities; this can then be removed, leaving a clear liquid.

Cleaver A small, sharp chopper heavy enough to chop through bones.

Coating batter see *Batter*.

Cocotte A single-portion round dish, usually made of heatproof porcelain. Cocottes are used for baking eggs and other foods in the oven, usually as a first course.

Coddle A technique for cooking eggs so that the white is firm and the yolks are runny. The eggs are placed in a pan of water which has just boiled and allowed to stand for about 10 minutes.

Cômpote Fresh or dried fruits cooked in a heavy sugar syrup and usually served cold, perhaps enhanced with some liqueur.

Concassé A term which means coarsely chopped; often applied to tomatoes when skinned, de-seeded and chopped.

Confectioners' custard see *Crème Patissière*.

Consistency Term used to describe the appearance or texture of the mixture.

Conserves Preserves made with whole fruit.

Coquilles French word for scallops but also refers to any shell-shaped dishes used for baking seafood AU GRATIN.

Concentrate To increase the flavor and strength of liquids by fast-boiling a stock or sauce without a lid to reduce the water content.

Cordon Bleu The blue-ribbon award bestowed on proficient cooks graduating from the Ecole Cordon Bleu, the famous cookery school in Paris.

Cornstarch Very smooth, fine thickening agent made from very finely ground maize kernels.

Coupe A cup or goblet-shaped dish with a short stem used for serving desserts such as fruit salad and ice cream.

Court-bouillon A lightly flavored liquid used for poaching fish which usually has wine, onion, carrot, herbs and seasoning added to it.

Crackling Pork skin which is roasted at a high temperature to become very crisp. It is usually scored into strips, salted and brushed with oil before cooking.

Cream, to A method of blending ingredients together until they are well combined and creamy.

Crème patissière A filling made with milk, cornstarch, egg yolks and sugar used for sweet flans and pastries.

Crêpe French term for pancakes. These are made with a BATTER of eggs, flour and milk spooned into an oiled pan and fried until brown on both sides. Crêpe suzette is a very thin crêpe flavored with orange juice, sugar and a liqueur such as Grand Marnier.

Crimping This term refers either to a technique of decorating a pie-crust by pinching with the fingers or pressing with a spoon handle or making diagonal cuts in the skin of a fish to ensure even cooking.

Croquette These can be mixtures of cooked chopped fish, meat or poultry or potatoes bound together with eggs or a thick sauce and shaped into balls or rolls before being deep-fried.

Croûte The term Croûte can either be applied to a small piece of toast or fried bread used as a base for game, or savory tidbits, or to a pastry crust.

Croûtons Tiny cubes of fried bread used as a garnish for soups or stews.

Crown roast A joint of lamb consisting of two loins, CHINED and arranged in a circle and secured for roasting. The ends of the bones are cleaned and decorated after cooking with tiny paper frills. The center of the roast may be filled with a savory stuffing.

Crudités Small pieces of raw vegetable served with a dip or dressing as an appetizer.

Cube or dice, to To cut meat or vegetables into small regular pieces by cutting it into strips then chopping into even-depthed pieces.

Curdle When fresh milk or cream, a sauce or soup separates due to the presence of acid or too much heat.

Curing The preservation of foods by salting, smoking or drying.

Cut in, to The technique of combining fats and flour by using a PASTRY BLENDER.

Cutters, pastry Shaped metal or plastic cutters with sharp edges used for cutting out pastry shapes for biscuits, tartlets, and so on.

D

Dariole A small mold with narrow sloping sides used for setting savory or sweet mousses, creams and jellies.

Danish pastry see *Pastry.*

Darne A fat slice cut from the thickest part of fish such as salmon or cod.

Daube Braised meat cooked with red wine.

Deep-fry A method of cooking food in deep fat or oil at high temperature. The food must be completely immersed; the objective being to produce a crisp finish with the flavor of the food locked in.

Deglacer or deglaze To make a gravy or basis for a sauce by adding stock of water to pan juices after spooning off excess fats.

Demi-glace A brown sauce reduced to a syrupy coating consistency.

Devilled Hot spicy seasoning added to cuts of meat or poultry before roasting or broiling.

Dice see *Cube.*

Double saucepan Two saucepans which fit together. The outer pan contains water, and the smaller one fits into the outer one without touching the water level. Double saucepans are used for cooking sauces and so on which need to be kept below boiling point.

Dough A mixture of flour and liquid which is soft and workable and can be kneaded or rolled out. A dough may contain eggs or a rising agent such as yeast.

Drain To remove all liquids from cooked or uncooked foods.

Draw, to The removal of the entrails from poultry and game.

Dredge, to Applying an even coating of a dry ingredient such as flour or sugar to food either before cooking or after baking to improve appearance. A dredger is a metal or plastic jar-shaped utensil with a perforated lid.

Dress, to This term can either be applied to the process of plucking, singeing and drawing poultry or game ready for cooking, or to the technique of decorating food, usually cold dishes, for the table.

Dripping Melted fat obtained from roasting meat or RENDERING down raw fats.

Dropping consistency A term used to describe the texture of a mixture such as cake or pudding batter. A filled spoon of the mixture should fall freely from the tilted spoon within a few seconds without dribbling or sticking.

Dumpling A small ball of dough made with flour and chopped suet and usually cooked in the liquid of a stew or soup.

Dust, to To lightly sprinkle food with flour, sugar or other dry ingredients.

Duxelles A mixture of finely chopped mushrooms or mushroom stalks, chopped shallot or onion, herbs and seasonings gently SWEATED in butter. It is used for flavoring stuffings, soups, sauces and stews.

E

Emulsion A suspension of oil or fats held in some form of liquid usually assisted by vigorous beating or gentle heat. An example of this is mayonnaise where oil is held in suspension by egg yolks to form an emulsion.

En croûte Food wrapped in a pastry case before cooking; the term is usually applied to meat cuts which can be roasted, and a savory stuffing is often added.

En papillote Food wrapped in parcels of waxed paper or cooking foil before cooking.

Entrecôte A beef steak cut from the sirloin.

Entreé A hot or cold savory course, which tradionally follows the fish and precedes the roast dish. It can consist of chops, steaks, joints of poultry or even dishes of vegetables and eggs and is served complete with its accompaniments, sauces and garnish.

Epigramme Refers to a dish of boiled and boned breast of lamb which has been sliced into thin strips, dipped in egg and breadcrumbs and fried.

Epicure A person who is highly interested in and appreciative of good food and drink.

Escalope A thin cut of meat, usually pork or veal, taken from the upper leg. It is beaten out until wafer thin then coated in flour or egg and breadcrumbs and fried.

Espagnole 'Spanish' sauce – one of the classic rich brown sauces which form the basis for a number of different recipes.

F

Fines herbes A classic mixture of finely chopped fresh herbs which should include parsley, chives, tarragon and chervil.

Fish kettle or steamer A long narrow pan big enough to poach a whole or large piece of fish. It has a close-fitting lid and a removable grid with handles for lifting out the cooked fish.

Fish slice A long-handled tool with a wide, flexible blade with slots to allow fats or liquids to drain. It is used for removing fish, meats, eggs, vegetables from frying pans or poaching liquid.

Flake, to The separation of cooked fish into small pieces.

Flambé The technique of pouring warmed alcohol over foods and igniting it. Flaming reduces the strong alcohol taste and leaves the flavor of the spirit or liqueur to enhance the food.

Flan ring see *Baking equipment*

Fleurons Tiny pieces of cooked flaky pastry, often cut in crescent shapes, used to garnish fish and meat dishes.

Florentine Refers to dishes containing cooked spinach.

Fold in, to A technique of combining ingredients with minimum stirring movements so that the texture of the mixture is not broken down and the maximum air remains trapped for a light and fluffy result. Whisked egg whites are gently folded in when making soufflés or some cakes; a meal spoon or palette knife should be used to fold, with a lifting and cutting movement.

Fondue A style of dish cooked over a spirit burner at the table. A Swiss cheese fondue consists of melted cheese mixed with wine into which cubes of bread are dipped on long-handled forks. Fondue Bourguignonne consists of cubes of meat (usually beefsteak) cooked in deep oil.

Food mill A circular sieve-like utensil with interchangeable disks through which soft foods can be pressed.

Food mixers and processors Electric food mixers combine equipment for mixing, beating and whisking using a detachable bowl and tools. Attachments are also available for blending and puréeing, mincing, coffee grinding and juice extraction, depending on the make. Food processors combine most of the functions of the food mixer without the necessity of different attachments but with merely a change of blade or disk.

Forcing bags and nozzles A tunnel-shaped bag made of closely woven cloth, nylon or plastic used with a series of nozzles. These are used for piping pureéd foods, pastry, cake mixtures and icing.

Forks Two or three stainless steel forks with long, sturdy prongs are essential in the kitchen. A 'cook's fork' refers to a large, long-handled fork with just two prongs.

French dressing A mixture of oil and vinegar or lemon juice often flavored with garlic and/or herbs and seasoning, and used as a salad dressing.

Fricassée A stew of white meat or poultry in a rich sauce containing egg yolks or cream, or both.

Fritter Sweet or savory foods coated in BATTER and deep-fried until crisp.

Frosting Various sugar coatings given to cakes and pastries. Icing ranges from the simple GLACÉ ICING consisting of confectioners' sugar and water; *butter icing* made from butter and confectioners' sugar creamed together with flavoring; *American frosting* uses sugar boiled to 240°F, beaten into whisked egg whites until the mixture stands in stiff peaks; *Royal icing* is made by beating confectioners' sugar with egg whites until smooth and glossy – GLYCERINE is sometimes added to give a soft finish; *Fondant icing* consists of boiling sugar to a thick syrup then working it until it cools into a dense, opaque mixture.

Frying The method of cooking food in shallow or deep hot oil or fat.

Fumet Essentially this is a concentrated flavoring obtained by reducing stock. The term frequently specifically refers to concentrated fish stock made by boiling fish heads, bones and trimmings.

G

Galantine Poultry (or sometimes joints of meat) which is boned, stuffed, and reshaped before being poached in stock. A galantine is usually served cold with salad and can be coated in ASPIC or a CHAUD-FROID sauce.

Game The term used to describe wild birds or animals hunted for the table.

Garnish Decorative trimmings added to a dish after it has been cooked.

Genoese A whisked cake mixture with melted butter added, used for making rich sponges and gâteaux.

Giblets This term covers the heart, liver, gizzard and neck of a chicken or other type of poultry, retained for making stock.

Glaze A coating used to give a shiney finish to cooked foods. It can be egg white, milk, meat jelly or sugar syrup.

Glycerine A viscous substance derived from animal fats and oils added to sweets and icing to give a soft consistency.

Goujons Fillets of flatfish cut into narrow strips, coated with flour or egg and breadcrumbs and fried.

Goulash A rich Hungarian stew made with beef and flavored with paprika.

Grater A grater can be made from sturdy plastic or stainless steel; tinned steel should be avoided as it tends to rust. A food processor grates food quickly and easily.

Grease, to To rub the inside of a container with fat to prevent sticking. It is a good idea to do this even when using a non-stick container. When greasing a cake tin, use a different fat to the one used in the mixture.

Griddle A heavy, flat metal plate used for cooking various types of breads and cakes on top of the stove; it usually has a hooped handle. Very good for scones..

H

Hachinette A small, heavy wooden bowl with half-moon shaped cutter designed for chopping herbs.

Hachoir A curved, broad-bladed knife with double handles used for chopping.

Hang, to Term applied to game and meat hung up to tenderize it and improve the flavor.

Haute cuisine The very highest standard of professional cookery.

Hollandaise A rich sauce made from egg yolks and butter cooked very gently in a DOUBLE SAUCEPAN and served with vegetable and fish dishes.

Hors d'oeuvres A selection of savory side dishes served as appetizers.

Hot pot A slow-cooked stew of lamb or mutton layered with potatoes and a thick, crisp crust of potatoes on top.

Hull To remove the calyx from fruit or the outer shells or pods of vegetables such as beans and peas.

I

Icing see *Frosting*.

Infuse The technique of STEEPING ingredients, generally herbs, vegetables and spices, in liquid to extract the flavors.

J

Joint A cut of meat which is generally cooked by roasting.

Jug, to Traditionally refers to the preparation of a strong dark stew by long, slow cooking in a stewing jar or jug. The term jugged is now generally applied to a casserole of hare, often including a little port as flavoring.

K

Kebab Small pieces of meat, poultry, fish or vegetable threaded onto thin steel SKEWERS and broiled or barbecued. Meat is often MARINADED before cooking to help tenderize it and add flavor.

Kedgeree A dish originating in India which consists of boiled rice, hard-boiled eggs and curried or smoked fish.

Knead The action of working dough; the outside of the mixture is stretched and folded over the inside until the correct consistency is reached.

Knives Good cutting implements are essential to the kitchen. Always buy good-quality stainless-steel knives; although not as sharp as traditional carbon-steel knives, they are less likely to discolor or rust. Knives can be sharpened with either a 'steel' or a piece or carborundum. Types of kitchen knives available include paring knives with short hollow ground blades for preparing vegetables; chopping knives with heavy triangular blades which come in a range of sizes; boning knives are fairly large and curved with a dagger-like handle; filleting knives are very long and thin; carving knives come with a variety of blades and handles depending on the cook's preference or the meat being carved but normally they have a long, broad blade which may be flat ground, or serrated. A ham knife has a very long narrow blade which is the same width throughout and has a rounded tip; this type of knife is also used for slicing smoked salmon. Other useful knives include the bread knife with a long, even-widthed blade and serrated edge; a freezer knife has a saw-like blade designed for cutting through blocks of frozen food; a potato peeler with an angled blade; a palette knife which has no sharp blade but is wide and flexible and used for lifting and scraping, or spreading cream or icing evenly.

Knocking back A second kneading given to bread dough

after it has been allowed to rise initially.

Knocking up Finishing a pie crust by pressing the blade of a knife into the pastry edge horizontally to make a layer of cuts all the way round.

L

Larding A method of basting lean meat by threading thin strips of fat through it with a larding needle. The strips of fat are known as lardons.

Liaison An ingredient used for thickening sauces, soups or stews, such as flour, cornstarch, arrowroot or a mixture of heavy cream and egg yolks.

Loaf tins see *Baking equipment*.

M

Macédoine Even-sized cubes of vegetables or fruit which may be served hot or cold, cooked or raw. A macédoine of vegetables may be served with a white sauce; fruits may be served in a jelly.

Macerate To flavor or soften foods by steeping them in a liquid, for instance dried fruits may be steeped in brandy or a liqueur to swell them and give flavor before being used in puddings and cakes.

Maître d'hotel The head waiter or manager of a restaurant. The term also refers to a style of serving fish dishes or entrées garnished with butter flavored with chopped fresh parsley and lemon juice.

Mandoline An adjustable slicer, commonly made of wood with a steel blade, used for vegetables.

Marbled Meat which has streaks of fat running between the layers of muscle tissue.

Marinade A mixture of oil, vinegar or wine, herbs and spices which is used to flavor meats before cooking and assist with tenderizing.

Marmite A large pot, either made of earthenware or metal, used to make stocks and stews.

Mask, to To coat cooked foods such as cuts of meat, poultry or fish with a cold sauce or jelly.

Medallions Cuts of meat or fish cut into small rounds.

Meunière, à la Food cooked in the style of the 'millers wife' – usually refers to fish cooked in butter and sprinkled with seasoning, lemon juice and fresh chopped herbs.

Microwave ovens Electric ovens which cook food very quickly by producing electro-magnetic waves which cause the water molecules in food to vibrate and give off heat. The waves, which are reflected off the metal walls of the oven cavity, are able to pass through glass, china or paper containers without affecting them, heating only the food.

Milanese à la Usually refers to escalopes cooked in the Milan style: coated in egg and breadcrumbs and fried in butter. The dish may be served with pasta flavored with tomatoes and Parmesan cheese.

Mirepoix A mixture of chopped vegetables used as a base for braising meat or for flavoring soups, stocks and stews.

Mixers see *Food processors, mixers*.

Mocha or mocca Can either refer to a fine blend of coffee or to a blend of coffee and chocolate flavors.

Mold A shaped container made in plastic, glass, china or metal used for forming baked foods or gelatin mixtures.

Mornay, à la Eggs, fish or vegetable dishes served with a coating of fairly thick white sauce flavored with cheese.

Moule a pâté A hinged mold used for cooking pâtés and pies cooked with a crust.

Mouli grinder-grater A hand utensil consisting of a revolving drum within an open 'box' which is used for grinding or grating cheese, breadcrumbs or nuts.

Mouli-légumes see *Food mill*.

Moulinette see *Food Mill*.

Mousse A light fluffy cold dish, which may be sweet or savory, usually made with cream, whisked egg whites and set with GELATIN.

N

Napolitaine, à la Dishes, often pasta, served with a tomato and herb sauce.

Navarin A stew containing lamb, root vegetables and often tomatoes.

Normande, à la Dishes cooked Normandy style – usually poultry or game flavored with apples, cream and cider or calvados.

Noisette Tender cuts of meat trimmed and shaped into small rounds.

O

Ovenproof Dishes which are heat resistant and can be placed in the oven.

P

Palette knife see *Knives*.

Panada A thick mixture made of flour, butter and milk or stock used as a base to bind other ingredients.

Pancakes see *Crêpes*.

Pan broil A term to describe frying meat in its own fat, which helps cut down on calories.

Papillote see *En papillote*.

Parboil A method of partly cooking foods in boiling water before being finished in another way.

Pare, to To thinly peel or trim the outer skins from fruits or vegetables with a knife.

Pastry blender A kitchen tool consisting of a handle to which are attached several thick wires used for rubbing fat into flour when making pastry.

Pastry wheel A small wheel mounted on a wooden handle which cuts a zig-zag pattern when run across pastry.

Pasty A small pie filled with meat and vegetables.

Pâté A savory mixture of meat (usually pork or veal) and liver or game flavored with herbs and seasoning and cooked in a MOLD or TERRINE.

Patty A small heavy savory round pie, often made with flaky or puff pastry.

Patty pan A mold for patties or tartlets.

Paunch, to A term used to describe the removal of the entrails of rabbits or hares.

Paupiette A thin slice of fish or meat, stuffed and rolled then poached or braised in a sauce.

Pestle and Mortar The mortar is a bowl, made of wood, marble or steel; the pestle is a heavy, club-shaped tool used to grind spices within the mortar.

Petits fours Very small cakes and biscuits, elaborately decorated, served at the end of a formal dinner.

Pilaff An Eastern dish based on rice flavored with chicken or fish and vegetables and cooked in a slow oven.

Pipe, to To shape foods with a paste-like consistency by forcing them through a nozzle in a FORCING BAG. The term can be applied to icing cakes, decorating dishes with shaped purées of vegetables or desserts with cream and various other uses.

Piquant An agreeably sharp, pungent flavor.

Pit, to To remove the stones or seeds from fruit.

Pith The white fibrous layer between the rind and flesh of citrous fruits.

Poach, to A method of cooking food in liquid in an open pan, keeping the temperature just below boiling point.

Pot au feu A joint of beef cooked slowly with vegetables in a deep, earthenware casserole.

Pot roasting A cooking method where meat and vegetables are first browned in fat or oil before being cooked very slowly in a covered pan on top of the stove with very little liquid.

Potted Cooked meat or fish preserved in the form of a spread by pounding it to a paste and sealing it in a jar with melted butter,

Preheat Usually refers to heating an oven to a required temperature before baking.

Pressure cooker A cooking pot used on the top of the stove which cooks food quickly by sealing in steam which raises the cooking temperature. A useful method of saving fuel and retaining nutrients and flavor.

Prove, to The second rising given to doughs made with yeast to allow the dough to recover its shape and to ensure an even texture.

Provençale, à la Dishes cooked with tomatoes and garlic.

Purée Cooked or raw vegetables or fruit liquidized or sieved to form a thick, smooth pulp.

Q

Quenelle A mousse-like savory dumpling made with finely minced meat, chicken or fish bound with eggs, then poached.

Quiche A savory tart baked in a pastry case.

R

Ragoût A rich, well-seasoned stew of meat and vegetables.

Ramekins Small ovenproof dishes used for cooking individual savories or soufflés.

Rechauffé To recook or to prepare dishes made with previously cooked foods, for instance rissoles and fish cakes.

Reduce, to The reduction and concentration of liquids by fast boiling.

Refresh, to A technique of retaining the color of vegetables by immersing them in cold water before reheating.

Remoulade A mayonnaise flavored with finely chopped capers, gherkins, tarragon, parsley and chervil.

Render, to The extraction and clarification of fat from meat by heating.

Roast, to The cooking of meat in dry or direct heat.

Rind The outer skin of fruits and vegetables or the hard coating on the outside of cheese.

Roe The eggs of a fish. Soft roes are the milt of a male fish.

Rolling pin see *Baking equipment.*

Rôtisserie An electric spit for cooking small joints of meat or poultry.

Roulade A term which can refer to a roll of meat, rolled soufflé mixture or a chocolate cake.

Roux A mixture of flour and fat cooked together to form the basis for a sauce.

Royal icing see *Icing.*

Rub in The term used to describe the techique of mixing solid fat into flour by rubbing with the fingertips.

S

Salad basket A collapsible wire basket used for drying leaf vegetables for salads.

Salmis A stew made by part-roasting game before completing the cooking in a rich, red wine sauce.

Sauté To lightly fry food by tossing it in shallow fat until browned.

Saucepans The choice of pans depends on your budget but generally it is better to buy a few good-quality pans than a whole set of cheap ones. Choose heavy-gauge pans with level, thick bases. Aluminum is one of the most popular metals for pans as it is a good heat conductor and is long lasting. Stainless steel is durable and easy to clean but it is expensive and to be effective requires a good bonded base of either aluminum or copper. Enamelled steel or aluminum pans have an attractive appearance but need to be good quality to avoid discoloration or chipping. A good cast-iron casserole is a useful pan as it can be used on top of the stove as well as in the oven; copper is traditionally regarded as the best material for pans as it is an excellent conductor but it must be coated with tin or aluminum inside and it is also very expensive. Ceramic and glass pans are now available but they tend to cook unevenly. Non-stick finishes are useful for milk pans but they need careful handling to keep the coating in good condition.

Saw A small, fine-toothed saw is needed for CHINING meat joints or cutting through large bones.

Scald, to The heating of milk to just below boiling point. It can also refer to the immersion of fruit or vegetables in boiling water in order to peel them more easily.

Scales A set of accurate scales is an important piece of equipment; they should be easy to use and store away. Wall-hung scales which fold away are probably the most convenient type of everyday use.

Scissors A heavy pair of stainless-steel scissors with serrated blades are useful for all types of jobs, from snipping the ends from mange toute and beans to removing the rind from bacon.

Score, to To make small cuts across the surface of food to assist the cooking process.

Scramble A method of cooking eggs in butter to form creamy flakes.

Sear To apply heat to meat in order to brown the surface and seal in the juices.

Seasoning Salt, pepper, herbs or spices used to enhance the flavor of cooked dishes.

Shears A twin-bladed scissor-like tool used for cutting up poultry.

Shortening Fat used for cake and pastry making.

Shuck To remove vegetables such as peas and beans from their pods.

Sift, to To pass dry ingredients through a strainer to remove any lumps.

Simmer To keep liquids just below boiling point, so that there is only an occasional bubble.

Singe The removal of hairs from the skins of poultry and game birds by using a lighted taper.

Skillet Choose a large sized, heavy-based pan with a lid for shallow frying. Non-stick skillets are best avoided as the surfaces tend to break down with strong heat after a time and food then tends to glue itself to the bottom. Reserve a small heavy pan for omelettes and pancakes; this should not be washed in detergent but merely wiped out after use.

Skim, to To remove scum, fat or other unwanted matter from the surfaces of cooked foods.

Soufflé dish A deep, straight-sided ovenproof dish used for cooking soufflés.

Souse, to To cook or STEEP foods, especially oily fish, in spiced vinegar or wine.

Spit see *Rôtisserie.*

Spoons A range of wooden and metal spoons in different sizes is needed for different tasks such as measuring, cutting and folding, or stirring. A large spoon with a slotted bowl is very useful for lifting cooked foods out of liquids; a long-handled spoon is useful for BASTING. Wooden spoons are needed for use with non-stick surfaces.

Steam, to A method of cooking food by exposing it to steam by suspending it over a pan of boiling water in a metal colander, or in a perforated container forming the top half of a steamer. An advantage of steaming is that valuable vitamins and nutrients are retained.

Steep, to To immerse food in a liquid to give flavor and to improve the texture (see MARINADE).

Stewing, to A long, slow process of cooking whereby foods are cooked until tender in liquid, either in the oven or on the top of the stove.

Stir-fry, to A method of cooking foods by cutting them into small dice or tiny strips and stirring them and tossing them in a little fat or oil over very high heat.

Stock The liquid produced after simmering fish, meat or vegetables to extract their flavor.

Strain, to The removal of liquids from solid foods by pouring it through a perforated container or strainer.

Sweat, to A term used to describe the gentle cooking of foods such as vegetables or mushrooms in a little butter in a covered pan until the juices run.

T

Terrine An ovenproof dish with a lid used for cooking savory meat mixtures, either minced (PÂTÉS) or layered, when the cooked mixture is also known as a terrine.

Thermometers Kitchen thermometers have a higher scale than ordinary thermometers and are useful for gauging the temperatures of fat or oil for deep frying or when making sugar syrup. Special meat thermometers can be obtained which are inserted into joints to see if they are cooked.

Timbales Small molds with sloping sides, generally used for savory mousses, and creams.

Tins see Baking tins.

Truss, to To secure the legs and wings of poultry and game birds into a good shape with string or skewers.

Turn out, to To remove foods from the dish or mold in which they were cooked or set by loosening the sides and inverting.

U

Unflavored gelatin An ingredient sold in powder form by boiling down animal bones and waste tissue. When reconstituted with water and allowed to cool, it forms a strong, flavorless jelly.

V

Velouté A classic white sauce made with flour, fat and stock.

Véronique Refers to dishes prepared with grapes.

Verte, sauce A mayonnaise flavored with watercress or green herbs.

Vichy, à la Refers to dishes cooked or garnished with carrots, often glazed with sugar and butter.

Vinaigrette see *French dressing.*

Vol-au-vent Circular or oval puff pastry cases wth a rich, savory filling.

W

Whisks Mainly used for incorporating air into mixtures or single ingredient. A balloon whisk is the most effective, and is best for whisking egg whites. Electric whisks, either free-standing or hand-held, can save a lot of time and energy.

White sauce see *Béchamel*

Wok A curved-bottomed pan used mainly for stir-frying.

Z

Zabaglione A dessert consisting of egg yolks, sugar and marsala beaten over hot water until thick and creamy.

Zest The outer rind of citrus fruit which contains oils used in flavoring.

SOUPS

Without doubt, the secret of making any soup is to start with a really good basic stock. A stock can be made from meat and poultry bones; fish heads, bones and trimmings, or vegetables. All stocks freeze well and it is worth making a large quantity and storing it in the freezer, either in blocks or, more conveniently, concentrated in cubes.

White stocks
The simplest of these is chicken stock made from the carcase of a cooked chicken – never throw these bones away. The flavor will not be as strong as stock made from fresh, uncooked chicken bones and meat, but combined with a mushroom or two and a few vegetables it will certainly give you an acceptable stock for little cost.

Your butcher, fish or poultry seller will probably supply you with fresh chicken giblets (necks, crops and hearts) or chicken 'backs' at a very low cost – these make an excellent white stock.

To make chicken stock, put about 1lb of chicken bones and giblets into a large saucepan with two carrots, peeled and roughly chopped, a stalk of celery, parsley stalks, a bay leaf, a sprig of thyme and some black peppercorns. It is best not to add salt unless you know exactly what you are going to use the stock for – it can always be added later. Unless you require a very highly flavored white stock avoid using onions as they make the stock very strong and can make meat-based stocks spoil quickly.

Pour in enough cold water to cover the ingredients (about 7½ cups for every 2lb of meat and bones) and bring the water to the boil. Skim off any scum rising to the surface with a slotted spoon, reduce the heat and simmer gently for 2-3 hours. Strain the stock through a fine strainer or through a cheesecloth and allow to cool. If the stock has reduced it should form a jelly when refrigerated and the fat will form a firm crust on top which can be removed easily. This jellied stock will keep in the refrigerator for several days. If you intend to freeze it, boil it until much of the water evaporates and the stock reaches a reduced, syrupy consistency. Cool this liquid, pour it into an ice-cube tray and fast-freeze. Once the stock is frozen, the cubes can be stored in a sealed polythene bag until needed. To use, simply add the cubes to boiling water until the right flavor and quantity is reached.

Veal bones can be used for white stock, but pork stock is rather too strong in flavor. A stock should give a background flavor but not dominate the taste of the whole dish.

Brown stocks
Beef bones for stock are readily obtainable from most butchers, often for no charge. If you want a particularly meaty, flavorful brown stock, buy ½lb of shin or shank of beef to give body. Roast the meat and bones in a hot oven for about half an hour or until they are browned and place them in a large saucepan. Add a similar combination of vegetables and herbs as for chicken stock, using mushroom stalks and peelings for extra-delicious flavor and color. Follow the method given for chicken stock, but simmer the stock for longer, between 4-5 hours.

Vegetable stocks
Nowadays, as more and more people are preferring to eat meatless meals, stocks made from vegetables are an increasingly important element in vegetable and fish cookery. Certainly, stocks made purely from a vegetable base need not be any less flavorful. Try a combination of carrots, leeks, celery, potatoes, turnips, rutabega [not too much of these last two as they are fairly pungent] with a handful of pearl barley or lentils, a bay leaf, black peppercorns and a glass of sherry. Cover with cold water and boil for about ½ hour. For an interesting bouillon why not try infusing a fresh bunch of herbs including sorrel, lovage, marjoram, thyme, parsley, a touch of tarragon and green peppercorns in boiling water with a glass of dry white wine.

Fish stocks

A good stock is as essential in fish cookery as for meat casseroles and stews, sometimes more so. A court-bouillon is normally used for poaching fish, particularly whole fish such a salmon, salmon trout, fresh-water trout and other species. This can be simply a pint of water, a tablespoon or two of lemon juice, a sprig of parsley, a bay leaf, a small sliced carrot, an onion or shallot and a few peppercorns. A glass of white wine will enliven this simple stock considerably.

For a more tasty stock, make a fish *fumet* of the trimmings (heads, tails, fins and bones) of filleted fish – your fresh fish-seller will probably be glad to give you these. Put them in a large saucepan, add any combination of the ingredients given for court-bouillon and cover with water. Bring to the boil and simmer for about 30 minutes in a well-ventilated kitchen. Strain through a fine strainer or a cheese cloth and cool until ready for use.

Chicken Consommé

This simple but fascinating clarifying process turns a dull, cloudy stock into a marvellously clear soup in minutes.

2 egg whites with their shells, crushed	5 cups good chicken stock, well strained

Preparation time: 5 minutes
Cooking time: 20 minutes

Whisk the egg whites until they are frothy. Pour the stock into a large pan and add the egg whites and crushed shells. Bring the stock up to the boil, whisking continuously with a balloon whisk, until the froth begins to rise up the sides of the pan. Remove the pan and lower the heat. Return the pan to the heat and simmer very gently for 5 minutes without whisking.

Allow the stock to cool a little and strain through cheese cloth.

Serving suggestion: Season and flavor with sherry, white wine or port and garnish with tiny julienne strips of carrot, leek or cucumber. Make chicken-noodle soup by simmering it with vermicelli and adding tiny pieces of chicken meat and thinly sliced mushrooms. Use chicken consommé for the following recipe for Chinese Egg Flower soup.

Variation: Beef stock can be clarified in the same way as chicken stock.

Chinese Egg Flower Soup

A simple soup to make but deliciously refreshing and very attractive with its lacy pattern of egg and contrasting snippets of green scallion.

5 cups unseasoned, clarified chicken stock (see Chicken consommé)	1 egg, beaten
1 tbspn soy sauce	1 scallion
1 teasp wine vinegar	1 tbspn tbspn sherry
salt and pepper	

Preparation time: 10 minutes
Cooking time: 10 minutes

Bring the stock to the boil. Add the soy sauce, wine vinegar and seasoning to taste. Return to the boil then remove from the heat.

Pour the beaten egg into the stock in a thin steady stream. Whisk well and return the pan to the heat. Add the sherry and snipped green part of the scallion and bring back to the boil. Serve immediately in warmed bowls. (Illustrated overleaf.)

Cream of Mushroom Soup

12oz fresh button mushrooms	1¾ cups milk
1 small onion, peeled and finely chopped	pinch of nutmeg
2 tbspns butter	salt and pepper
1 tbspn flour	**Garnish:** 3-4 mushroom caps, thinly sliced; chopped parsley; 3 tbspns heavy cream
3¾ cups good chicken stock	

Preparation time: 15 minutes
Cooking time: 20 minutes

Wipe and trim the mushrooms and chop them finely, reserving 3-4 for garnishing. Using a large, heavy-based pan, sauté the onion and mushrooms in the butter for 4-5 minutes. Stir in the flour and cook for a further minute. Take the pan off the heat, add the stock and milk and stir well. Return the pan to moderate heat and cook, stirring continuously, until the soup thickens. Add the nutmeg, season to taste and allow the soup to simmer, covered, for about 15 minutes.

Serve in warmed bowls, garnished with a swirl of cream, mushroom slices and chopped parsley.

Clockwise from left: Chillied Tomato Soup; Cream of Mushroom Soup; Chinese Egg Flower Soup.

Chillied Tomato Soup

16oz can tomatoes

1 large carrot

1 large potato

1 medium onion

1 celery stalk

1 clove garlic, crushed

2 tbspns oil

1 tbspn tomato paste

2 teasps sugar

1 bay leaf

chilli powder (about ⅛ teasp)

dash Worcestershire sauce

salt to taste

3¾ cups chicken stock

Garnish: 2 tbspns heavy cream; finely chopped or snipped chives

Preparation time: 15 minutes
Cooking time: 30-35 minutes

Strain the tomatoes, with the juice, to remove the pips. Peel, trim and chop the vegetables. Heat the oil in a large, heavy-based pan, add the vegetables (except the tomatoes) and sweat with the lid on for 5-6 minutes, stirring occasionally. Add the tomatoes, tomato paste, sugar, bay leaf, seasonings and stock and bring to the boil. Reduce the heat and simmer for about 25-30 minutes until the carrot, potato and celery are tender. Take out the bay leaf and work in an electric blender until smooth. Serve very hot with crusty bread; swirl cream in each bowl or snip chives over to decorate.

French Onion Soup

1lb onions

¼ cup butter

5 cups good beef stock

1 glass white wine

1 teasp brown sugar

salt and freshly ground black pepper

4 slices French bread

1 cup grated Gruyère or Cheddar cheese

Garnish: chopped parsley

Preparation time: 20 minutes
Cooking time: 50-60 minutes

Peel and slice the onions thinly. Melt the butter in a large, heavy-based pan and fry the onions gently until they turn golden, stirring occasionally.

Stir in the stock, wine, brown sugar, salt to taste and a generous amount of black pepper. Bring to the boil, then simmer for 40 minutes.

When the soup is almost ready, toast 4 slices of French bread, sprinkle with grated cheese and toast until the cheese has melted.

To serve, spoon the soup into heated bowls and float a piece of bread with toasted cheese on top.

Soupe de Poissons

2 tbspns olive oil	1 teasp sugar
1 large onion, peeled and chopped	bouquet garni (see page 126)
1-2 fat garlic cloves	salt and pepper
2 large carrots, peeled and chopped	1lb white fish (coley, cod, haddock, halibut, or sole)
16oz can tomatoes	2 tbspns fresh parsley, chopped
3 cups water	
⅔ cup white wine	

Preparation time: 25 minutes
Cooking time: 45-50 minutes

Heat the oil in a large, heavy-based pan and sauté the fresh vegetables until they begin to turn golden. Coarsely chop the tomatoes and add them to the sautéd vegetables together with the juice from the can. Add the water, wine, sugar, bouquet garni and salt and pepper and cook for 20 minutes.

Skin and slice up the fish, removing any large bones and add to the vegetables. Bring to the boil, reduce the heat and simmer for a further 25-30 minutes.

Remove the bouquet garni and blend the soup in a blender until smooth. Return to the pan and reheat. Just before serving, stir in the chopped parsley. Serve with croûtons or crusty bread.
Variation: For a special occasion stir in ⅓ cup peeled shrimp after blending and heat through thoroughly.

Mussel Soup

5 cups fresh mussels in the shell	¼ cup flour
2½ cups water	1 tbspn chopped fresh parsley
⅔ cup dry white wine	⅔ cup creamy milk
2 shallots, peeled and chopped	salt and black pepper
1 fat garlic clove, crushed	**Garnish:** 12 mussels in their shells
¼ cup butter	

Preparation time: 30-40 minutes
Cooking time: 15 minutes

As soon as you have brought the mussels home, put them in a bucket of fresh water and stand in a cool place. They will keep satisfactorily overnight like this, provided that they were freshly picked when you bought them.

To prepare the mussels: Discard any shells which are broken or open shells which do not close when sharply tapped with a knife. Scrub each one well (a plastic pan-scourer is good for this job) and scrape off any barnacles or other clinging marine life with a knife. Also pull away the hairy 'beard.' Rinse the mussels 2 or 3 times in bowls of clean water and, lastly, place in a strainer under running water for a few minutes, then drain them. They should all smell fresh and sweet.

Put the water, wine, shallots and garlic into a very large pan, bring to the boil and cook for 5 minutes. Tip in the mussels and cover. Cook for 4-5 minutes over a high heat until all the shells have opened wide. Discard any shells which have not opened. Remove the pan from the heat and spoon out the mussels onto a dish or plate. Strain the liquor through a fine strainer and reserve.

Rinse out the pan and melt the butter in it. Add the flour, cook for 1 minute and stir in the mussel liquor and parsley. Bring to the boil, stirring, reduce the heat and simmer for 5 minutes.

Meanwhile, remove all the mussels except 12 from their shells. Stir the cooked mussels into the soup and heat through. Adjust seasoning to taste and serve in wide soup plates garnished with the mussels still in their shells.

Vichyssoise

A traditional winter soup with a sophisticated, smooth texture and subtle flavor. Vichyssoise is delicious hot or cold.

4 large leeks	pinch of ground cinnamon
1lb potatoes	salt and pepper
¼ cup butter	⅔ cup light cream
3¾ cups well-flavored chicken stock	**Garnish:** chives cut with scissors; croûtons

Preparation time: 20 minutes
Cooking time: 35 minutes

Cut the root bases and green tops from the leeks. Slice the white stems into pieces and wash well in a strainer under running water to remove any grit. Drain the leeks well. Peel and chop the potatoes.

Melt the butter in a heavy-based pan and fry the leeks and potatoes until soft but not colored. Stir in the stock and bring to the boil. Reduce the heat, season to taste and simmer for about 30 minutes. Purée the vegetables in a food processor or an electric blender; or rub through a sieve until smooth. If serving hot, return the soup to the pan and reheat. Add the cinnamon and check the seasoning and stir in the cream just before serving in warmed bowls.

If serving cold, chill in the refrigerator for 2-3 hours and stir in the cream just before serving. Garnish with chives and crisp croûtons.

Creamy Avocado Soup

An elegant soup for summer parties with a delicate taste and pretty color.

2 ripe avocados
1 shallot, finely chopped
2½ cups chicken stock
⅔ cup natural yoghurt
1 tbspn lemon juice
2 tbspns heavy cream
salt and pepper
Garnish: scissored chives

Preparation time: 15 minutes
Chilling time: 2 hours

Cut the avocados in half and remove the stones. Scoop out the flesh taking care to scrape away all the dark green part next to the skin as this gives the color to the soup.

Put the avocado flesh into a blender with the shallot, stock, yoghurt and lemon juice. Work until smooth. Season to taste and stir in the cream. Chill for 2 hours and serve sprinkled with chives.

Spiced Carrot Soup

2lb carrots

1 large onion

2 medium potatoes

¼ cup butter

6¼ cups chicken stock

1 bay leaf

1-2 teasps hot curry paste

2 teasps tomato paste

salt and pepper

½ cup heavy cream

Garnish: chopped parsley, crushed poppadums or croûtons

Preparation time: 20 minutes
Cooking time: 25-30 minutes
Chilling time: 2-3 hours

Peel and coarsely chop the carrots, onion and potatoes. Melt the butter in a large pan and sweat the vegetables with the lid on for 5-6 minutes, stirring occasionally.

Add the stock, bay leaf, curry paste and tomato paste and pepper and salt to taste. Simmer for 20 minutes or until the vegetables are tender.

Remove the bay leaf and work the soup in an electric blender or food processor until smooth. Check the seasoning, adding more curry paste mixed with a little water, if liked. Chill the soup for 2-3 hours. Add the cream and serve in chilled bowls garnished with chopped parsley, crushed poppadums or garlic-flavored croûtons.

Spiced carrot soup is also very good served hot with crusty garlic bread.

Chilled Cucumber Soup

2 large cucumbers

1 shallot, peeled and chopped

1 large garlic clove, crushed

⅔ cup natural yoghurt

1¼ cups milk

2 teasps wine vinegar

salt and freshly ground pepper

Garnish: cucumber slices and croûtons

Preparation time: 10 minutes
Chilling time: 1½-2 hours

Peel and roughly chop the cucumber (reserving about 8 thin slices with the peel still on for garnishing). Place the cucumber and shallot in an electric blender with the garlic, yoghurt, milk, wine vinegar and salt and pepper to taste. Blend at high speed until smooth. Check the seasoning (you may find that you need quite a lot of salt) and chill thoroughly for 1½-2 hours. Serve garnished with cucumber slices and crisp croûtons.
Tip: This soup should be served icy cold. If you are short of chilling time, try putting it in the freezer for about ¾ hour or until crystals start to form round the edges of the container. Whisk thoroughly until smooth and serve in chilled bowls.

Watercress Soup

The pepperiness of watercress gives a unique flavor to this delicious summer soup.

2 bunches of watercress

3 medium potatoes

1 medium onion

2 tbspns butter

3¾ cups chicken stock

⅔ cup heavy cream

Garnish: chopped fresh watercress leaves

Preparation time: 20 minutes
Cooking time: 25 minutes
Chilling time: 2-3 hours

Wash the watercress well and chop coarsely (reserving a few sprigs for garnishing). Peel and chop the potatoes and onion. Melt the butter in a heavy-based pan and 'sweat' the potatoes and onion for 4-5 minutes. Stir in the stock, and bring to the boil. Reduce the heat and simmer for 10 minutes or until the potato is tender. Add the watercress and cook for another 10 minutes.

Work the soup in a blender or food processor until smooth. Season to taste and chill for 2-3 hours. Stir in the cream and serve in chilled bowls garnished with chopped watercress.

Gazpacho

Serves 4-6

This traditional Spanish iced soup, served with a fresh vegetable garnish, is wonderfully refreshing on a hot summer day.

1 lb ripe tomatoes	1 tbspn wine vinegar
⅔ medium cucumber, peeled and chopped	3 tbspns olive oil
1 red or green pepper, deseeded and chopped	⅔ cup iced water
1 fat garlic clove, peeled and chopped	⅔ cup tomato juice
½ small onion, peeled and chopped	salt and pepper
2 slices white bread with the crusts removed	**Garnish:** ⅓ cucumber, chopped; 1-2 large tomatoes, deseeded and chopped finely; 1 small pepper, cut into thin strips; croûtons
1 teasp sugar	
1 tbspn lemon juice	

Preparation time: 30 minutes
Chilling time: 2-3 hours

Pour boiling water over the tomatoes in a bowl and leave for 2-3 minutes until the skins come away easily. Peel and chop the tomatoes into quarters and deseed. Place all the vegetables together with the bread, sugar and lemon juice into an electric blender and work to a purée. Gradually add the wine vinegar and olive oil until the mixture is smooth. Add the iced water and tomato juice and season to taste.

Chill the soup in a refrigerator for 2-3 hours (it must be really cold). Serve in chilled bowls with separate side dishes of chopped cucumber, deseeded and chopped tomato, sliced green or red pepper and croûtons.

Clockwise from left: Spiced Carrot Soup; Chilled Cucumber Soup; Gazpacho.

Chicken and Corn Soup

A good idea for using up leftover cooked chicken to make a substantial soup for lunch or supper.

¼ cup butter	¾ cup frozen whole kernel corn
1 medium onion, peeled and finely chopped	salt and freshly ground black pepper
⅓ cup flour	1 tbspn chopped parsley
2½ cups well-flavored chicken stock	3 tbspns heavy cream
1¼ pints milk	
1¼ cups cooked chicken, chopped	

Preparation time: 15 minutes
Cooking time: 30-35 minutes

Melt the butter in a large, heavy-based pan and sauté the onion until it is soft but not brown. Stir in the flour and cook for 1-2 minutes. Remove the pan from the heat and stir in the stock and milk. Add the chicken and whole kernel corn, bring to the boil then reduce the heat and simmer for 25-30 minutes. Just before serving, season to taste and stir in the parsley and cream.

Variation: For a stylish occasion hand round finely chopped green sweet peppers in a separate bowl.

Country Garden Soup

1lb carrots
2 large potatoes
2-3 turnips
½ small rutebaga
2 celery stalks
1 large onion
¼ cup butter
1 tbspn tomato paste
5 cups good vegetable stock
bouquet garni (see page 126)
1 bay leaf
salt and pepper
1 tbspn chopped fresh parsley

Preparation time: 20-30 minutes
Cooking time: 30 minutes

Peel and chop all the vegetables into very small dice. Melt the butter in a heavy-based pan and 'sweat' the vegetables for about 5 minutes, stirring occasionally. Add the tomato paste, stock, herbs and seasoning and bring to the boil. Reduce the heat and simmer for about 25 minutes or until the vegetables are tender. Stir in the chopped parsley just before serving.

Oxtail Soup

A very hearty, warming soup for cold winter days

1 whole oxtail (about 1½lb)	bouquet garni (see page 126)
3 tbspns oil	6¼ cups brown stock
1 large carrot, peeled and finely chopped	¼ cup flour
1 large onion, peeled and finely chopped	1 tbspn soy sauce
1-2 turnips, peeled and chopped (optional)	dash Worcestershire sauce
1 bay leaf	**Garnish:** grated carrot

Preparation time: 15 minutes
Cooking time: 3-4¼ hours

Trim as much fat as possible from the oxtail and brown it in 1 spoon of the oil in a heavy-based skillet. Remove the oxtail with a slotted spoon and put it in a deep casserole, then fry the vegetables in the pan until golden brown. Transfer the vegetables to the casserole and add the water and herbs and seasoning (not too much salt at this stage).

Cook the oxtail and vegetables in the oven at a low temperature (300°F) for 3-4 hours until the meat is tender and well browned. Allow to cool (preferably overnight) and skim off the fat. Take out the oxtail, fork the meat from the bones, chop finely and reserve. Heat a little of the fat and stir in the flour. Cook for 1 minute. Stir in the juices, made up to 4½ cups with water if necessary and bring to the boil, stirring until they have thickened slightly. Add the meat, vegetables, soy sauce and Worcestershire sauce and return to the boil. Adjust the seasoning and simmer for a further 10 minutes.

Serve on heated soup plates garnished with grated carrot. Hand round slices of crusty bread.

Country Vegetable Soup (left); Chicken and Corn Soup.

Shrimp Gumbo

An exotic Creole main-course soup with a bite to it, ideal as a filling lunch or supper dish.

¼ cup butter	1 cup canned okra, drained and sliced
1 medium onion, peeled and finely chopped	⅔ cup rice
2 celery stalks, trimmed and finely chopped	1 cup peeled shrimp
2 bacon slices, with rind removed and chopped	pinch of marjoram
1 garlic clove, crushed (optional)	1 teasp sugar
1 small green pepper, deseeded and finely chopped	salt
¼ cup flour	cayenne pepper to taste
6¼ cups well-flavored chicken stock	**Garnish:** chopped parsley
16oz can tomatoes, chopped	

Preparation time: 35 minutes
Cooking time: 25-30 minutes

Melt the butter in a heavy-bottomed pan and sauté the onion, celery, bacon, garlic and green pepper for 3-4 minutes. Stir in the flour and cook for a further minute. Stir in the stock, tomatoes and their juice, okra, rice, peeled shrimp, marjoram and sugar. Bring to the boil, adding a little water if the soup appears to be very thick, and then reduce the heat and simmer for about 20 minutes or until the rice is tender. Season to taste with salt and cayenne pepper (it should have a peppery 'bite').

Serve in heated bowls and generously sprinkle with chopped parsley. Hand round thick chunks of crusty bread.

New England Clam Chowder

16oz can of clams	2 tbspns flour
2 tbspns butter	3¾ cups milk
⅔ cup salt pork or bacon, diced	freshly ground black pepper
1 medium onion, peeled and chopped	**Garnish:** crumbled, crisply fried pork or bacon;
2 medium potatoes, peeled and chopped	chopped parsley

Preparation time: 20 minutes
Cooking time: 20 minutes

Drain the juice from the clams and make up to 1¼ cups with water. Chop the clams finely and reserve.

Melt the butter in a large, heavy-based pan and fry the pork or bacon until it is crisp and brown. Take out the pieces with a slotted spoon, strain them on kitchen paper and set aside.

Add the vegetables to the fat and fry gently for 3-4 minutes but do not allow them to brown. Stir in the flour and cook for 1 minute. Pour in the clam juice and milk and stir. Add the clams, half the pork or bacon pieces and a generous amount of black pepper; cook gently for 10-15 minutes.

Serve in warmed bowls garnished with crisp bacon, crumbled up, and chopped parsley. Hand round crackers or hot toast.
Variation: Manhatten Clam Chowder. Prepare recipe as above to stage of adding flour. Drain and reserve the juice from one 16oz can tomatoes. Add tomato juice to the juice from the clams and make up to 4½ cups with water. Add this liquid in place of the milk after stirring in the flour. Coarsely chop the tomatoes and add them, together with some chopped fresh parsley, to the chowder and continue recipe as above.

Shrimp Gumbo.

Codfish Chowder

2 tbspns butter	2½ cups milk
1lb potatoes, peeled and cut into small dice	1 bay leaf
1 large onion, peeled and finely chopped	salt and freshly ground black pepper
½ cup chopped ham	2 tbspns heavy cream (optional)
1lb cod fillet, skinned and cut into cubes	**Garnish:** chopped parsley; crumbled crackers
1 cup whole kernel corn	
1¼ cups fish stock (made with fish skin and trimmings) or water	

Preparation time: 15 minutes
Cooking time: 20 minutes

Melt the butter in a large, heavy-based pan and gently cook the potatoes, onion and ham for 3-4 minutes, stirring occasionally. Add the fish and stir-fry for 2-3 minutes. Add the stock or water, bay leaf, corn, a little salt and a generous amount of black pepper. Cook gently for 15 minutes.

Stir in the milk and cream and adjust the sea-soning. Do not allow the chowder to boil at this stage or the milk and cream may curdle. If it does, take the chowder off the heat, stir well and add a little more cream – the curdling will not spoil the flavor, just the look, of the chowder.

Serve in hot bowls, sprinkled with chopped parsley and crumbled crackers.

APPETIZERS

Smoked Mackerel Pâté with Horseradish

A slimmer's fish pâté which is very quick to make in a food processor or blender.

1 smoked mackerel (about 8oz)	½ small onion, grated
1 cup cream cheese	1 tbspn creamed horseradish
2 tbspns heavy cream	pinch cayenne pepper
Rind of 1 lemon plus 1 tbspn of the juice of the lemon	**Garnish:** thin slices of tomato and 4 lemon wedges

Preparation time: 20 minutes

Remove the skin and bones from the mackerel. Combine all the ingredients in a food processor or blender or pound well until smooth.

Chill in the refrigerator for at least an hour. Garnish with tomato slices and lemon wedges and serve with hot toast.

Taramasalata

A smooth, creamy fish pâté originating from Turkey. If you have only tasted the pink, commercially made version, try making your own as it has a totally different taste and is far more flavorful.

8oz smoked cod's roe (in the piece or preserved in a jar)	6-7 tbspns olive oil
1 small onion, grated	3-4 tbspns lemon juice
1 garlic clove, crushed (optional)	½ teasp sugar
4 thick slices soft white bread, without crusts	freshly ground black pepper
4 tbspns natural yoghurt	**Garnish:** sliced stuffed olives; parsley sprigs

Preparation time: 25-30 minutes
Chilling time: 1 hour

If using roe in the piece, scoop it out of the skin. Put the roe in a bowl and pound it with the grated onion and garlic until smooth.

Grate the bread into the yoghurt. Mash well until the bread is well softened and mix it into the cod's roe mixture. Pound with a pestle or beat well with a spoon. Once the mixture is smooth gradually begin to start adding trickles of oil and lemon juice alternately, beating well until the mixture becomes creamy. Check the seasoning, adding the sugar, a generous quantity of black pepper and a little more lemon juice and yoghurt if liked. If you prefer a smoother mixture pass it through a strainer.

If you have a blender or a food processor you can speed up the preparation process. Work all the ingredients, except the oil and lemon juice, until smooth. Gradually add the lemon and oil in a thin, steady stream until the mixture is thick and creamy. Add black pepper to taste.

Chill for at least an hour and serve garnished with sliced stuffed olives and parsley sprigs. Hand round thick toast or warmed pitta bread.

Marinaded Kipper Fillets

10-12oz frozen kipper fillets	1 tbspn olive oil
juice of 2 lemons	1 teasp wine vinegar
	black pepper
	Garnish: thin onion rings; chopped parsley

Preparation time: 15 minutes
Marinading time: 24 hours

While the kipper fillets are still frozen peel off the skin (it comes off easily) and slice the fish diagonally into thin slices. Lay the slices in a shallow dish.

Mix together the lemon juice, oil, and vinegar and pour over the kippers. Sprinkle with freshly ground black pepper and cover the dish with foil or plastic wrap. Refrigerate for 24 hours.

Garnish with onion rings and chopped parsley and serve with thinly sliced brown bread and butter.

Marinaded Kipper Fillets (left); Smoked Mackerel Pâté with Horseradish (right).

Smoked Haddock and Egg Mousse

Serves 6

12oz smoked haddock fillets

2 hard-boiled eggs, peeled and chopped

1¼ cups milk

1 bay leaf

2-3 slices onion

sprig of parsley

5 black peppercorns

2 tbspns butter

¼ cup flour

1 envelope unflavored gelatin

⅔ cup water (or cooking liquid from the haddock if not too salty)

3 tbspns mayonnaise

1 egg yolk, beaten

1 tbspn lemon juice

1 tbspn chopped fresh parsley

⅔ cup heavy cream, lightly whipped

1 egg white whisked to peaks

salt and freshly ground black pepper

Garnish: Lemon slices or twists; parsley sprigs

Preparation time: 45 minutes
Cooking time: 15-20 minutes
Setting time: 2-3 hours

Poach the haddock fillets in water for about 10-15 minutes until the fish is tender and cooked through. Drain (reserving some cooking liquid if not too salty) and cool the fish; remove the skins and bones and flake the flesh.

Heat the milk gently (do not boil) with the bay leaf, onion, parsley sprig and peppercorns for about 5 minutes and strain. Melt the butter in a pan and stir in the flour. Cook gently for about a minute; do not allow it to brown. Take the pan off the heat and stir in the milk. Return it to the heat and cook gently, stirring until the sauce has thickened, then cool it slightly in a large bowl.

Dissolve the gelatin in the water or fish stock over a low heat. Stir the flaked fish, chopped egg, mayonnaise, egg yolk, lemon juice, and chopped parsley into the sauce then mix in the gelatin. Fold in the whipped cream and whisked egg white carefully. Check the seasoning adding salt, pepper and more lemon juice if necessary. Turn into a soufflé dish and allow to set in the refrigerator for 2-3 hours. Before serving, decorate with lemon slices or twists and sprigs of parsley.

Hot Shrimp Ramekins

Serves 6

¾ cup cooked pasta wheels, short-cut macaroni or any other short pasta

½ cup peeled shrimp

2 eggs, beaten

3 tbspns sour cream

salt and pepper

4-5 tbspns breadcrumbs

2 tbspns butter

Preparation time: 10 minutes
Cooking time: 20 minutes

Stir together the cooked pasta, shrimp, eggs and sour cream until well mixed. Season to taste and spoon into greased ramekin dishes.

Sprinkle a covering layer of breadcrumbs over each ramekin and dot with butter. Bake for 15-20 minutes at 375°F. Serve immediately. A delicious light starter.

Devilled Whitebait

These tiny fishes, crisply fried, make a simple but fairly substantial appetizer, ideal as a beginning to a cold salad meal.

1lb whitebait	oil for deep frying
1 cup flour	pinch of cayenne pepper
3 teasps mustard powder	**Garnish:** lemon wedges
salt	

Preparation time: 10 minutes
Cooking time: 10-15 minutes

Rinse the fishes under cold running water in a strainer, picking out any seaweed or other detritis. Shake well to remove excess moisture and spread out on a clean teacloth.

Put the flour, mustard powder and salt into a bowl.

Half-fill a deep-frying pan with oil, and heat to about 375°F. You can gauge the correct temperature by using a cube of stale bread – if it turns golden brown in about 1 minute then the oil is ready for cooking the fish. Coat a double handful of fish with flour by shaking in the bowl (be careful when handling them as they are very delicate). Remove surplus flour by shaking in a strainer and put straight into the hot oil in a frying basket. Do not cook too many at a time or they will stick together and be soggy. Cook for 2-3 minutes until they have turned light brown in color, taking the basket out now and then and shaking occasionally to separate the fishes. Drain the cooked fish on absorbent kitchen paper and keep warm.

Repeat the flouring and frying process until all the fishes are cooked (about 4-5 batches). Check the temperature of the oil again with a bread cube and put all the fishes in the frying basket and cook for another minute or two until they crisp up and look an appetizing golden color. Sprinkle with cayenne pepper.

Serve immediately, garnished with plenty of lemon wedges and hand around thin slices of brown bread and butter.

Variation: Sprats and sardines can also be cooked in this way but require slightly longer cooking time.

Devilled Whitebait.

Tomato Orange Cocktail

⅔ cup freshly squeezed orange juice

2 cups tomato juice

1 tbspn lemon juice

1 teasp sugar

salt to taste

Garnish: orange slices

Preparation time: 15 minutes
Cooking time: 1-2 hours

Strain the orange juice and put it with all the other ingredients into a blender and blend at high speed for about 1 minute.

Chill well and serve in large chilled cocktail glasses garnished with a slice of orange.

Carrot, Celery and Tomato Cocktail

2 large carrots

1 large celery stalk

1¼ cups tomato juice

salt

Tabasco sauce

Garnish: leafy celery stalks; lemon twists; straws

Preparation time: 15 minutes
Cooking time: 1-2 hours

Peel and coarsely grate the carrots. Trim the celery, remove the 'string' and chop the stalk into strips.

Put the vegetables into a blender with 4-5 tablespoons water and blend to a pulp. Press the pulp through a fine strainer then repeat the process to remove any fibers which may have been pushed through.

Stir in the tomato juice, salt, a few drops of Tabasco to taste and chill well. To serve, pour the cocktail over crushed ice in highball glasses and garnish with leafy celery stalks, lemon twists and straws.

Three-Fruit Cocktail

1¼ cups pineapple juice

2 ripe peaches, peeled and sliced

2 cups ripe strawberries, washed and hulled (save 4 for garnishing)

2½ tbspns grenadine

1 teasp castor sugar

Garnish: strawberries, sprigs of mint and straws

Preparation time: 15 minutes
Chilling time: 1-2 hours

Put all the ingredients into an electric blender and work until smooth. Strain through a fine strainer and chill well.

Serve the cocktails in frosted highball glasses or large wine glasses garnished with strawberries, sprigs of mint and straws.

Left-right: Tomato Orange Cocktail; Three-Fruit Cocktail; Carrot, Celery and Tomato Cocktail.

Guacamole

2 large ripe tomatoes	1 teasp wine vinegar
2 ripe avocados	½ teasp chilli powder (or to taste)
1 tbspn lemon juice	dash of Worcestershire sauce
1 fat garlic clove, crushed	salt to taste
2 teasps onion, grated	

Preparation time: 15 minutes
Chilling time: about an hour

Put the tomatoes in a bowl and pour on boiling water. After 3-4 minutes the skins will peel off easily. De-seed the tomatoes and chop up the flesh. Halve the avocados, take out the stone and scoop out as much of the flesh as possible, especially the bright green part next to the skin which adds color to the mixture.

Mash the avocados with the tomatoes, lemon juice, garlic and onion until you have a creamy but slightly lumpy pulp. Stir in the wine vinegar, chilli powder, Worcestershire sauce and plenty of salt to taste.

Chill in the refrigerator for an hour or so – if the guacamole discolors a little, stir it with a fork.

Serve with tacos or hot toast or sliced fresh vegetables (see Crudités, page 32).

Avocado with Spiced Crab

2 large ripe avocados

1 teasp lemon juice
1 tbspn mayonnaise
1 teasp catsup
dash Worcestershire sauce
pinch of chilli powder
salt to taste
½ cup cooked crabmeat
Garnish: 4 crab legs (if available); parsley sprigs; paprika

Preparation time: 10 minutes

Halve the avocados and take out the stones. Spoon out about half the avocado flesh from each skin and mash in a bowl with the lemon juice, mayonnaise, catsup and seasonings. Once you have a fairly smooth creamy mixture, check the seasoning, adding more lemon juice and chilli powder if desired.

Fold in the crabmeat and spoon into the avocado halves. Sprinkle with paprika and decorate with parsley sprigs and crab legs if available.

Crudités

Carrot sticks: Scrub or peel, cut into small sticks.
Celery sticks: Scrub the stalks and trim off the coarse 'string' and cut into sticks.
Scallions: Trim the tops and bottoms, and with sharp scissors cut the tops into fine fronds. Place in cold water and the fronds will curl back, making pretty tassels.
Cauliflower florets: Separate the cauliflower head into individual florets.
Cucumber: Wash and cut into sticks.
Mushrooms: Use tiny fresh button mushrooms speared on cocktail sticks, or sliced larger ones.
Radishes: Wash, top and tail and make little cuts downwards at one end with a sharp knife. Immerse the radishes in cold water for an hour or so and these cut slices will bend backwards, forming 'roses.'
Sweet peppers: Wash and cut into wedges.

Dips: Make mayonnaise (see page 130) and flavor it with garlic, freshly chopped herbs, curry paste, horseradish, tomato paste or cooked meats or fish.

Garlic Mushrooms

24 (approximately 1-1¼lbs) medium mushrooms
½-⅓ cup butter
1 tbspn olive oil
2 tbspns chopped parsley
2 garlic cloves, crushed
black pepper
dried breadcrumbs

Preparation time: 5 minutes
Cooking time: 7-10 minutes

Remove the stalks and wipe the mushroom caps. (The stalks can be used to make duxelles, page 63). Melt a quarter of the butter with the oil in a pan. Put in the mushrooms, cover and sweat for 3-4 minutes. Drain the caps, arrange on a heatproof gratin dish and leave to cool.

Meanwhile, cream the remaining butter with the garlic and parsley. When the mushrooms have cooled, fill each cap with butter mixture and sprinkle over with breadcrumbs.

Heat under the broiler until the butter has melted and begins to bubble. Serve very hot with masses of crusty French bread.

Deep-fried Mushrooms with Tartare Sauce

Quickly cooked after the style of Japanese *tempura*, the crisp batter coating seals in the flavor and juices of the mushrooms making them succulent and delicious.

16 medium button mushrooms	1 egg beaten with 1 egg yolk
seasoned flour for coating	¾ cup half milk and half water
oil for deep-frying	**Tartare sauce:**
4 lemon wedges	⅔ cup mayonnaise
Batter:	2 teasps each of chopped capers, gherkins and parsley
1 cup flour	1 teasp wine vinegar
pinch of salt	

Preparation time: 15-20 minutes
Cooking time: approx 20 minutes

To make the batter, sieve the flour with the salt and stir in the beaten egg. Pour in half the milk and water and beat well until you have a smooth mixture. Beat in the remainder of the liquid and allow the batter to stand while you prepare the tartare sauce and mushrooms.

Cut the stalks of the mushrooms level with the caps and wipe with a damp cloth. Prepare the tartare sauce by mixing all the ingredients together.

Half-fill a deep-frying pan with oil and heat to about 375°F. Test the temperature by frying a cube of stale bread – this will turn golden brown in about a minute when the oil is at the correct temperature. Spear the mushrooms on a fork, roll in seasoned flour, dip in the batter and coat evenly. Place in the hot oil and deep-fry until golden brown (about 2-3 minutes), turning once. Lift out the cooked mushrooms with a slotted spoon, drain on kitchen paper and keep hot. Do not try to cook too many at once or the temperature of the oil will drop and the results will not be so good. If you need to keep them hot for some time, they can be crisped up by returning them to the hot oil and frying for a further minute. Serve hot with lemon and tartare sauce.

Cheese-stuffed Tomatoes

4 large, ripe tomatoes	salt and freshly ground black pepper
½ cup curd cheese	2 eggs, hard-boiled
1 tbspn mayonnaise	1 celery stalk
dash anchovy essence	**Garnish:** parsley sprigs

Preparation time: 20 minutes
Chilling time: 1 hour

Cut the tomatoes in half, as shown in the photograph, and carefully cut out the cores and flesh from the centers. Discard the pips and cores but chop the flesh and put it in a bowl with the cheese, mayonnaise, anchovy essence, salt and pepper to taste and mix well. Chop up the eggs and celery fairly finely and stir into the cheese mixture. Spoon the stuffing into the tomato halves and chill for about an hour. Decorate with parsley sprigs before serving.

Potted Meats and Fish

This is a handy way of using up left-over meats such as ham, chicken, turkey and beef, or fish such as salmon, salmon trout or smoked trout. Potted meats and fish keep for a few days in the refrigerator if they are well sealed with butter.

For each cup of minced meat or flaked fish use ¼-½ cup of butter. Pound the butter and meat or fish into a smooth paste. Season to taste, adding a pinch of nutmeg to meat mixtures and a pinch of dried dill to fish mixtures.

Press the mixture into small pots carefully so that there are no gaps or holes and seal the surface with melted butter.

Serve in individual ramekins with hot toast or on crackers as canapés to accompany drinks. Potted meats and fish are also very useful as sandwich fillings.

Game Terrine

1lb gamebird meat (1 pheasant, or 1 partridge, or 2 grouse, or the breasts from 3-4 pigeons or a combination of different game meats)	pinch dried thyme
	pinch dried parsley
8oz fat pork belly, salt pork or bacon	1 tbspn brandy
1 garlic clove (optional)	salt and pepper
1 small onion	4oz bacon slices
½ cup sausage meat	

Preparation time: 35 minutes
Cooking time: 2 hours

Slice the meat off the bones and reserve the breasts. Mince any scraps of meat and the tougher meat of the legs with the pork, garlic and onion. Mix in the sausage meat, thyme, parsley, brandy and seasoning with the minced meat. Use the bacon slices (stretched gently with the back of a spoon) to line the inside of a 3¾-4 cup capacity terrine. Cut the breast meat into thin strips and lay alternate layers of the minced meat mixture and the breast meat in the terrine. Cover the dish with a layer of cooking foil and put on the lid. Place the dish in a baking pan containing about 1in of water and cook in a medium oven (325°F) for about 2 hours.

Use a heavy object to weigh down the terrine and compress it (preferably overnight). Refrigerate for at least 24 hours before serving. To serve, cut into slices, and serve with toast.

Quick Chicken Liver Pâté

8oz chicken livers	⅛ teasp ground coriander
4oz bacon or cooked ham	1 tbspn brandy
1 small onion, finely chopped	salt and black pepper
½ cup butter	

Preparation time: 20 minutes
Cooking time: 10 minutes

Trim any fat or skin from the chicken livers and slice up the larger ones. If using bacon, remove the rind and cut into small pieces. Sauté the chicken livers, bacon and onion gently in ⅛ cup butter until the chicken livers are well cooked (about 10-15 minutes). Add the ham (if using) and work the mixture finely in a food processor or blender with the sherry, brandy and seasoning and ¼ cup of melted butter. Melt the last piece of butter and use it to seal the pâté in a small pot. Chill for at least 1 hour but it is best stored overnight in the refrigerator.

Creamy Chicken Liver Pâté

8oz chicken livers	⅔ cup milk
8oz bacon slices	1 egg, beaten
1 small onion, peeled and chopped	1 tbspn sherry
1 garlic clove (optional)	pinch of thyme
1 slice of bread	salt and freshly ground black pepper
2 tbspns butter	2-3 bay leaves
¼ cup flour	

Preparation time: 35 minutes
Cooking time: approx 2 hours
Cooling and standing time: 24-48 hours

Mince the chicken livers with the bacon (reserving 2-3 slices for lining the base of the pâté dish or terrine), onion, garlic and bread.

Melt the butter in a pan and stir in the flour. Cook for about 1 minute and take the pan off the heat. Stir in the milk and return to the heat, stirring continuously until the sauce has thickened. Let it cool slightly then beat it into the meat mixture with the egg, sherry, thyme and seasoning.

Carefully grease a 4 cup capacity pâté dish or terrine and line it with the bay leaves and bacon slices (stretched slightly with the back of a spoon). Pour in the meat mixture, cover with cooking foil and put on the lid. Place the dish in a baking pan containing about 1 inch of water and cook in a medium oven (350°F) for about 1½ hours. Remove the lid and place a weight on top of the foil (2-3 large cans of food will do) and allow the pâté to cool, preferably overnight. Store in the refrigerator for at least 12 hours before serving.

Cheese-stuffed Tomatoes.

Chicken, Mushroom and Spinach Terrine

Serves 6-8

1 × 3lb roasting chicken	black pepper and a little salt
4oz bacon, plus 3-4 extra slices with rinds removed	2 cups button mushrooms
	2 tbspns butter
1 small onion or shallot, peeled	1lb leaf spinach
1 slice bread	2-3 bay leaves
½ cup sausage meat	
pinch of marjoram	

Preparation time: 40 minutes
Cooking time: 1½-2 hours

With a sharp knife, slice the breast meat off the chicken, cut it into thin slices and set it aside. Cut off the legs and slice off the meat and mince it coarsely. Then mince the bacon (except the extra slices), the onion and finally the bread. Mix all the minced ingredients with the sausage meat, marjoram and seasoning (take care with the salt as the bacon may be salty) and set aside.

To prepare the mushrooms: Wipe clean, slice and 'sweat' them in the butter for 4-5 minutes. Drain well (use the juice for flavoring stocks or soups) and reserve.

To prepare the spinach: Wash the spinach in several changes of water and remove the coarse ribby stalks. Drain and place in a pan with a pinch of salt and a teaspoon of sugar and cook over fairly high heat, in only the water still clinging to the leaves, for 6-7 minutes. Drain into a strainer, pressing gently with the back of a spoon to remove as much water as possible.

To layer the terrine: Using a 5 cup capacity terrine or pâté dish, start with a layer of minced mixture followed by a single layer of mushroom slices then a layer of chicken breast followed by a layer of spinach. Repeat the layers and cover with bacon slices and a row of bay leaves down the center. Cover with a sheet of foil, put on the lid and stand the terrine in a baking tin containing about 1in of water.

Cook in a moderate oven (325°F) for 1½-2 hours until the terrine has shrunk away from the sides of the pot and the top feels firm and crusty. Take off the lid and put a heavy weight on the top of the pâté. Leave for several hours (preferably overnight) in a cool place then store in the refrigerator until needed.

This makes a substantial starter served with hot toast and garnished with sliced tomato and watercress or lettuce, or a delicious buffet lunch dish served with salad.

Chicken, Mushroom and Spinach Terrine.

Satay

4 chicken breasts, boneless	1 fat garlic clove, crushed
Marinade:	1 tbspn soft brown sugar
1 tbspn soft brown sugar	1 tbspn molasses
2 tbspns soy sauce	2 teasps tomato paste
1 fat garlic clove, crushed	chilli powder to taste
1 tbspn lemon juice	1 tbspn lemon juice
1 tbspn olive oil	1 tbspn soy sauce
Peanut sauce:	2-3 tbspns natural yoghurt
½ cup unsalted peanuts, roasted, shelled and peeled (see Tip at the end of the method)	**Garnish:** scallion tassels
3 tbspns olive oil	

Preparation time: 20 minutes
Cooking time: 15 minutes (plus previous 50-60 minutes baking time for peanuts)
Marinading time: 2 hours

Skin the chicken breasts and cut into small dice (about ¾in) and put into a bowl. Mix all the ingredients for the marinade together and pour over the chicken. Leave in a cool place for at least 2 hours.

Meanwhile make the sauce. Put the peanuts, 2 tbspns olive oil, garlic, sugar, molasses and tomato paste and chilli into a food processor or electric blender (or alternatively chop the peanuts and beat into the rest of the ingredients) and work until smooth, adding a tablespoon or so of water if necessary.

Thread the chicken pieces on to 8 thin skewers (wooden or bamboo skewers are available from most Chinese supermarkets) and broil the chicken for 2-3 minutes each side under fairly high heat. While the chicken is cooking, fry the peanut paste in the remaining oil and stir in the lemon juice, soy sauce and yoghurt.

Arrange the skewers on a warmed dish and garnish with scallion tassels. Serve the sauce separately in one or two small bowls.

Tip: To roast peanuts, spread on a baking tray and bake for about 50-60 minutes at 300°F (cool oven). Once roasted, the brown peanut skins will rub off easily.

Sushi-style Fish

8oz cod or haddock fillet (must be very fresh)	1 garlic clove, crushed
1 teasp sesame oil	dash tabasco sauce
2 teasps soy sauce	½ teasp sugar
2 tbspns lemon juice	freshly ground black pepper
1 tbspn sherry	small pinch dried dill
	Garnish: scallion tassels and radish 'roses'

Preparation time: 10 minutes
Chilling time: 24 hours

Skin the fish and cut it diagonally into very thin slices. Lay the slices in a shallow dish. Mix together all the other ingredients, except the black pepper and dill, and pour this marinade over the fish. Sprinkle with the dill and black pepper. Cover with foil or plastic wrap and refrigerate for 24 hours.

Garnish with scallion tassels and radish 'roses.' Serve with brown bread and butter.

Arrange individual portions of fish Japanese-style on tiny mounds of cooked rice and garnish the plates delicately with different types of raw vegetable.

SEAFOOD DISHES

Seafood, with all its wide range of species, offers the best variety of tastes and textures of all the protein-based foods. It makes very healthy eating, being low in carbohydrates and is rich in minerals and vitamins such as A and D. Even the fats present in the 'oily' fish such as mackerel and herring are safer to eat than animal fats as they contribute little to high cholesterol levels.

Buying fish
It is important to make sure that fish is very fresh when you buy it and it should be prepared and eaten on the day that it is purchased.

White and flat fish fillets: Fish such as cod, haddock, halibut, and flounder are frequently sold as fillets, cutlets or steaks and it is difficult to see clearly the condition of the fish. A good sniff, however, will tell you a fair amount – odor should be minimal – do not buy if there is a distinctly fishy smell. The flesh should have a translucent, glossy look and appear firm, not flabby. Do not buy if the flesh is falling into flakes.

Whole fish: When purchasing whole fish, you will have a better chance to judge its freshness. If the fish is on open display, use this opportunity to touch it (Chinese ladies never buy a fish without handling it). Press the body – it should feel firm and the flesh should immediately spring back into shape. The tail should be stiff. Avoid fish with sunken eyes and dull, dry-looking skin – possibly shedding scales. The eyes and skin should be bright and shiny and the gills a bright red color. There should be little odor.

Shellfish and crustacea: It is essential that these are purchased fresh as they deteriorate rapidly when kept, particularly in warm weather. Fresh shellfish such as mussels and clams should be tightly closed – do not buy if you see a large number of the batch gaping open. Uncooked shrimp, lobster and crab should be sold live to ensure freshness. When buying cooked shellfish or crustacea, do not buy if there is any hint of an ammonia odor – the only smell detectable in fresh shellfish is a faint odor of the sea.

To fillet and skin flat fish
1) Lay the fish down flat and, with a sharp knife, cut around the head and down the dorsal (central) line of the fish towards the tail.
2) Slide the blade of the knife under the flesh near the head. Cut downwards and along the bones to slice off the first fillet. Then remove the other fillet in the same way. Repeat with the other 2 fillets on the other side.
3) To skin the fillets, lay them skin-downwards and, holding the tail end firmly at an angle, remove the flesh by cutting from side to side, as close to the skin as possible.

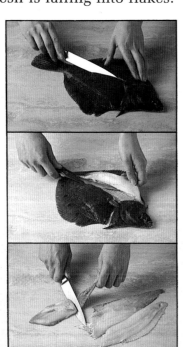

Boning round fish
1) With a sharp knife, cut off the fins and head. Make a cut along the belly to remove the entrails.
2) Open out the fish, flesh-side downwards, and press firmly with the fingers or fist along the back of the fish to loosen the backbone.
3) Turn the fish over and, starting at the head end, ease out the backbone with finger and thumb, holding down the flesh with the knife. Cut it off at the tail end.

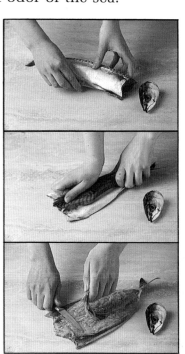

Mackerel with Lemon Butter

4 medium mackerel, cleaned	freshly ground black pepper
½ cup butter	1 tbspn chopped fresh parsley
juice and grated zest of 1 lemon	

Preparation time: 5-10 minutes
Cooking time: 8-10 minutes

Wash the mackerel and pat dry with kitchen paper. Make 2-3 slashes diagonally along the sides of the fish to allow the heat to penetrate quickly. Brush a wire grid with oil to prevent sticking and lay the mackerel on top.

Mix the grated zest of the lemon into ⅓ cup of butter with a palette knife until it is well blended. Form the lemon butter into 4 pats and chill in the refrigerator.

Melt the remaining 2 tbspns of butter and use it to brush the sides of the mackerel. Spoon the lemon juice into the body cavities and over the top of the fish, sprinkle black pepper over the mackerel and place under a moderate broiler. Broil on each side for 4-5 minutes until cooked through. Arrange on a serving dish or individual plates, top each fish with lemon butter and sprinkle with chopped parsley. Decorate with twists of lemon.

Variations: Instead of the lemon butter, top with peanuts or flaked almonds fried for a minute or two in butter until golden. Mackerel is also delicious served with a purée of gooseberries: simmer 2 cups of gooseberries with ½ cup of sugar and about a cup of water and 2 tbspns butter until soft, then rub through a strainer to remove the pips.

Rosemary-stuffed Red Snapper or Red Mullet

4 × 8-12oz red snapper or red mullet, cleaned and scaled but left whole	salt and black pepper
2 tbspns olive oil	4 sprigs of fresh rosemary
1 tbspn lemon juice	**Garnish:** lemon wedges

Preparation time: 10 minutes
Cooking time: 10-15 minutes

Wash the fish well, inside and out, and pat dry. With a sharp knife, make 2 or 3 slashes diagonally along both sides of each fish. Mix together the oil and lemon juice and seasoning and brush the fishes liberally with this basting liquid.

Stuff the body cavity of each fish with a sprig of rosemary. Place a sheet of cooking foil on a broiler pan, brush with the basting liquid and lay the fishes on it. Broil the fishes under moderate heat for 5-6 minutes each side until the fishes are cooked through. Baste with the oil/lemon juice occasionally. Serve garnished with lemon wedges. Serve hot with a green salad of watercress, lettuce and cucumber and Hot Potato Salad (see page 135). Small snapper or red mullet also make a very impressive first course garnished with lemon wedges and watercress and served with warm wholemeal rolls.

Rosemary Stuffed Red Mullet.

Cheese-topped Codfish Steaks

4×6-8oz codfish steaks or cutlets, skinned and boned if preferred

¼ cup butter

2 medium onions, peeled and sliced into rings

4 slices Cheddar cheese

Preparation time: 5 minutes
Cooking time: 10-15 minutes

Place fish steaks on a wire grid (brushed with oil) and dot with half of the butter. Broil under moderate heat for 5-7 minutes (depending on the thickness of the steaks). Then turn the fish over and broil the other side for slightly less time. While the fish is cooking, fry the onions in the rest of the butter until browned. Remove the grid from the broiler and top each steak with a slice of cheese and return to the heat. Cook until the cheese melts and begins to bubble. Arrange fried onion rings on each steak and serve immediately. **Variations:** Instead of the fried onions, try a broiled bacon slice with each steak. Alternatively you could top the cheese with sliced green or red peppers, tomatoes, chutney or tomato relish.

Baked Codfish Steaks with Mushrooms and White Wine

4 codfish steaks, about 1in thick, skinned and boned if preferred

4 tbspns butter

approx. ½ cup milk

¼ cup flour

1 wineglass dry white wine

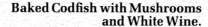

1¼ cups button mushrooms, wiped and sliced

salt and freshly ground black pepper

2 tbsps heavy cream

Garnish: watercress or parsley sprigs

Baked Codfish with Mushrooms and White Wine.

Preparation time: 15-20 minutes
Cooking time: about 40 minutes

Rinse the codfish steaks, pat dry with kitchen paper and lay in a shallow greased ovenproof dish. Dot with half the butter and bake for about 15-20 minutes at 375°F until firm. Drain off the juice and make up to a good ⅔ cup with milk. Cover the steaks with foil and keep warm while you make the sauce.

Melt the remaining butter in a pan and stir in the flour. Cook for about 1 minute without allowing it to color. Take the pan off the heat and gradually stir in the milk and fish liquid and white wine. Return the pan to a moderate heat and cook, stirring continuously, until the sauce thickens. Add the mushrooms to the sauce and simmer gently for about 10 minutes. Season to taste, take the sauce off the heat and stir in the cream.

Pour the sauce over the cod steaks and serve garnished with watercress or parsley sprigs.

Baked Flounder with Shrimp and Leek

8×4 defrosted if frozen flounder fillets, skinned

salt and freshly ground black pepper

⅔ cup dry white wine

8oz leeks

¼ cup butter

½ cup shrimp, peeled

salt and pepper

paprika pepper

Preparation time: 20 minutes
Cooking time: 30 minutes

Pre-heat oven to 400°F.

Wash the fish fillets, season and fold into three. Place in a shallow, ovenproof dish and pour the wine over the fish. Cover and bake for 15-20 minutes.

Trim the leeks and cut them in half lengthways and wash thoroughly. Slice very thinly and sauté in the butter until just cooked. Stir in the shrimp and season with salt and pepper.

Pour the wine liquor from the fish into the pan containing the leeks and shrimp. Reheat quickly, check the seasoning and spoon the dressing over the fish. Sprinkle with paprika and serve at once.

Haddock Florentine en Chemise

1lb cod fillets, skinned and cut into 2in pieces

1lb leaf spinach

2 tbspns butter

¼ cup flour

⅔ cup milk

salt and black pepper

puff pastry made with 3 cups flour

1 egg, beaten

Preparation time: 40 minutes
Cooking time: 35-40 minutes

Wash the spinach thoroughly in several changes of water and remove any coarse stalks. Drain the leaves and place in a pan with a pinch of salt and a teaspoon of sugar. Cook for 5-6 minutes until it is just tender. Drain the spinach in a strainer, pressing it with the back of a spoon to remove excess water, and allow to cool.

Melt the butter in a pan, stir in the flour and cook gently for 1 minute. Take the pan off the heat and gradually stir in the milk. Return to the heat and cook until the sauce thickens, stirring continually. Allow the sauce to cool.

Roll out the pastry into a large rectangle and cut it in half to make two smaller rectangles. Preheat the oven to 400°F. Pat the fish dry with kitchen paper and arrange it on one of the pastry rectangles, leaving a ¾in border. Season the fish with salt and pepper and lay the spinach over the top. Then spoon over a coating of white sauce. Brush the border of the pastry with beaten egg and cover with the other pastry rectangle. Fold over the edges and seal by making indentations with a spoon handle. Make 3 or 4 diagonal slashes with a knife across the top and brush with beaten egg. Bake for 25-30 minutes until the pastry has risen and is golden brown. Serve hot with ratatouille (see page 107) and lots of crusty French bread.

Baked Bass with Black Bean Sauce

1 × 3-4lb sea bass, cleaned and descaled but left whole	3 tbspns dry white wine
2 tbspns butter	1-2 parsley sprigs
1 large sheet of foil	black peppercorns
1 teasps lemon juice	**Garnish:** scallion tassels (see page 32); orange slices

Preparation time: 10 minutes
Cooking time: 45 minutes-1 hour

Black Bean Sauce:

1 piece of fresh ginger root (about 2ins square)	1 teasp brown sugar
1 scallion	1 tbspn sherry
1 fat clove garlic	1 tbspn cornstarch
1 tbspn corn oil	⅔ cup chicken stock
1 teasp sesame oil	1-2 tbspns canned salted black beans
1 tbspn soy sauce	

Preparation time: 10 minutes
Cooking time: 10 minutes

To cook the bass: Preheat the oven to 350°F. Wash the fish well inside and out and make sure that any dark blood clots along the spine are removed (these can taste bitter). Pat dry with kitchen paper. Use the butter liberally to grease the sheet of foil, lay it in a large roasting pan and place the fish on it. Fold up the sides of the foil and pour over the lemon juice and wine. Place the parsley sprigs and a few peppercorns in the body cavity. Loosely fold over the foil on top and seal. Make sure that there is plenty of air space around the fish. Bake in the oven, allowing about 15 minutes per lb cooking time.

To prepare the sauce: Mince or very finely chop the ginger, scallion and garlic and fry gently in the oils for 2-3 minutes. Take off the heat and allow to stand. Meanwhile in a bowl mix together the soy sauce, brown sugar, sherry, cornstarch and a little of the stock. Return the pan with the ginger, onion and garlic to the heat and stir in the soy sauce mixture. Add the remaining chicken stock and heat gently until the sauce thickens. Rinse the black beans to remove some of the saltiness and add to the sauce. Simmer very gently for 3-4 minutes.

Put the fish on a large, warmed, serving dish, pour over the sauce and decorate with scallion tassels and orange slices. Serve with boiled rice and Stir-fried Vegetables (see page 114).

Baked Bass with Black Bean Sauce.

Flounder Provençale

8 flounder fillets, skinned

16oz can tomatoes

2 tbspns butter

1 medium onion, peeled and finely chopped

1 garlic clove, crushed

1 wineglass dry white wine

pinch of dried basil

1 teasp sugar

salt and pepper

Garnish: chopped parsley or chopped fresh basil, 1-2 parsley sprigs

Preparation time: 15-20 minutes
Cooking time: 20-25 minutes

Preheat the oven to 350°F. Wash and pat dry the fish fillets and roll them up or, if they are fairly large, fold them in half or into three. Lay them in a greased ovenproof dish and put a small dot of butter on each one.

Push the tomatoes, with the juice, through a strainer to remove the pips. Melt the butter in a pan and gently fry the onion and garlic for 1-2 minutes. Stir in the tomatoes, wine, basil, sugar and salt and pepper to taste. Boil this sauce rapidly for about 10 minutes then pour it round the fish fillets. Bake in the oven for 20-25 minutes or until the fish fillets are cooked through. Serve very hot, straight from the oven, sprinkled with chopped parsley and decorated with an extra sprig or two of parsley.

Serve with boiled new potatoes or Duchesse potatoes (see page 52) and French beans. Alternatively, this dish is also delicious served cold with a crisp, fresh, green salad and crusty bread.
Variation: You can use sole fillets instead of flounder.

Bacon-stuffed Trout with Cucumber Sauce

4 fresh trout, cleaned and washed

melted butter for basting

Stuffing:

½ cup mushrooms

6 bacon slices

¼ cup butter

1 tbspn fresh parsley, chopped

1 tbspn lemon juice

freshly ground black pepper

Cucumber sauce:

½ cucumber, peeled and finely chopped

2 tbspns butter

2 tbspns flour

1 shallot, peeled and finely chopped

1¼ cups milk

salt and pepper

Garnish: parsley or watercress sprigs; lemon wedges

Preparation time: 40-50 minutes
Cooking time: 20 minutes

To prepare the stuffing: Wipe the mushrooms and chop finely. Remove the rinds from the bacon and chop finely. Sauté the mushrooms and bacon in the butter for 5 minutes, remove from the heat and stir in the parsley, lemon juice and pepper.

Bone the fish as shown on page 38 and fill the body cavities with the stuffing. Preheat the oven to 400°F. Lay the stuffed trout on a greased baking sheet and brush with melted butter. Bake for about 20 minutes, until firm.

While the fish is cooking prepare the sauce.

Cook the cucumber in a little salted water until soft, drain and reserve. Melt the butter in a pan, stir in the flour and cook gently for about 1 minute. Take the pan off the heat and gradually stir in the milk. Return to the heat and cook, stirring continuously, until the sauce thickens. Stir in the cucumber and shallot and simmer gently for a further 10 minutes stirring occasionally. Pass the sauce through a strainer or blend until smooth. Reheat, season to taste and serve separately with the stuffed trout.

Butter-fried Trout with Almonds

4 × 8oz trout, cleaned but left whole	½ cup slivered almonds
½ cup butter	**Garnish:** parsley or dill sprigs and lemon slices or twists
¾-1 cup flour seasoned with salt and freshly ground black pepper	

Preparation time: 10 minutes
Cooking time: 10-15 minutes

Wipe the trout inside and out, removing any black blood next to the backbone as this gives a bitter tang to the flesh. Roll the fish in seasoned flour spread on a plate and shake off any excess.

Melt the butter in a large skillet and fry the fish over moderate heat for about 5 or 6 minutes each side or until the skin is crisp and golden and the fish are cooked through. Remove the trout from the pan, place on serving dish and keep warm. Put the almonds in the pan and fry them, turning from time to time, until golden. Add a little extra butter if necessary. Remove the almonds with a slotted spoon and sprinkle over the fish and serve, garnished with parsley and lemon slices or twists.

Old English Witches

1 egg yolk	1 egg white
1 tbspn dry mustard powder	oil for deep frying
1 teasp wine vinegar	**Garnish:** orange slices
salt and freshly ground black pepper	
4 × 8oz witch or flounder fillets, skinned and cut in half lengthways	
seasoned flour for dusting	
4oz cooked ham, sliced	
cocktail sticks	
Coating batter:	
¾ cup flour	
pinch of salt	
1 tbspn oil	
⅔ cup water	

Preparation time: 30 minutes
Cooking time: 20 minutes (total)

Mix together the egg yolk, mustard powder, wine vinegar and salt and pepper into a smooth paste.

Lightly dust the fish fillets with flour and spread one side of each fillet with the paste. Trim the ham slices to the size of the fish and lay a piece on each fillet. Roll up and secure with a cocktail stick.

To prepare the batter: Sift the flour with the salt into a bowl and gradually beat in the oil and water until smooth. Whisk the egg white into stiff peaks and fold into the batter with a metal spoon.

Heat the oil to 375°F or until a square of stale bread turns golden in 1 minute. Dip the rolled fillets into the batter and deep fry for 8-10 minutes until golden brown. Do not try to cook too many witches at once or the oil temperature will drop too low for successful frying. Drain the witches well on kitchen paper and serve immediately garnished with orange wedges and accompanied by a crisp green salad and sautéd potatoes.

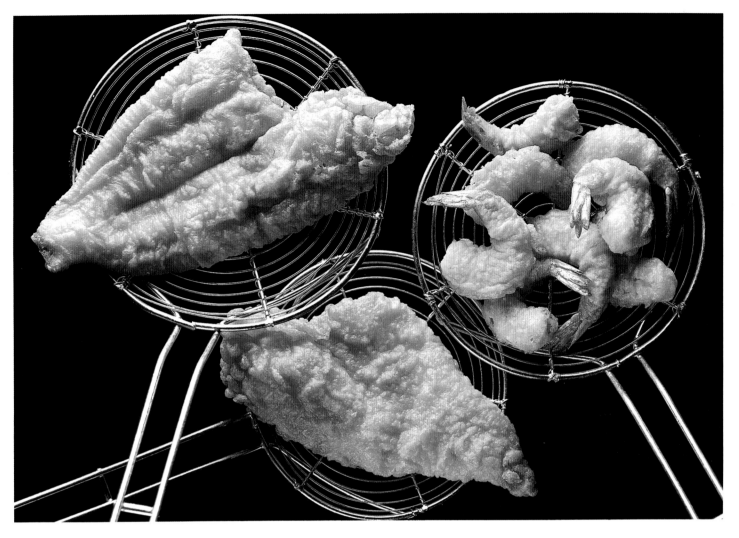

Deep-fried Fish and Shrimp.

Deep-fried Fish

4×6-8oz fillets of white fish; cod, haddock, coley, halibut or flounder	1 large egg
flour seasoned with salt and pepper	⅔ cup milk
oil for deep frying	pinch of salt
Batter:	**Garnish:** lemon wedges
1 cup flour	

Preparation time: batter: 15 minutes plus 30 minutes standing time
Cooking time: 6-10 minutes

To make the batter: sift the flour into a bowl with the salt. Make a well in the center and pour the egg into it. Beat the egg, gradually drawing the flour into it. Add half the milk and beat well until air bubbles rise. Beat in the rest of the milk and allow to stand for 30 minutes.

Rinse the fish fillets and pat dry. Coat the fish pieces in seasoned flour spread on a plate – this will help the batter to coat the fish properly. While you are flouring the fish, heat a pan half-filled with oil to 375°F or until a stale cube of bread turns brown within a minute. Dip a piece of fish into the batter and once it is well coated hold the fish over the bowl to let any surplus run off. Then carefully place the fish into the hot oil and cook for 6-10 minutes, depending on the size of the fish. Repeat with the remaining pieces of fish. Do not cook too many pieces of fish at once, as this will lower the temperature of the oil and give poor results.

Variation: Deep-fried shrimp are succulent and take just 1-2 minutes to cook.

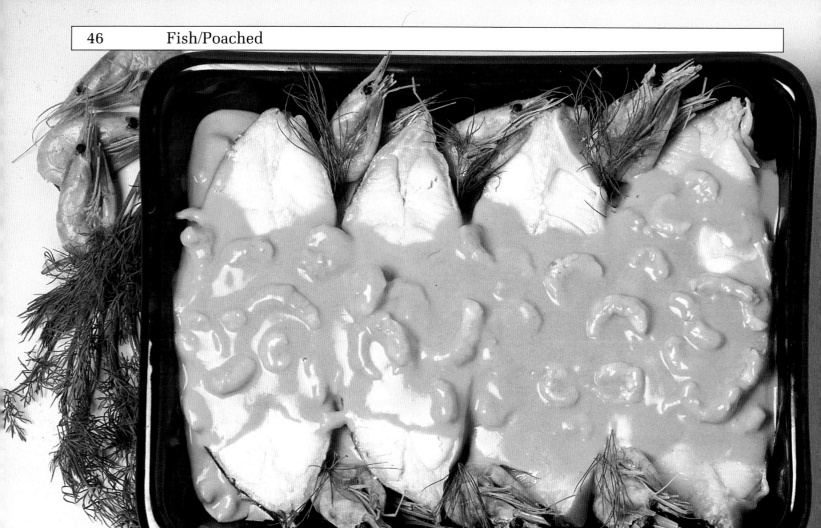

Halibut with Shrimp Sauce.

Poached Halibut with Shrimp Sauce

1½-2lb halibut steaks	⅔ cup milk
1 thick slice of onion	2 tbspns butter
bay leaf	¼ cup flour
black peppercorns	2 teasps tomato catsup
parsley sprig	½ cup peeled shrimps
Shrimp sauce:	**Garnish:** shrimps in the shell, sprigs of dill
1 wineglass dry white wine	

Preparation time: 20 minutes
Cooking time: 30 minutes

Wash the steaks and place in a pan with the onion, bay leaf, a few black peppercorns, parsley sprig and wine. Add just enough cold water to cover the fish and slowly heat until it is almost boiling. Reduce the heat, cover and simmer very gently for 15-20 minutes or until the fish is firm, white and comes away from the bone easily. Lift out the fish on to a warmed serving dish and keep warm.

Pour the milk into a measuring jug and make up to a good 1¼ cups with strained liquor from the fish. Melt the butter in a pan, stir in the flour and cook for about 1 minute. Take the pan off the heat and stir in the liquid then return to the heat and cook, stirring continuously until the sauce thickens. Stir in the catsup and shrimps and cook for a further 5 minutes.

Pour off any additional juice which has collected in the serving dish with the halibut and pour the shrimp sauce over it. Serve garnished with shrimps in the shell and sprigs of dill.

Salmon Trout with Lemon and White Wine

Serves 6-8

1 × 4lb salmon trout or salmon, cleaned but left whole	parsley sprig
1¼ cups white wine	black peppercorns
1¼ cups cold water	**Garnish:** lettuce leaves; watercress; lemon slices; cucumber slices
2 tbspns lemon juice	
celery stalk	

Preparation time: 10 minutes
Cooking time: about 40 minutes

Wash the fish and scrape away any blood lying next to the backbone (this would make the flesh next to it bitter). Lay the fish with the rest of the ingredients in a fish kettle or large pan. If you do not have a pan which is large enough you can use the method for baked bass on page 42.

Cover the pan and slowly heat to just below boiling point. Reduce the heat and poach very gently for about 40 minutes (10 minutes per lb) or until the flesh is cooked through.

To serve hot: Drain the fish, remove the skin and serve garnished with watercress on a warmed dish accompanied by a Hollandaise Sauce (page 125).

To serve cold: prepare and garnish as for Baked Salmon on page 138.

Fish Mousseline with Watercress Sauce

1lb cod, haddock or hake fillets, skinned	**Watercress sauce:**
1 teasp lemon juice	1 bunch fresh watercress
3 medium eggs, separated with two yolks reserved for the sauce	1 shallot, peeled and finely chopped
dash of anchovy essence	¼ cup butter
salt and freshly ground black pepper	2 tbspns flour
pinch of dried dill	1¼ cups milk
1¼ cups heavy cream, whipped	2 tbsps heavy cream
Garnish: watercress sprigs	2 egg yolks (see above)
	salt and black pepper

Preparation time: 40 minutes
Cooking time: 30-35 minutes

To prepare and cook the mousseline: Preheat the oven to 350°F. Remove any bones from the fish and finely mince or chop in a food processor. Place the prepared fish in a bowl and then add the lemon juice, one egg yolk, anchovy essence, dill and seasoning. Beat well until smooth. Stir in the cream. Whisk the egg whites into stiff peaks and fold them carefully into the mixture with a metal spoon. Spoon the mixture into 8 small buttered molds. You can use dariole molds, custard cups or any other suitable small molds. Alternatively you can use one large mold or a baking dish. Cover each mold with a circle of buttered waxed paper and place in a baking tin containing about 1in water. Poach in the oven for about 20 minutes until firm. Meanwhile, make the sauce.

Watercress Sauce: Wash the watercress and remove any coarse stalks and leaves. Reserve a few good sprigs for garnishing. Chop the watercress and shallot and 'sweat' in the butter for 2-3 minutes. Stir in the flour and cook for about 1 minute. Take the pan off the heat and gradually stir in the milk. Return to the heat and cook, stirring continuously until the sauce has thickened. Pour it into an electric blender together with the cream, egg yolk and seasoning and work at high speed for about 1 minute (alternatively you can sieve the sauce and beat in the cream, egg yolk and seasoning). Reheat gently without boiling, or it may curdle.

Once the mousseline is cooked, unmold it on to a warmed serving dish, pour over the watercress sauce and garnish with watercress sprigs.

Mediterranean Fish Stew with Aioli

This Bouillabaisse-style stew is a real feast of a dish to enjoy with friends and family, especially if you like garlic!

2-3 red snapper, cleaned	salt and freshly ground black pepper
1lb cod fillet	⅔ cup white wine
1lb baby squid	1-2 tbspns fresh parsley, chopped
2 tbspns butter	slices of French bread, toasted and dried in the oven
2 carrots, peeled and diced	**Aioli:**
1 large onion, chopped	A simple garlic mayonnaise, ideal for flavoring fish soups and stews and vegetables.
2 celery stalks, diced	3 fat garlic cloves, crushed
2 garlic cloves, chopped	2 egg yolks
3 medium potatoes, diced	⅔ cup olive oil
16oz can tomatoes, chopped	salt to taste
bouquet garni (see page 126)	
bay leaf	
1 teasp sugar	

Preparation time: 40-50 minutes
Cooking time for the fish stew: 40-50 minutes

Cut the heads off the red snapper and fillet them (see photographs and instructions on page 38). Skin the cod fillet and remove any large bones remaining and cut into spoon-sized chunks. Put the snapper heads, bones and the cod skin and trimmings into a pan with 3¾ cups water and bring to the boil. Reduce the heat and simmer for about ¾ hour.

To clean the squid, gently pull away the heads from the bodies and cut off the tentacles just below the eyes. Turn the bodies inside out and wash away any membranes or roe under running water. Cut the bodies into rings. Store all the raw fish and squid in covered bowls in the refrigerator.

Next, melt the butter in a large pan and sauté the vegetables for about 5 minutes. Add the canned tomatoes with their juice, the bouquet garni and bay leaf, sugar, salt and black pepper. Pour in the wine, strained fish stock and add the prepared squid.

Bring to the boil then reduce the heat and simmer for about 20 minutes. All this preparation can be done well in advance. About an hour before serving pour the contents of the pan into a large pre-heated ovenproof casserole such as a marmite. Heat the stewed vegetables and squid through, add the cod chunks and cook for a further 15-20 minutes.

About 15 minutes before serving, check the seasoning and lay the snapper fillets on the top of the stew to poach. Just before serving stir in the chopped parsley.

To prepare the Aioli: Put the crushed garlic in a bowl with a little salt. Add the egg yolks and beat thoroughly. Beat the olive oil slowly and gradually into the mixture until you have a thick creamy mayonnaise. Taste and add more salt if necessary.

To serve the fish stew with aioli: place 2-3 slices of toasted French bread in warmed bowls and spoon the aioli generously on to the bread. The stew is then ladled on to the bread and aioli, ensuring that each person has a snapper fillet. Serve a side salad with this dish and warm, crusty, French bread.

Lobster

Buying lobsters

The size of a lobster varies from about 1lb up to as much as 10lb. For 4 people, 2×1lb or one 2lb lobster will suffice. Lobsters are often sold ready-cooked but you have no way of knowing how fresh they are or, indeed, whether they have been frozen, a process which detracts considerably from their texture and flavor, making them rather dry. The best way to buy lobster is to order a live one. If you cannot bear the thought of killing it by boiling, you can ask the shop to kill it for you, provided that you are able to take it home *immediately* and cook it.

Boiling and dressing lobster

Fill a large pan with enough water to cover the lobster, add 3 slices of onion, a glass of dry white wine, a tablespoon spoon of lemon juice, a bay leaf and salt to taste. Bring this simple court bouillon to the boil and add the lobster. Boil a 1lb lobster for 15-20 minutes; 1½-2lb lobster for 20-30 minutes. When cooked, lift it out and allow it to cool.

When the lobster is cold, twist off the claws and legs and lay the body down with the back uppermost. Using a sharp knife, split the lobster in half lengthways from head to tail. Remove the black intestinal vein, the stomach sac (which is in the head) and the gills. Keep any orange roe or 'coral' if present and the greeny liver known as tomalley, as these are considered to be delicacies.

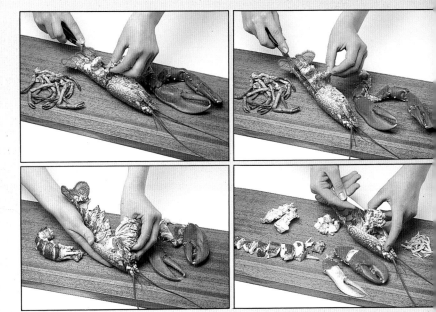

Crack the claws and legs and remove the meat. If you are serving lobster mayonnaise, lift the tail meat out of the half-shells and slice into fork-sized pieces and arrange in the opposite half of the shell upside down. Pile the claw meat into the head, arrange the shells on a serving dish garnished with salad and hand mayonnaise separately. Alternatively, once the meat is arranged in the shell, brush it with melted butter and broil it for about 5 minutes. Serve with more melted butter.

Lobster a l'Americaine

1×2lb lobster, prepared as above	1 wineglass dry white wine
3 large, ripe tomatoes	1 tbspn chopped fresh parsley
3 tbspns clarified butter	1 teasp sugar
1 small onion, peeled and finely chopped	salt and freshly ground black pepper
pinch of dried basil	1 tbspn brandy

Preparation time: 15-20 minutes
Cooking time: 15 minutes

Soak the tomatoes in boiling water for 2-3 minutes, drain and peel. Cut into quarters, remove the cores and strain to remove the pips but save the juice. Chop the flesh finely. Heat 2 tbspns of the clarified butter in a skillet and sauté the onion for 3-4 minutes. Add the tomato flesh and juice, basil, parsley, white wine, sugar and seasoning and simmer until reduced to a sauce-like consistency. If the coral and liver are available, push them through a strainer and add to the sauce. Stir in the chopped parsley and keep warm.

Pour the remaining butter into a small skillet and sauté the prepared lobster for 2 minutes. Pour the brandy into a large, hot metal spoon, set alight and pour over the lobster. Stir-fry for another minute then transfer the lobster on to a warmed serving dish. Spoon over the sauce and serve immediately.

Crab

To dress crab

1 Twist off the claws and legs. Remove the body by knocking the edge of the shell sharply on a board. Press the underside of the shell outwards to free the body.

2 Discard the stomach sac from behind the body together with the greyish gills (dead man's fingers). Cut the body into 4 and remove the meat with a skewer.

3 Use a teaspoon to scoop out the brown meat from inside the shell. Crack the claws and legs to remove the white meat.

Crab mayonnaise

Place the white meat from the body and claws in a bowl and pick it over to ensure that there are no shell fragments mixed in. In a separate bowl, cream the brown meat with half a teaspoon of mustard powder, a dash of Worcestershire sauce, salt and pepper and a spoon or two of dry breadcrumbs.

Taking the top shell of the crab, break off the pieces of under-shell, which is divided naturally into sections, and thoroughly scrub and dry the shell. Pile up the white meat on each side in the shell and spoon the brown meat down the center. Strain the yolk of a hard-boiled egg over the brown meat and sprinkle with chopped fresh parsley.

Crab Soufflé

This makes an extra-special starter for 4 people or a gourmet supper dish for 2 with a salad.

2 tbspns butter	4 large, fresh eggs
2 tbspns flour	¾-1 cup prepared crabmeat
⅔ cup milk	1 tbspn chopped fresh parsley
1 teasp dry mustard powder	1 tbspn heavy cream
1 dash Worcestershire sauce	

Preparation time: 20 minutes
Cooking time: 20 minutes

Preheat the oven to 400°F.

Melt the butter in a pan and stir in the flour. Cook gently for about a minute and take off the heat. Stir in the milk and mix well. Return to moderate heat and cook, stirring continuously until the sauce thickens. Add the mustard powder and Worcestershire sauce. Take the sauce off the heat and allow to cool slightly.

Separate the eggs and beat the yolks into the sauce. Stir in the crabmeat, parsley and cream and pour into a large bowl. Butter the inside of a 2½-3¾ cup soufflé dish and set aside.

Whisk the egg whites by hand with a wire whisk until they form a firm snowy bulk but are not dry-looking (ie do not over-whisk). Stir a spoonful of egg white into the sauce to soften it and then fold and cut the rest in quickly with a palette knife, turning the sauce over the whites so that they become part of the mixture but still keep their lightness and bulk. Do not overmix. Now turn the soufflé mixture into the buttered dish and bake for about 20 minutes in the middle of the oven until the soufflé has risen and the outside is firm to the touch while the center remains creamy. Serve immediately.

Fried Jumbo Shrimp with Garlic and Ginger

Serve this Peking-style shrimp dish as an exciting starter or part of a main course with other Chinese dishes.

1 piece fresh root ginger (1in), sliced	8 raw jumbo or Pacific shrimp
2 tbspns soy sauce	2-3 tbspns oil
1 tbspn sherry	1-2 garlic cloves, finely chopped
1 teasp brown sugar	1 scallion, finely chopped

Preparation time: 10 minutes
Cooking time: about 10 minutes

Wash the shrimp and trim off the whiskers. Drain and pat dry with kitchen paper.

Heat the oil in a heavy skillet — a black cast-iron pan is good for this as it makes a dramatic serving dish. Stir in the garlic, scallion and ginger and stir-fry for 1 minute. Add the shrimp (unshelled) and fry them for 3-4 minutes over moderate heat. Stir in the soy sauce, sherry and brown sugar and cook for another 2 minutes. Serve straight from the pan.

Coquilles St Jacques Mornay

A classic dish of tender scallops simmered gently in an aromatic court-bouillon and served in a creamy cheese sauce on the shells in nests of Duchesse potatoes.

8-12 large scallops, prepared but with four deep shells reserved	⅔ cup milk
1 wineglass dry white wine	¼ cup Parmesan cheese, grated
1 teasp lemon juice	½ cup Gruyère cheese, grated
1 bay leaf	2 tbspns heavy cream
1 sprig parsley	**Duchesse potatoes:**
black peppercorns	¾lb potatoes, boiled
2 tbspns butter	1 egg yolk, seasoning and milk
1¼ cup flour	**Garnish:** parsley sprigs

Preparation time: 20 minutes
Cooking time: 20-30 minutes

Wash the scallops, removing any grit, and put them (with the orange roe or 'coral') in a pan with the wine, lemon juice, bay leaf, parsley and peppercorns. Poach *very gently* without boiling for about 10 minutes or until the scallops are firm but still tender to slice. Do not overcook or they will toughen and shrink.

Strain off the poaching liquid and reserve. Slice the scallops into fork-sized pieces and divide them among the four deep shells.

To make the sauce: melt the butter in a pan and stir in the flour. Cook for 1 minute and take the pan off the heat. Pour in the poaching liquid and the milk and return to the heat, stirring continuously until the sauce has thickened. Stir in the Parmesan and half of the Gruyère cheese and cook until it has melted. Take the pan off the heat and stir in the cream. Thin the sauce with a little extra milk if necessary to make a good covering consistency.

Mash the potatoes, and add the egg yolk and sufficient milk to moisten. Using a large piping bag with a star nozzle, pipe the potato round the rims of the shells. Spoon the warm sauce over the scallops, sprinkle with the remaining cheese and place the filled shells under a fairly hot broiler until the sauce begins to bubble and the top is nicely browned. Serve at once garnished with parsley sprigs.

Serve as a light main course accompanied by a side salad and crusty bread or allow one scallop per person and 2-3oz of sliced mushrooms added to the sauce for a starter.

Breaded Clams.

Moules Marinière

This classic dish may be lengthy to prepare but it is very quick to cook and the taste of the succulent shellfish cooked in white wine is reward enough for your labors.

4 pints of mussels in the shell
2 tbspns butter
1 shallot, finely chopped
1 garlic clove, crushed
⅔ cup dry white wine
salt and freshly ground black pepper
2 tbspns fresh parsley, chopped

Preparation time: 35-45 minutes
Cooking time: 10 minutes

Prepare the mussels as described on page 18. Melt the butter in a large saucepan and cook the onion and garlic for 2-3 minutes over fairly gentle heat. Add the wine, ⅔ cup of water, and seasoning and bring to the boil. Put the mussels in the pan all at once and cook over high heat, covered. Shake the pan from time to time to ensure that the mussels cook evenly. When all the mussels have opened (it takes about 5 minutes) use a slotted spoon to transfer them into a warmed, deep serving dish or into 4 large bowls. Discard any shells that have not opened. Boil the liquid left in the pan with the parsley for a minute or two and pour it over the mussels. Avoid pouring out the last spoonful as it may contain grit from inside the mussel shells.

Serve immediately accompanied by lots of crusty French bread.

Breaded Clams

36 medium-sized hard-shelled clams, shelled	oil for deep fat frying
seasoned flour for dusting	1 lettuce, washed
2 eggs, beaten	**Garnish:** lemon slices, tomato wedges, parsley sprigs
1-2 cups fresh breadcrumbs	

Preparation time: 15 minutes
Cooking time: 15-20 minutes

Dust the clams in the seasoned flour. Then dip them in the beaten eggs and coat in the breadcrumbs.

Half-fill a deep skillet with oil and heat it to 375°F or until a square of stale bread turns golden in about 1 minute. Cook the clams in 3-4 batches (otherwise the temperature of the oil will drop too low) until they are light golden brown. Drain each batch on kitchen paper and keep warm. When all the clams are cooked, check the temperature of the oil again and return the clams to the deep-fryer for 1-2 minutes to crisp up.

Serve immediately as an appetizer on a bed of lettuce leaves garnished with lemon slices, tomato wedges and parsley sprigs.

SAVORY PIES AND PASTRIES

So many people say 'Oh I can't make pastry' and tend to resort to the ready-made frozen pastries for all their flans, tarts and pies. Certainly many of the modern commercially made pastries are very good for most baking purposes but it is very satisfying to be able to make your own and it always tastes that little bit better, especially if you use some butter in your mixture. If time is your problem you can make up a double or treble quantity of dough and freeze it – most types of pastry freeze well.

Tips for pastry-making
Basically, practice makes perfect when it comes to pastry-making, but there are certain general rules which, if you stick to them, should give you good results. Use the exact proportions of ingredients specified in the recipe. Always make sure that the kitchen, utensils and ingredients are cool – avoid using runny fats and lukewarm water. Also, speed is the essence of good pastry-making (this is where plenty of practice helps). Handle the ingredients and dough as little as possible as over-working makes pastry hard. Do not carry on rubbing in for longer than necessary as it may make the pastry greasy.

Be careful not to add too much water to the mixture – if it becomes wet it will be sticky to roll out and will probably shrink quite a lot during cooking. If, however, the pastry is too dry, it will be crumbly and awkward to handle and may crack. Don't forget to allow time for the pastry to 'rest' in a cool place before using it. When rolling out it is a good idea to do it directly on to your laminated work surface (if your style of kitchen has one), as this is cooler than a wooden board; it must be spotlessly clean of course. Finally, make sure you remember to preheat the oven before baking. *Bon chance!*

Lining a flan ring or case
Flans are usually baked in flan rings placed on baking trays, shallow sandwich tins, or deeper porcelain flan cases (often fluted).

Roll out the pastry in an approximate circle (about ⅛in in thickness) and check the size by placing the ring or case over the top. You should make sure that the pastry circle is about 2in wider than the ring or case. Lift the pastry by laying it over the rolling pin and lower it into a greased case. Gently push the pastry down into the shape of the case with your fingers, being careful not to handle the pastry too much or stretch it. Once the pastry is in position, without any air pockets present between the sides of the case or ring and the pastry, hold the surplus pastry upwards and trim it off evenly with a knife or a pair of scissors ⅛in higher than the case, using your other hand for support. This little extra height will allow for any shrinkage. If using a fluted case, make sure that you press the pastry into the ridges and trim off surplus by rolling over the top with the rolling pin. Prick the inner surface lightly with a fork.

Blind baking
Often pastry cases need to be 'baked blind' or empty so that they are partially or fully cooked before the filling is put in. This is particularly so for sweet dessert flans and tarts.

When baking an unfilled case you need to stop the pastry rising so that the case keeps its shape. There are two ways of doing this. The first method is to prick the inside of the pastry lining all over with a fork and then bake for about 10 minutes in a fairly hot oven (400°F). The second method is to cut out a circle of foil or waxed paper roughly the size of the pastry lining, lay this in the flan case and weight it with dried beans such as haricots. Bake the flan in a moderately hot oven (375-400°F) for 10-15 minutes. Pastry cases baked blind for quiches and savory tarts should not be cooked for too long – they should be pale gold in color because they will brown further when they are baked with the filling.

Flaky Pastry

Makes 8oz

| 2 cups flour |
| pinch of salt |
| ⅓ cup butter |
| ⅓ cup shortening |
| iced water to mix |

Preparation time: 35 minutes plus 45 minutes resting time for the pastry

Sift the flour and salt into a bowl. Divide the butter and lard each into two halves so that you have 4 portions of fat. Take one portion of butter and rub it into the flour. Then mix in enough water to make a soft dough (about 4-5 tbspns).

On a lightly floured surface, roll out the dough into a neat rectangle. Soften a portion of the shortening with a palette knife and use it to dot ⅔ of the surface of the pastry, leaving the remaining third bare. Fold this bare ⅓ over half the buttered pastry and fold up the other third over the top so that the pastry is then in three folded layers. Turn an open end towards you, seal both ends with the rolling pin and roll out into another rectangle. Using the last portion of butter, again dot ⅔ of the pastry. Fold over the sides to make three layers as before, and seal the ends. Rest in a cool place wrapped in plastic wrap or in a plastic bag for 15 minutes.

Roll out the pastry again into a rectangle and use the lard (shortening), the last portion of fat, to dot the pastry and repeat the folding and sealing. Wrap the pastry and rest for a further 30 minutes in a cool place. The pastry is then ready for use.

Rough Puff Pastry

This is a good alternative to flaky pastry which can be made when time is short by using the same ingredients as given above. Cut the fat into small (approximately ¾in) pieces and mix with the sieved flour and salt. Stir in enough cold water to make a stiff dough. Roll out the dough on a floured board into a rectangle and fold into three layers, seal and rest as for the Flaky Pastry method given above. The rolling and folding process should be carried out a total of 4 times. Rest in a cool place for another 30 minutes and the pastry is ready for use.

Note: Flaky and rough puff pastry should be cooked at an oven temperature of 425°F.

Savory Shortcrust Pastry

Weights and proportions
Generally in shortcrust pastry, the proportions used are half the quantity of fat to flour. The recipe given is for 2 cups of pastry but if you need a smaller or larger quantity simply adjust the proportions, i.e. for 1½ cups of pastry you will need 1½ cups flour to ⅜ cup fat. The amount of fat can be increased in some cases to give a richer pastry.
Reminder: Unless otherwise stated, the flour used in recipes throughout this book is all-purpose flour.

| 2 cups flour |
| pinch of salt |
| ¼ cup butter |
| ¼ cup vegetable fat, or shortening |
| iced water (about 3-4 tbspns) |

Preparation time: 15 minutes

Sift the flour with the salt into a mixing bowl. Cut the fat into small pieces and add to the flour. Rub the fat into the flour by picking up flour and fat with just the tips of your fingers and rubbing your thumb across your finger tips so that tiny portions of the fat are coated by the flour. Keep on repeating this until all the fat is rubbed in. The fat/flour mixture should look rather like fine breadcrumbs, which cling together when pressed between fingers and thumb. It is important to use only the tips of your fingers as the mixture should be kept as cold as possible. Shake the bowl from time to time to bring any bigger lumps to the top of the mixture.

When the rubbing-in is completed, add about 3 tablespoons of iced water, cutting it into the 'crumbs' with a palette knife. If the mixture remains crumbly, add a little more water. When the dough begins to leave the sides of the bowl, you should then be able to form a soft ball of dough. Do not knead it or handle it overmuch. Wrap it in plastic wrap and chill it for 30 minutes, and then roll out as required.
Variations: for a richer, savory shortcrust pastry add an egg yolk beaten with about 2 teaspoons of cold water to the crumb mixture.

Shortcrust pastry for sweet pies, flans and tarts
Follow the recipe above but add 2 tbspns superfine sugar to the 'breadcrumb' stage and stir in a beaten egg instead of the water. Follow the rest of the method given.

Smoked Salmon Flan

shortcrust pastry made with 1½ cups flour (see page 55)	2 teasps lemon juice
	freshly ground black pepper
2 large eggs	½ cup smoked salmon pieces
⅔ cup light cream	pinch of nutmeg
2 tbspns milk	

Preparation time: 15 minutes (plus 45 minutes extra for making and chilling the pastry
Cooking time: 30-40 minutes

Preheat the oven to 375°F.

Roll out the pastry and use it to line a 8-9in flan case or ring. Whisk the eggs in a bowl and stir in the cream, milk, lemon juice and black pepper. Trim any bones or skin from the smoked salmon and cut into small pieces. Spread the fish out on the pastry base and pour over the egg mixture. Sprinkle the top with nutmeg and bake for about 30-40 minutes or until the filling has set and the top is an attractive golden brown. The flan is equally good served hot or cold.

Variations using the same pastry base:

Spinach tart: Cover the pastry base evenly with 1lb leaf spinach cooked with salt and 1 teasp sugar, pressed in a strainer and chopped finely. Pour over a mixture of ¾ cup cream cheese beaten with 2tbspns creamy milk or light cream and added to 2 beaten eggs. Season to taste. Bake for 30-40 minutes in a moderately hot oven (375°F) until the pastry is golden and the filling is set.

Alsace creamy onion tart: Cook 1lb sliced onions gently in ¼ cup of butter until pale gold (20-30 minutes). Spread evenly over the pastry case. Beat 2 large eggs with 1¼ cups heavy cream and season to taste. Pour over the onions and sprinkle with grated nutmeg and bake in a moderately hot oven (400°F) for 30-40 minutes until the filling is firm to the touch and the pastry is golden.

Tuna and Leek Quiche.

Egg and Bacon Tartlets

Perfect bite-sized tarts to accompany cocktails and also popular at children's parties and picnics. Makes about 36 tartlets.

savory shortcrust pastry made with 3 cups flour (see page 55)

4oz bacon slices, with rinds removed

1 small onion or shallot, peeled

2 tbspns butter

3 eggs

⅔ cup heavy cream

pinch of dried thyme

salt and pepper

Preparation time: 20 minutes plus an extra 45 minutes for making and chilling the pastry
Cooking time: 20-30 minutes

Roll out the pastry thinly and cut out circles with a fluted pastry-cutter (3-3½in in diameter). Prick them all over with a fork and use them to line greased tartlet or patty tins. bake at 400°F for about 7-10 minutes until firm but not brown. Leave to cool slightly.

Mince or finely chop the bacon and onion and cook gently in the butter for 3-4 minutes. Beat the eggs with the cream, add the thyme and seasoning and stir in the bacon and onion. Spoon this filling into the tartlet cases and bake for about 20 minutes or until the pastry is golden and the filling has set and is beginning to brown on top.

Tuna and Leek Quiche

Serves 4-6

savory shortcrust pastry made with 2 cups flour (see page 55)

2 tbspns butter

8oz leeks, trimmed, well washed and thinly sliced

3 eggs

1¼ cups milk

1 teasp mustard powder

salt and freshly ground black pepper

½ cup Cheddar cheese, grated

7oz can tuna fish in brine, drained and flaked

Preparation time: 25 minutes plus 45 minutes extra for making and chilling the pastry
Cooking time: 50 minutes

Roll out the pastry on a lightly floured surface and use it to line a 10in fluted flan tin. Bake blind for 15 minutes in a moderately hot oven (400°F).

Meanwhile, melt the butter and gently fry the leeks until just soft. Whisk together the eggs, milk, seasonings and cheese. Arrange the leeks and flaked tuna fish in the flan case. Pour the egg mixture carefully on top then bake in the oven for about 30 minutes until the filling is firm and golden. Serve warm or cold.

Fish Jalousie

1½ tbsps butter	1 teasp tomato paste
1½ tbsps flour	rough puff pastry made with 3 cups flour (see page 55)
⅔ cup milk	beaten egg to glaze
1 small onion, peeled and finely chopped	**Garnish:** lemon and cucumber slices
8oz cooked white fish, flaked	

Preparation time: 25 minutes
Cooking time: about 30 minutes

Melt the butter, stir in the flour and cook gently for about a minute. Remove the saucepan from the heat and stir in the milk, return to the heat and cook over moderate heat, stirring continuously until the sauce thickens. Season the sauce and stir in the cooked flaked fish, onion and the tomato paste. Cover this mixture and put aside to cool.

Preheat the oven to 450°F. Halve the pastry and roll out the halves to form two rectangles. Place one rectangle on a greased baking sheet and spread with the cooled fish mixture, leaving a small border around the edge of the pastry. Taking the second rectangle, fold this piece of pastry in half lengthways and make a series of diagonal cuts down the folded edge to within about ½in of the cut edge so that when the pastry is unfolded there is a herringbone pattern down the center. Brush lightly with egg around the edge and lay the pastry over the fish mixture, sealing the two pastry edges. Knock up the edges of the pastry parcel with a knife and glaze with beaten egg. Bake for about 30 minutes until the pastry has risen and is golden brown.

Shrimp Puff Pastries

These small pastries are ideal for a buffet as they can be kept warm until needed. The ingredients make approximately 12 pastries.

8oz boneless haddock or cod fillets, skinned	1 teasp onion, finely chopped
2 tbspns butter	1 tbspn chopped parsley
1 tbspn oil	salt and pepper
2 tbspns flour	2 hard-boiled eggs, chopped
⅔ cup milk	rough puff pastry or flaky pastry made with 3 cups flour (see page 55)
⅔ cup light cream	
1½ cups frozen shelled shrimp, defrosted	1 egg, beaten

Preparation time: 40 minutes (plus 45 minutes extra for making pastry)
Cooking time: about 50 minutes

Place the fish fillets in a saucepan, cover with water and poach gently for 15 minutes. Skin and flake the fish and set aside. Heat the butter and oil in a saucepan and stir in the flour. When it begins to bubble, remove from the heat and gradually add the milk, stirring briskly. When all the milk has been added, return to the heat and cook, continuing to stir until the sauce thickens. Stir in the cream, flaked fish, shrimp, onion, parsley and seasoning. Cook over very low heat for 10 minutes. Add the eggs and allow the mixture to cool.

Preheat the oven to 400°F. Roll out the pastry fairly thinly and cut into circles measuring about 5-6in across. Spoon the shrimp mixture on to the pastry circles and brush milk round the edges. Fold the pastry across the filling and seal the edges by crimping with a spoon handle. Cut two small slits across the top and paint with beaten egg to glaze. Bake for about 25-30 minutes until the pastries are golden brown. Serve warm.

Fish Jalousie.

Chicken and Mushroom Patties

1½lb fresh chicken joints	1½ tbspn cornstarch
sprig of parsley	pinch dried mixed herbs
slice of onion	¼ cup milk
bay leaf	salt and pepper
1 cup button mushrooms, sliced	savory shortcrust pastry made with 3 cups flour (see page 55)
1-2 slices of bacon with rind removed, chopped	
1 tbspn butter	
1 small onion, peeled and chopped	

Preparation time: 40 minutes (plus extra 45 minutes for making and chilling pastry)
Cooking time: boiling time 30-35 minutes; baking time 25-30 minutes

Wash the chicken joints and trim off any fat. Place in a saucepan with the parsley, onion and bay leaf and add water to cover. Bring to the boil and remove any froth with a slotted spoon. Cover and reduce the heat. Simmer for about 30 minutes or until the chicken is tender and comes off the bone easily. Remove from the stock and allow to cool. Reserve the stock for making the sauce.

Gently sauté the mushrooms and bacon in the butter with the onion, without coloring. Strain off 1¼ cups of the stock and use a little to mix with the cornstarch in a cup. Pour this into the pan with the mushrooms and onion and add the milk and the remaining stock. Stir well over moderate heat until the sauce has thickened. Add the mixed herbs and cook gently for 4-5 minutes. While this is cooking cut the chicken off the bone into fork-sized pieces. Add the chicken to the sauce and season to taste. Allow the mixture to cool.

Preheat the oven to 400°F. Roll out the pastry to about ⅛in thick and use to line, and make lids for, 4 individual pie or patty tins. Divide the filling between the 4 pies and cover each one with a lid and pinch the edges together to seal. Make 2 small slashes in the top to let out steam and brush the tops with beaten egg. Bake for about 25-30 minutes until the tops are an appetizing golden brown.

Bacon and Apple Roll

Filling:	Pastry:
12oz bacon, with rind removed and chopped	2 cups self-rising flour
1 large onion, peeled and chopped	pinch of salt
2 tbspns butter	⅞ cup ground suet
1 large cooking apple, peeled, cored and grated	iced water to mix
1 teasp soft brown sugar	beaten egg to glaze
freshly ground black pepper	

Preparation time: 40 minutes
Cooking time: 45 minutes

Prepare the filling by cooking the bacon and onion together in the butter for about 10 minutes. Remove from the heat and add the apple, sugar and pepper. Leave to cool. Preheat the oven to 375°F.

To make the pastry, sift together flour and salt and add the suet. Mix together and add enough water to give a stiff dough. Knead lightly on a floured work-surface and roll out to give a rectangle measuring 10in×8in. Spread the cold filling over the pastry leaving a 1in border. Brush the border with beaten egg and roll up like a swiss roll.

Place the roll with the join hidden on the underside onto a greased baking sheet and brush with egg. Bake for 30 minutes until golden.

Lamb and Vegetable Pasties

Equally good either hot or cold, these satisfying savory pastries are useful for family suppers, picnics or packed lunches.

8-12oz lamb (boned chops, shoulder, leg or fillet)	pinch of mixed herbs
4oz potatoes, peeled and finely chopped	salt and pepper
1 large carrot, peeled and finely chopped	2-3 tbspns stock
1 small onion, peeled and finely chopped	savory shortcrust pastry made with 3 cups flour (see page 55)
2 tbspns butter	1 egg, beaten

Preparation time: 40 minutes plus 45 minutes extra for making pastry and chilling
Cooking time: 35 minutes

Cut off any fat from the lamb, slice the meat into little slivers and set aside. Cook the vegetables gently, stir-frying, in the butter until softened (about 5-6 minutes). Take the pan off the heat and allow the vegetables to cool. Mix in the meat, herbs, salt and a generous amount of freshly ground black papper. Moisten the mixture with a little stock.

Preheat the oven to 425°F. Roll out the pastry and, using a saucer or small plate as a guide, cut out 4 circles (approximately 7in across). Divide the filling between the pastry circles, spooning it into the centers. Brush beaten egg round the edges of the pastry circles and lift 2 sides up over the filling and seal them together, crimping the edges with a spoon handle. Brush each pastry all over with beaten egg and bake for 10 minutes. Turn the oven down to 375°F and bake for a further 25-30 minutes.

Variation: Use sliced or ground beef steak instead of lamb; include 2-3oz rutabega instead of the carrot. Alternatively you could omit the meat entirely and make an all-vegetable pasty.

Bacon and Apple Roll.

Turkey and Ham Pie

Serves 3-4

1 tbspn butter	pinch of dried thyme
1 tbspn flour	freshly ground black pepper and salt
⅔ cup turkey or chicken stock	savory shortcrust pastry made with 2 cups flour (see page 55)
1 cup cooked turkey, minced	
½ cup cooked ham, minced	beaten egg for glazing
1 small onion, peeled and minced or finely chopped	

Preparation time: 30 minutes plus 45 minutes extra for making and chilling pastry
Cooking time: 40-45 minutes

Melt the butter in a pan and stir in the flour. Cook for a few moments and take off the heat. Stir in the stock, return to the heat and cook, stirring continuously, until the sauce thickens. Add the turkey, ham, onion, thyme, black pepper and very little salt (depending on the saltiness of the ham). Cook over gentle heat for 6 or 7 minutes. Take off the heat and allow to cool.

Preheat the oven to 400°F. Cut the pastry into equal halves. Roll out one piece fairly thinly and use to line a 8in shallow pie plate. Roll out the second piece and cut out a lid, brushing the edge with beaten egg or milk. Spoon the filling into the pie base and cover with the pastry lid. Seal the edges decoratively and top with pastry leaves or twists. Brush with beaten egg to glaze and make 2-3 small slashes in the top to let steam escape. Bake for 30-35 minutes until the pie is golden. This freezes well, so make a big batch as a standby.

Beef and Oyster Pie

2lb stewing beef, chuck steak or braising steak cut into 1½in squares	2 cups beef stock
	bouquet garni (see page 126)
2 tbsps oil	salt and freshly ground black pepper
1 large onion, peeled and chopped	4½ oz can of smoked oysters
1 large carrot, peeled and chopped	flaky or rough puff pastry made with 2 cups flour (see page 55)
2 slices bacon, with rinds removed, diced	
1 tbspn flour	beaten egg for glazing

Preparation time: 35 minutes
Cooking time: 1½-1¾ hours plus 30 minutes for making pastry

Heat the oil in a heavy, ovenproof pan and brown the beef quickly over high heat. Remove the meat with a slotted spoon and set aside. Brown the vegetables and bacon in the pan used for the beef, adding a little more oil if necessary. Stir in the flour, cook and add the stock, stirring until the sauce thickens. Return the beef to the pan and add the bouquet garni, pepper and a little salt (the bacon will probably be salty so taste first).

Cook in a low oven (300-325°F) for 1½-1¾ hours or until the meat is tender. If you prefer a thicker sauce, drain off the meat juice and cook it briskly over high heat until it reduces.

Raise the oven temperature to 400°F. Roll out the pastry and use a 3¾ cup capacity pie dish to mark out the pastry lid. From the trimmings cut a strip long enough to make a double rim. Put a pie funnel into the dish (this stops the pastry sinking into the filling and also allows the steam to escape and prevents the pastry from going soggy). If you have no pie funnel you can use a china egg-cup upside down and put a couple of slashes across the pastry top. Spoon in the filling. Slice the oysters into 2 or 3 pieces and scatter evenly over the filling. Dampen the edge of the pie dish and cover with the pastry rim. Brush the pastry rim with beaten egg and cover with the lid. Pinch the pie rim firmly to make a decorative edge. Brush the lid with egg and bake for 30 minutes until the pastry has risen and is golden brown.

Lamb Cutlets en Croute

Delectable pastry parcels containing tender lamb cutlets spread with a savory duxelles of mushrooms – truly a pastry dish to impress.

8 even-sized lamb cutlets	pinch dried thyme
oil for grilling	black pepper
1 cup button mushrooms	flaky or rough puff pastry made with 3 cups flour (see page 55)
1 small onion, peeled	
2-3 slices bacon, with rinds removed	1 egg, beaten
2 tbspns butter	

Preparation time: 45 minutes
Cooking time: 10 minutes plus 15-20 minutes baking time

Trim the cutlets, removing bone splinters and any excess fat. Leave about ¾in of the end of the bone bare of meat. Brush the cutlets with oil and broil for 3-4 minutes (depending on thickness) each side. Allow to cool.

Wipe the mushrooms and chop finely. Mince or finely chop the onion and bacon. Melt the butter in a pan and sauté the mushrooms, onion and bacon gently for about 5 minutes with the thyme and black pepper. If there is quite a lot of juice present in the pan, heat slowly for a little longer to reduce the liquid. Allow the mixture to cool slightly then press equal amounts on top of the cutlets.

Preheat the oven to 400°F. Roll out the pastry into a rectangle and cut into 8 equal pieces. Roll out each piece into thin rectangles (⅛in) thick and trim each one roughly into an oval shape. Place a cutlet on one half of each oval, paint round the pastry edges with beaten egg and fold the other half over the top. Seal the edge, making folds and tucks as necessary, leaving the bone end out of the parcel. Repeat with all the other chops. Using the trimmings, roll out the remaining pastry and cut out decorative leaf shapes. Stick these on each parcel with beaten egg and paint the whole of the visible part of the parcels with the remainder of the egg.

Transfer the pastries to a greased baking sheet and bake for about 15 minutes or until the pastry has risen and is golden brown.

Lamb Cutlets en Croute.

Burgundy Beef

1½-2lb stewing beef or chuck steak	1¼ cups red wine
2 slices bacon, with rinds removed and chopped	16oz can tomatoes
2 tbspns oil	¾ cups water
8oz carrots, peeled and sliced	bouquet garni (see page 126)
1 large onion, peeled and sliced	1 teasp sugar
1 fat garlic clove, crushed	salt and freshly ground black pepper
1 celery stalk, trimmed and chopped	**Garnish:** Crisp triangles of fried bread
1 tbspn flour	

Preparation time: 25 minutes
Cooking time: 2-2¼ hours

Trim any fat or gristle from the beef and cut into cubes. Brown the beef and bacon quickly in the oil over fairly high heat. Remove from the pan and place in a casserole. Fry the vegetables in the pan for 2-3 minutes, adding more oil if needed, and transfer to the casserole. Stir the flour into the pan juices and cook for a few moments. Add the red wine, stir until it thickens then add this liquid to the casserole. Coarsely chop the tomatoes and add them to the meat and vegetables with their juice. Add the rest of the ingredients and cook at 325°F for 1¾-2 hours. Serve with triangles of fried bread.

New England Boiled Dinner.

Country Beef Casserole

Serves 4-6

2lb stewing beef or chuck steak	2 cups unseasoned beef stock
oil for frying	1 tbspn tomato paste
2 large carrots, peeled and diced	salt and freshly ground black pepper
2 medium onions, peeled and sliced	pinch of dried thyme
2oz smoked bacon, with rinds removed and cut into small squares	bay leaf
1 rounded tbspn flour	**Garnish:** chopped fresh parsley

Preparation time: 25 minutes
Cooking time: 1¾-2 hours

Wipe the beef and cut it into cubes, removing any fat or gristle. Brown it in the oil over fairly high heat in a large skillet. Transfer the meat into an ovenproof casserole with a slotted spoon. Fry the vegetables and bacon in the pan for 2-3 minutes. Sprinkle the flour over and stir it into the pan juices. Add half the stock and the tomato paste and stir to mix in well. Cook for a few minutes until the stock has thickened. Pour the contents of the pan over the meat in the casserole and add the rest of the stock, the black pepper, thyme and bay leaf.

Cook the casserole in a low oven (325°F) for 1½-2 hours or until the meat is tender. Allow to cool slightly and spoon off any excess fat on the surface of the liquid. Sprinkle with the chopped parsley and serve with plenty of creamed potatoes and a green vegetable or root vegetable purée.

New England Boiled Dinner

Serves 6-8

3-4lb joint of rolled, corned brisket or boneless rump beef	1lb small turnips, peeled and left whole
bouquet garni (see page 126)	2lb small potatoes, peeled or scraped and left whole
8 peppercorns	1lb young beets
1½lb baby onions	1 small white cabbage, thickly sliced
1lb carrots (preferably new), scraped and sliced lengthways if large	

Preparation time: 20 minutes
Cooking time: 2-3 hours

Make sure that the meat is tied into a neat, round shape. Soak it in cold water for 2 hours then place the joint in a large saucepan and cover with cold water. Heat the water until it boils and simmer for 10 minutes. Drain away the water but check first how salty it is. If the water is very salty, repeat the boiling and draining process. Alternatively you can simply soak the joint overnight and proceed as follows.

Cover the joint with fresh cold water, add the bouquet garni and peppercorns and two of the onions, sliced, and again bring to the boil. Remove any scum as it rises, lower the heat until the liquid is barely trembling. Cook gently until the meat is tender, allowing 35 minutes per lb and 35 minutes over. About 45 minutes before the meat is ready add the vegetables (except the cabbage) and cook until they are tender. At the same time boil the beets separately in salted water.

Transfer the meat to a serving dish, slice it, surround with the vegetables and keep warm. Bring the cooking liquid to the boil and add the cabbage and cook it quickly until tender. Serve the cabbage and beets in separate serving dishes along with the sliced meat and vegetables and creamed horseradish.

Chile con Carne

Serves 4-6

An easy, low-calorie lunch or supper dish which is popular with the whole family. The meat mixture freezes well and makes a good basis for pasta dishes and cottage pie, so cook up a larger quantity and spoon out some freezer portions before adding the chilli powder and beans.

1½lb lean ground beef	1 tbspn tomato paste
1 large onion, peeled and finely chopped	1 teasp sugar
1 fat garlic clove, crushed (optional)	salt to taste
1 large green or red pepper, washed, de-seeded and finely chopped	chilli powder to taste (approx ½ teasp)
1 celery stalk, trimmed and finely chopped	16oz can red kidney beans (approximate measure)
16oz can tomatoes	
3-4 tbspns beef stock or water	

Preparation time: 20 minutes
Cooking time: 1-1½ hours

In a flameproof casserole or a large skillet fry the beef in its own fat over medium heat until it is well browned and separated. Add the onion, garlic, pepper and celery and cook for about 3-4 minutes, stirring from time to time. Add the tomatoes, coarsely chopped, with their juice, the stock or water, sugar, salt and chilli powder to taste.

Cover and cook in a moderate oven (350°F) for 1-1¼ hours. About 10 minutes before serving, add the kidney beans with a little of the juice, depending on how dry the meat mixture is – do not make it too liquid. Check the seasoning again before serving.

Serve with tacos, crackers or plain boiled rice and a green side salad.

Carbonnade of Beef

This rich, dark stew is ideal for cold winter nights – make more than you need and freeze it.

2lb stewing beef	1 teasp wine or malt vinegar
2 tbspns lard or beef drippings	1 teasp brown sugar
2 large onions, peeled and thickly sliced	salt and a generous quantity of freshly ground black pepper
¼ cup flour	
⅔ cup strong beef stock	6 slices stale French bread or 6 triangles of white bread
1¼ cups brown ale or stout	French mustard

Preparation time: 15-20 minutes
Cooking time: 2 hours 45 minutes

Melt the fat in a large skillet and quickly brown the beef over fairly high heat. Transfer the meat to an ovenproof casserole and put the onions in the pan adding more lard or a little oil if necessary. Fry the onions until golden, and sprinkle with the flour. Cook, stirring for a minute then add the stock, and cook until the liquid begins to thicken. Pour over the meat and add the beer, vinegar, sugar and seasoning.

Cook the casserole in a low oven (375°F) for about 2 hours.

Spread the bread liberally with mustard and float it on the surface of the casserole to absorb any fat. Return the casserole to the oven uncovered, turn up the heat to 375°F and cook for a further 30-40 minutes until the bread is appetizingly brown and crusty.

Serve with creamed potatoes or buttered egg noodles and fresh seasonal vegetables.

Goulash

This rich, mouth-watering combination of lean beef, sweet paprika pepper and tomatoes topped with sour cream makes a perfect winter dinner-party dish.

1½lb lean stewing beef	1lb fresh tomatoes, peeled and chopped
2 tbspns oil	1 teasp sugar
2 medium onions, peeled and sliced	4oz garlic sausage in the piece
1 tbspn flour	salt to taste
1 tbspn paprika pepper	3-4 tbspns soured cream
1¼ cups beef stock	

Preparation time: 30 minutes
Cooking time: 1½-1¾ hours

Trim any fat or gristle from the meat and cut it into 1in squares. Brown the beef over high heat in the oil in a flame-proof casserole. Remove the meat from the casserole and fry the onions for about a minute. Sprinkle over the flour and paprika and cook for another minute. Stir in the stock and cook, stirring continuously, until the sauce thickens. Return the meat to the casserole and add the tomatoes. Cook in a moderate oven (350°F) for 1½-1¾ hours or until the meat is tender. About half way through the cooking time add the garlic sausage, thinly sliced. Before serving check the seasoning and add salt to taste.

Spoon the sour cream over the top and serve with buttered noodles and salad.

Goulash.

Navarin of Lamb

Serves 4-6

2lb chops, cubed	1lb tomatoes, peeled and quartered
4oz bacon, with rind removed and chopped	1½lb whole, tiny new potatoes, scraped
oil for frying	1 tbspn flour
1 teasp sugar	2 cups chicken stock
8oz pickling onions, peeled	bouquet garni (see page 126)
2 celery stalks, trimmed and chopped	salt and freshly ground black pepper
1lb new baby carrots, scraped	1 cup fresh garden peas
1 fat garlic clove, crushed	**Garnish:** Chopped fresh parsley

Preparation time: 40 minutes
Cooking time: approx 1-1½ hours

Brown the lamb and bacon in oil, in a large frying pan, over fairly high heat and transfer to a large, deep casserole or marmite. Add a spoonful or 2 of oil to the pan and the sugar and lightly brown the onions, celery, carrots and garlic. Add these to the meat, together with the tomatoes and potatoes. Stir the flour into the pan juices and add half the stock, stirring well until it thickens. Cook for 2-3 minutes then pour into the casserole. Add the rest of the stock, the bouquet garni and seasoning.

Cook in a moderate oven (350°F) for about 1 hour. 15 minutes before serving add the peas.

Lamb Hot Pot

8 lamb loin chops or approximately 2lb stewing lamb
1 tbspn oil
2 lambs' kidneys, skinned, cored and sliced (optional)
1 large onion, peeled and sliced
1½lb potatoes, peeled and thickly sliced
freshly ground black pepper
pinch of dried parsley
salt to taste
1¼ cups chicken stock

Preparation time: 15 minutes
Cooking time: 2½ hours

Trim any fat from the lamb and wipe it over to remove any bone fragments. Fry the meat and kidneys, if using, quickly in the oil, remove from the pan and set aside. Fry the onions until golden brown and remove from the heat.

In a deep casserole place a layer of potatoes then a layer of meat and kidney, onion and black pepper. Repeat these layers until the meat is used up. Pour over the stock, salted to taste and top with the parsley and a layer of potatoes decoratively overlapping. Brush the potatoes with a little oil and cover the casserole with a lid. Cook

Moussaka

This spicy, savory casserole of eggplant and lamb with its creamy topping makes a satisfying family supper, either on its own or with a crisp green salad.

4 medium eggplants, peeled and thickly sliced

oil for frying eggplants

Lamb Hot Pot.

in a fairly low oven (325°F) for 2½-3 hours. About 20 minutes before the end of the cooking time, turn up the oven to 450°F, uncover the casserole and cook to crisp the top layer of potatoes. Serve with buttered cabbage or leeks.

| 1lb lean ground lamb |
| 2 slices bacon, de-rinded and finely chopped |
| 1 medium onion, peeled and finely chopped |
| 1 fat garlic clove, peeled and crushed |
| 2 tbspns olive oil or corn oil |
| 3 large ripe tomatoes, peeled and quartered |
| 1 tbspn tomato paste |
| pinch of dried oregano |
| 1 teasp ground coriander |
| ½ teasp ground cinnamon |
| 6 tbspns stock or water |
| salt and freshly ground black pepper |

Topping:

| 2 tbspns butter |
| ¼ cup flour |
| 1¼ cups milk |
| ½ cup grated Cheddar cheese |
| salt and pepper |
| 1 egg, beaten |

Preparation time: 45-50 minutes
Cooking time: about 1¼ hours

Lay the eggplant slices on a plate and sprinkle with salt, place another plate on top of them and let stand for about 30 minutes. This draws out some of the excess moisture and bitter flavor. Pat dry with kitchen paper and fry the slices in oil on both sides until golden.

Fry the lamb, bacon, onion and garlic in the oil in a large skillet or flame-proof casserole for 5-10 minutes until the meat and onion are browned. Add the tomatoes, tomato paste, oregano and spices, stock and seasoning, bring to the boil, reduce the heat and simmer gently for about 10-15 minutes.

Arrange layers of eggplant and lamb mixture alternately in a casserole and leave to stand while you make the custard topping.

Melt the butter in a pan and stir in the flour. Cook for about 1 minute without browning. Take off the heat and stir in the milk and cheese. Return the pan to the heat and cook, stirring constantly until the cheese melts and the sauce thickens. Season to taste and allow the sauce to cool slightly. Stir in the beaten egg slowly and when it is well mixed, pour the topping over the lamb mixture and eggplant. Bake in a medium oven 375°F for 45 minutes to 1 hour until the topping is firm and an appetizing golden brown color.

Boiled Ham or Bacon Joints

A piece of boiled ham or bacon is a most versatile joint of meat which can be served hot or cold. Any left over portions are an excellent basis for salads, pies, quiches, rice and pasta dishes. Cooked bacon and ham can be frozen but it tends to dry out and should not be stored for too long in the freezer.

To prepare ham and bacon cuts

All bacon or ham should be soaked to remove excess salt. Soak small joints (1-2lb) for 2-3 hours; medium-sized joints (2-4lb) for 4-5 hours and joints over 5lb overnight. If you are cooking a small piece of bacon and have no time to soak it, put the joint into a saucepan, cover with water and bring it to the boil. Simmer for about 15 minutes, drain off the water and commence cooking as if the joint was soaked.

General cooking method for ham and bacon

Cover the joint with cold water (1¼ cups of cider added to the water gives a good flavor) and add a bay leaf, an onion studded with 2 or 3 cloves, a peeled and sliced carrot and a bouquet garni (see page 126). Bring to the boil, then reduce the heat. For joints under 2lb allow about 1 hour cooking time; for joints over 2lb allow about 25 minutes to the lb.   **Cold Boiled Ham.**

Glazes and serving suggestions

Once cooked, ham or bacon joints can be finished in various ways depending on whether they are to be served hot or cold.

To serve hot: Boil the joint for about ⅔ of the cooking time. Remove from the cooking liquid and, when cool enough, use a sharp knife to strip off the skin. Score lines across the fat to make a diamond pattern and brush with honey, light corn syrup or molasses to glaze. If preferred, stud the corners of the diamond patterns with cloves and press brown sugar firmly into the fat with a palette knife. Once you have applied your chosen glaze, cook in a moderate oven (350°F) basting once, for the remainder of the cooking time.

Why not try an orange glaze for a special occasion? Mix together ¾ cup orange juice with 3-4 tbspns honey, the rind of a fresh orange and a pinch of ground mixed spice. Brush this glaze over the ham. Bake in the oven (350°F) for the remaining cooking time. Serve garnished with oranges, peeled and sliced.

To serve cold: Boil the joint for the necessary time according to its weight and allow to cool in the cooking liquid. Strip off the skin with a sharp knife and press toasted breadcrumbs into the fat.

Pork and Apple Casserole

2lb sparerib chops, loin chops or shoulder meat, boned, trimmed and cubed
oil for frying
1 medium onion, peeled and sliced
1lb dessert apples, peeled and chopped
2 tbspns flour
1¼ cups chicken stock
pinch of dried sage
salt and freshly ground black pepper
1 teasp brown sugar
3 tbspns heavy cream
Garnish: chopped fresh parsley

Preparation time: 15-20 minutes
Cooking time: 1½-1¾ hours

Brown the pork quickly in a large skillet in 2-3 tbspns oil over fairly high heat. Transfer the meat into a casserole. Fry the onions for 2-3 minutes and add to the pork with the apple. Sprinkle the flour on the pan juices and stir-fry for about 1 minute. Pour in the stock and cook for a few more minutes, stirring continuously, until the liquid thickens. Pour this sauce over the contents of the casserole and add the sage, salt, pepper and sugar.

Cover tightly and cook in a low-moderate oven at 325°F for 1-1½ hours or until the meat is tender. Just before serving, stir in the cream, heat through without boiling.

Sprinkle the dish with chopped parsley and accompany with boiled rice and buttered green beans.

Polish Sausage Stew

A tasty lunch or supper dish which is a complete meal – just serve with hot crusty rolls.

8oz pork, diced (shoulder or sparerib)	½ small rutebega peeled and chopped into small dice
oil for frying	16oz can tomatoes
4oz smoked Polish boiling ring with garlic	1 bay leaf
4oz paprika sausage	⅔ cup dry cider
4 frankfurter sausages	1¼ cups chicken stock
1 medium onion, peeled and sliced	freshly ground black pepper
2 celery stalks, trimmed and sliced	1 teasp sugar
2 large carrots, peeled and chopped into small dice	½ small white cabbage, thinly sliced
1 large potato, peeled and chopped into small dice	

Preparation time: 30 minutes
Cooking time: about 1 hour 10 minutes

Brown the pork in oil in a skillet and transfer to a large pan or ovenproof casserole. Add the sausage, cut into slices, and the frankfurters cut into ½in chunks and the fresh vegetables (except the cabbage). Add the tomatoes, coarsely chopped with their juice; the bay leaf, cider and stock; sugar and pepper. You will need little or no salt.

Bring to the boil and then simmer for about 1 hour or cook in the oven at 350°F. 20 minutes before serving, add the cabbage. Serve in heated bowls.
Tip: This casserole reheats well. It should not be frozen.

Cassoulet

Serves 4-6

2 cups dried white haricot beans (dried navy beans)	1 tbspn soft brown sugar
1 medium onion, peeled and sliced	salt and freshly ground black pepper
1-2 tbspns pork or bacon fat, duck fat or oil	2 cups chicken stock
8oz lamb cut from the leg or shoulder, cubed	8oz cooked duck
8oz pork, cubed	4oz smoked garlic sausage, sliced
2 celery stalks, trimmed and chopped	bouquet garni (see page 126)
1 tbspn tomato paste	dried breadcrumbs for topping
½ teasp mustard powder	

Preparation time: 25 minutes plus 12-14 hours soaking time
Cooking time: 5-5½ hours

Soak the beans overnight, drain and rinse well. Place in a saucepan with plenty of cold, salted water and a slice or two of onion. Bring to the boil then reduce the heat and simmer for about 2 hours. Remove from the heat, drain off the juice and set beans aside until needed.

Heat the fat or oil in a large, heavy-based skillet and brown the pork and lamb. Remove from the pan with a slotted spoon and reserve. Soften the rest of the onion and the celery in the pan adding a little more fat if necessary. Remove the vegetables and mix with the meat. Add a little water to the pan and stir well to mix in the juices. Stir in the tomato paste, mustard powder, sugar, black pepper and a little salt. Add about ⅔ cup of stock and cook for a few minutes.

Preheat the oven to 425°F.

Mix the cooked duck and sausage into the meat

Cassoulet.

mixture. Put a layer of beans at the bottom of a deep terracotta ovenproof pot or any other large casserole. Add a layer of the meat mixture. Alternate these layers until the ingredients are used up, finishing with the meat. Add the bouquet garni and the pan juices. Top up with more stock to moisten but do not make it too liquid. Cover tightly and place in the oven. After 15 minutes turn the oven down to 325°F and cook for 5 hours.

Check from time to time and add a little more stock if the casserole appears dry. Sprinkle a layer of breadcrumbs on top and cook for a further hour.

Serve with crusty French bread and a green side salad and plenty of good red wine.

Casseroling Chicken

Chicken must be the most versatile meat for casserole cooking. The delicately flavored flesh combines happily with a great range of vegetables, herbs, spices and wines and it is economical both in cost and cooking time.

Chickens can be cooked whole, jointed, boned or cubed. It is usual to buy birds labelled as 'roasting' for casserole cooking as the older boiling (stewing) fowl need a great deal of cooking and 'dressing-up' to make them really palatable. The following cooking methods and variations are based on a 3½lb chicken and will serve 4 people.

Jointing a chicken

If using a frozen chicken, make sure that it is fully defrosted (a 3lb bird will take about 10 hours to defrost at room temperature and 36 hours in the refrigerator). Once the chicken is thawed, cook it as soon as possible and under no circumstances refreeze it.

To joint a fowl, first remove the legs by pulling them away from the body and cutting through the joint. Cut through the joint joining the thigh and drumstick. Next cut the bird in half lengthways from tail to wings to separate the breast from the back. Cut along beside the backbone to divide the breast in 2 then cut each in half to give 4 pieces of breast meat. You should now have 8 pieces plus the back (which can be used for stock). Each serving can consist of a piece of breast and leg meat. If you have time to spare, try cutting the meat from the bones and cubing it, using the bones to make stock. This turns a casserole into a perfect fork-dish – ideal for serving with pasta or rice at a buffet. Cooked in cubes, the chicken tends to taste extra succulent and delicious.

Chicken Marengo

Serves 4-6

4lb roasting chicken	⅔ cup chicken stock
5 cups water	1lb tomatoes, peeled and quartered
bay leaf	1 tbspn tomato paste
2-3 onion slices	2 cups tiny button mushrooms, fresh or canned
sprig of parsley	1 teasp sugar
oil for frying	1 tbspn brandy
4 slices bacon, with rind removed and chopped	½ cup sherry
1-2 fat garlic cloves, peeled and crushed	bouquet garni (see page 126)
2 large carrots, peeled and sliced lengthways	a little salt and freshly ground black pepper
1 large onion, peeled and sliced	**Garnish:** chopped fresh parsley, 4-6 crayfish or 4-6 shrimp
2 stalks celery, trimmed and chopped	
1 tbspn flour	

Preparation time: 45 minutes
Cooking time: 2¼-2½ hours

Joint and skin the chicken and cut the meat off the bones into fork-sized pieces. Refrigerate the chicken and use the bones to make stock by placing in a pan with 5 cups water, a bay leaf, a slice or two of onion and a sprig of parsley. Bring to the boil and skim off the scum as it rises. Reduce the heat and simmer for about an hour.

Brown the chicken in oil over fairly high heat in a skillet; transfer to an ovenproof casserole (preferably earthenware).

Fry the bacon and vegetables (except the tomatoes) for 2-3 minutes adding more oil if necessary. Sprinkle with the flour and stir well to mix in with the pan juices. Add the stock and cook, stirring well until the juices thicken. Add this mixture to the chicken with the rest of the stock, the tomatoes, tomato paste, mushrooms, sugar, brandy, sherry, bouquet garni and seasoning. Cook in a low oven (325°F) for about 1½ hours or until the chicken is tender. If a thicker sauce is preferred, thicken with a spoonful of cornstarch mixed with a little water, or beurre manie (page 121). Sprinkle with chopped parsley to serve and garnish with the shellfish.

Basic cooking method

Dust the joints or cubes of chicken with 1 tbspn spoon of seasoned flour and brown in 1-2 tbspns oil. If using a whole chicken, brown the bird without flouring. Remove from the pan and transfer to an ovenproof casserole. Add the ingredients for the recipe of your choice and cook the casserole in a low-medium oven (325°F) for about an hour or until the chicken is tender. The juices can be thickened if preferred using *beurre manie* (see page 121), plain flour or cornstarch mixed with water. Whole chickens should be carved and coated with the thickened sauce.

Add the following ingredients to the prepared chicken:

Coq au vin: Add to the pan 4oz diced bacon, 1 medium onion, peeled and sliced, 1 fat garlic clove (crushed), 1 carrot, peeled and sliced; adding more butter or a little oil if necessary. Brown these ingredients lightly and add to the chicken in the casserole together with 1¼ cups of red wine, bouquet garni (see page 126) and seasoning. Serve garnished with chopped parsley.

Chicken chasseur: Sauté 8 baby onions and 1 cup button mushrooms, wiped, and transfer to the casserole. Add ⅔ cup dry white wine; ⅔ cup chicken stock; 1 tbspn tomato paste; a bouquet garni (see page 126) and seasoning.

Paprika chicken: Brown 4oz diced bacon; 1 medium onion, peeled and sliced; 1 fat garlic clove, crushed and 1 tbspn paprika in the pan, adding more butter or oil if necessary. Stir in 1 large can (16oz) of tomatoes, chopped, with their juice and ⅔ cup of chicken stock, 1 teasp sugar and salt to taste. To serve, swirl in some soured cream.

Chicken Marengo.

Game Casserole

2 grouse or 1 pheasant	⅔ cup well-flavored stock
1 tbspn seasoned flour	⅔ cup white wine
¼ cup butter	6 juniper berries
1-2 tbspns oil	bouquet garni (see page 126)
1 medium onion, peeled and chopped	black pepper and salt
2 stalks celery, trimmed and chopped	**Garnish:** Crisp croûtons, chopped parsley
¼ cup chopped ham	

Preparation time: 30 minutes
Cooking time: about 2 hours

Joint the grouse or pheasants. Pat dry with kitchen paper and sprinkle with flour. Brown the joints in the butter and oil in a skillet; transfer into a casserole. Add the vegetables to the pan and fry for 2-3 minutes. Add the vegetables to the casserole with the ham and pour over the stock and wine. Lightly crush the juniper berries with a spoon and add to the casserole with the bouquet garni and seasoning.

Cook in a slow oven at 300°F for about 1¾-2 hours or until the game is tender. Sprinkle with crisp croûtons and parsley.

Serve with braised celery or leeks, creamed potatoes and redcurrant or rowan jelly.

Game Casserole.

Rabbit Dijon

1 whole rabbit (about 1½lb)	2 cups well-flavored stock
4-6oz bacon	1 tbspn Dijon mustard
2-3 tbspns oil	black pepper and salt
2 medum onions, peeled and sliced, or 8-12 baby onions, peeled	bouquet garni (see page 126)
	2 tbspns heavy cream
1 large carrot, peeled and thinly sliced	1 egg yolk
1 tbspn flour	

Preparation time: 30 minutes
Cooking time: about 1¾ hours

Joint the rabbit and pat dry with kitchen paper. De-rind the bacon, cut it into squares and fry it in a little oil until the fat runs and it is crisp. Remove the bacon from the pan, reserve a little for garnish and place the rest in a casserole dish (preferably earthenware).

Fry the rabbit in the oil and bacon fat, adding more oil if necessary, until the meat is lightly browned. Place the pieces of rabbit in the casserole. Fry the onions and carrots for 2-3 minutes and stir in the flour. Take the pan off the heat and stir in the stock. Return to the heat and cook, stirring until the sauce thickens. Add the mustard, pepper and very little salt and pour the sauce over the meat in the casserole. Add the bouquet garn and cook at 325°F until the meat is tender (1-1½ hours).

Just before serving, beat together the cream and the egg yolk and stir it into the casserole. Sprinkle with the reserved crisped bacon and serve.

Jugged Hare

1 hare dressed and cut into serving pieces	6 juniper berries, lightly crushed
2oz bacon with rind removed, chopped	rind and juice of 1 orange
oil for frying	bouquet garni (see page 126)
1 large onion, peeled and sliced	1 wineglass port or red wine (approx ¾ cup)
2 large carrots, peeled and cut up lengthways	salt and freshly ground black pepper
2 stalks celery, trimmed and chopped	1 tbspn redcurrant jelly
1 tbspn flour	**Garnish:** crisp croûtons cut into decorative shapes with pastry cutters.
2½ cups beef stock	

Preparation time: 30 minutes
Cooking time: 2½-3 hours

Brown the bacon and hare in the oil quickly in a large skillet over fairly high heat; place in a large casserole or marmite. Fry the vegetables for 2 or 3 minutes, adding more oil if necessary, and sprinkle with the flour. Stir well to mix in the flour and add half the stock. Cook for 2 or 3 minutes stirring until the juice thickens then pour it over the meat in the casserole. Add the juniper berries, orange rind and juice, bouquet garni, the port or red wine, black pepper and a little salt and the rest of the stock. Cover tightly and cook for 2½-3 hours, or until the meat is tender, at 325°F. Do not overcook otherwise the meat will break up.

About 10 minutes before serving, check the seasoning, adding more salt if necessary. if a thicker sauce is preferred, thicken with buerre manie (see page 121). Stir in the redcurrant jelly.

Serve garnished with croûtons and accompanied by buttered root vegetables and plenty of creamed potatoes and redcurrant jelly.

Variation: Wild rabbit is also good cooked in this way. It is a perfect way of cooking an elderly cock pheasant and adds character to a frozen chicken.

Calamar Casserole

A deliciously-rich dish with its own unique taste yet simple and fairly quick to cook.

2lb small squid (inkfish)	⅔ cup red wine
¼ cup butter	pinch of dried basil
1-2 fat garlic cloves, peeled and crushed	1 teasp sugar
1 medium onion, peeled and finely chopped	salt and freshly ground black pepper
1 celery stalk, trimmed and finely chopped	**Garnish:** chopped fresh parsley
1lb ripe tomatoes, peeled and quartered	

Preparation time: 30 minutes
Cooking time: about 1 hour

To prepare the squid: Pull away the heads from the bodies and discard the transparent 'pen.' Cut away the entrails from the tentacles just above the eyes. Turn the bodies inside out to remove the intestines and roe. Try to identify and keep 1 or 2 of the silvery ink sacs as these give added flavor and color to the dish. Slice the bodies into rings and the circles of tentacles into 2 if they are fairly large. Finally wash and drain the prepared squid.

Heat the butter in a skillet and gently sauté the garlic, onion and celery. Add the squid and cook for about 5 minutes, stirring occasionally. Transfer the vegetables and squid to an ovenproof casserole and add the tomatoes, wine, basil, sugar and seasoning. Crush the inksacs (if using) and add these to the pot.

Cook in a fairly low oven (325°F) for about 40 minutes or until the squid is tender. Sprinkle with chopped parsley to garnish. Serve on a bed of boiled rice with salad.

Tuna Noodle Bake

8oz dried ribbon egg noodles	7oz can tuna fish, drained and flaked into fork-sized pieces
1 tbspn oil	4 ripe tomatoes, peeled and sliced across
1 medium onion, peeled and sliced	salt and freshly ground black pepper
1 garlic clove, peeled and crushed	1½ cups Béchamel (see page 120)
2 celery stalks, trimmed and sliced	½ cup cheddar cheese, grated
pinch of dried basil	
2 tbspns butter	

Preparation time: 35 minutes
Cooking time: 35 minutes

Cook the noodles in plenty of fast-boiling salted water with the oil for about 5 minutes. Do not overcook. Drain and set aside.

Preheat the oven to 350°F.

Fry the onion, garlic, celery and basil in the butter for 2-3 minutes and remove from the heat. Put a layer of noodles in a medium-sized, ovenproof casserole followed by a layer of tuna and a layer of fried vegetables and tomatoes. Repeat, lightly seasoning each layer until all these ingredients are used up. Finish with a layer of noodles.

Pour the sauce over and sprinkle with grated cheese and bake for about 25-30 minutes.

Serve with green peas and buttered carrots.

Fisherman's Stew

5 cups of fresh mussels in the shell

¼ cup butter

1 fat garlic clove, crushed

1 medium onion, peeled and sliced

⅔ cup dry white wine

2 large carrots, peeled and cut into small dice

1 celery stalk, trimmed and sliced

16oz can of tomatoes, drained and pulped

bouquet garni (see page 126)

good pinch of cayenne pepper

1½lb firm white fish, filleted, skinned and cubed (use monkfish, cod, haddock, halibut, or similar)

1 tbspn flour

salt to taste

Garnish: chopped fresh parsley

Preparation time: 40 minutes
Cooking time: 35-40 minutes

Prepare the mussels for cooking as described on page 18.

Melt about 2 tbspns of butter in a large pan and fry the garlic and a slice or 2 of onion for a few minutes, until soft. Add the wine and bring to the boil. Tip in the mussels and cook, covered, over fairly high heat for 2-3 minutes. Shake the pan from time to time to ensure that the mussels cook evenly. When all the shells have opened, remove the pan from the heat. Set aside and keep warm. Discard any mussels which remain obstinately shut.

In a smaller pan, melt the rest of the butter and fry the remaining onion, carrot and celery for 2 or 3 minutes. Add the pulped tomatoes, the liquid from the mussels, bouquet garni and cayenne pepper and simmer for about 20 minutes or until the carrot and celery are soft.

Take the pan off the heat and thicken the liquid by adding the flour mixed to a smooth paste with a little cold water. Bring to the boil, stirring, and cook over reduced heat for a further 8-10 minutes, stirring occasionally. Add the fish, cover the pan and cook gently for between 5 and 10 minutes. Do not overcook the fish or it will disintegrate. Check the seasoning, adding a little salt and more cayenne if preferred.

Serve the fish stew with rice or French bread and salad, garnished with the mussels in their shells and sprinkled with fresh chopped parsley.
Tip: Monkfish is excellent for this dish as it has a good flavor and a very fine texture.

Fisherman's Stew.

ROASTING AND BROILING

Beef

When buying beef, particularly for roasting or broiling, look at the color of the fat. In good quality beef it should be creamy white. If it is yellow in color this probably denotes that it is past its prime. If the meat is bright pink or red then it may not be properly hung and if dark in color with a poor covering of fat then it may prove to be tough. Well-hung prime beef should be a deep, rich red, and the very best quality meat will have streaks or 'marbling' of pale fat running through it.

Joints for roasting

The cuts of meat and the joints vary from country to country but, essentially, the principles remain the same: only the most tender cuts on or near the bone are reserved for dry roasting.

The most tender piece of beef to choose is the tenderloin which lies under the ribs of the sirloin. This cut is mostly sold as steaks but can be roasted in the piece. It is very lean and should be barded with strips of fat if plain roasted. The best way of cooking tenderloin is to part-roast it and wrap it in pastry to finish cooking.

The sirloin is perhaps the tastiest cut, but is the most expensive. The cheaper standing ribs are popular, such as the wing or prime rib, or the smaller fore ribs. These can be cooked on the bone or boneless and rolled. For roasting times see the chart on page 220.

Steaks

Tenderloin: Tenderloin steak is the tenderest cut of all. It may include the ends of the tenderloin or be sold in the piece cut from the middle of the meat as Chateaubriand (about 4in) to serve 2 portions, or as individual steaks or tournedos (1-1½in thick). These steaks are usually broiled or pan-fried.
Sirloin and ribs: Cuts from these include sirloin, entrecôte, club, T-bone, and porterhouse. These can usually be cut into even-sized steaks for single servings except for the T-bone, which is a cut across the wing rib end of the sirloin – it generally makes 2 servings. Broil or dry-fry.

Rump: Steaks cut from the rump have more flavor than those cut from the rib areas but unless they are top-quality and well-hung, they can be a bit chewy. If you are unsure of the quality, it is a good idea to tenderize them with a meat mallet and brush with oil before cooking.
Cooking methods
Cooking time for steaks very much depend on the thickness of the cut, the heat of the broiler and how you like your steaks cooked but the chart below gives an approximate guide to the total amount of time needed:

Type of steak	Rare	Medium	Well done
Sirloin and rib steaks approx 1in thick	5 minutes	6-7 minutes	8-10 minutes
Tenderloin and tournedos approx 1-1½in thick	5-6 minutes	6-8 minutes	9-12 minutes
Rump steak approx 1-1½in thick	6 minutes	7-10 minutes	12-14 minutes

Roast beef with Yorkshire pudding and Red Wine Gravy

Serves 6-8

1 standing rib or wing rib of beef weighing from 5-7lb

salt and freshly ground black pepper

Red wine gravy:

1¼ cups beef or vegetable stock

1 wineglass red wine

1 teasp sugar

salt and freshly ground black pepper

Yorkshire pudding:

1 cup flour

pinch of salt

1 large egg

⅔ cup milk

⅔ cup water

beef fat from the roasting pan or lard for cooking

Preparation time: 5 minutes
Cooking time: see method

Preheat the oven to 425°F. Rub the beef with salt and sprinkle with pepper. Stand on a wire grid in a roasting pan so that the meat is clear of the fat and juices while cooking. Roast for 15 minutes then turn down the oven heat to 350°F. For rare beef cook for 15 minutes per 1lb and an extra 15 minutes. For medium-cooked beef roast for 20 minutes per 1lb plus 20 minutes.
Note: When calculating your cooking time, take into account the 20-30 minutes needed for the Yorkshire Pudding at a high temperature. To prevent the meat overcooking, take it out about 15 minutes before the end and keep it warm (residual heat will continue to cook it).
To prepare and cook the Yorkshire pudding: Sift the flour with the salt into a mixing bowl. Make a well in the center of the flour and drop in the egg. Mix the milk and water together and gradually add a little as you stir the flour into the egg. Add about half the liquid and beat well to incorporate air into the mixture. When air bubbles start to form, beat in the remaining milk and allow to stand for 30-40 minutes. Turn up the oven to

Preparation time: 20 minutes plus 30-40 minutes standing time
Cooking time: 20-30 minutes

preheat to 450°F (hot).
When you are ready to cook the Yorkshire pudding, put a teasp of hot fat from the beef roasting tin, or a knob of lard, in the bottom of individual Yorkshire pudding, patty or muffin tins. Place the tins in a high position in the oven for 4-5 minutes until the fat is hot. Take out of the oven and spoon in the batter. Bake for 20-30 minutes until risen and golden.
To prepare the gravy: While the Yorkshire puddings are cooking, pour off most of the fat from the meat roasting tin, leaving enough to soak up about a tablespoon of flour. Place the tin over a moderate heat and stir well to incorporate the crusty, meat juice sediment and cook the flour for 1-2 minutes. Add about 1¼ cups of beef or vegetable stock (reserved water from boiled vegetables if it is not too salty) and stir well. Add the wine and sugar and simmer for 5-10 minutes. Check the seasoning, strain and serve separately in a warmed gravy boat.

Roast Beef.

Tournedos with Pâté and Mushrooms

A version of the classic Tournedos Rossini – tender rounds of steak garnished with pâté de fois gras and mushrooms.

4 thick slices white bread	1 tbspn sherry or Madeira
oil for frying	salt and freshly ground pepper to taste
½ cup butter	4 tournedos (approx 1½in thick)
4oz button mushrooms, finely chopped	**Garnish:** 2oz button mushrooms, sliced and lightly sautéd in butter
1 small tin pâté de fois gras (approx 2oz)	
1 teasp chives, chopped	

Preparation time: 15-20 minutes
Cooking time: 10 minutes

Cut the slices of bread into circles, the same size as the steaks. Fry the bread until crisp and golden in a little oil.

Using a little less than half the butter, sauté the chopped mushrooms for about 2 minutes, add the pâté, mashed with a fork, the chives, sherry or Madeira and seasoning and cook for a further minute or two to blend the flavors. Keep the mixture warm while you then fry the steaks in the remaining butter for 2-3 minutes each side (or broil if preferred). Spread the pâté mixture on to the croûtons, place a steak on each and serve sprinkled with mushroom slices.

Tournedos with Pâté and Mushrooms (left); Beefsteak Kebabs (right).

Beefsteak Kebabs

1lb lean rump steak cut into 1in cubes	**Marinade:**
4 small tomatoes	5 tbspns olive oil
2 medium onions	5 tbspns red wine
1 green or red pepper, de-seeded and blanched in boiling water for 2 minutes	1 fat garlic clove, crushed
	1 bay leaf
8 medium mushrooms	1 tbspn chopped fresh parsley
	pinch of sugar
	salt and freshly ground black pepper

Preparation time: 25 minutes
Marinading time: 2-3 hours
Cooking time: 15-20 minutes

Mix all the ingredients for the marinade together in a bowl and add the cubed beef. Cover with plastic wrap and place in a cool pace for 2-3 hours.

Halve the tomatoes, cut the onion into quarters and cut the pepper into squares. Thread all the ingredients onto long skewers alternately, brush with the marinade and broil or barbecue for about 15-20 minutes, turning from time to time and brushing with the marinade. Serve with salad and boiled rice.

Scotch Steaks

Serves 2

2 sirloin or entrecôte steaks (approx 6-8oz each)	2 tbspns heavy cream
1 shallot or small onion, peeled and finely chopped	1 tbspn Scotch whisky
2 tbspns butter	salt and freshly ground black pepper

Preparation time: 5 minutes
Cooking time: 5-10 minutes

Preheat the broiler and cook the steaks to your liking. Fry the onion in the butter until soft, add the whisky and cook, stirring over high heat for about 1 minute. Stir in the cream and when it is heated through, season to taste and pour this over the steaks.

Accompaniments and garnishes for steaks (for 4 servings):
Garlic butter: Mix together 1 fat garlic clove (crushed) with ¼ cup softened butter and 1-2 tbspns chopped fresh parsley. Form into circular pats, chill and serve on top of broiled steaks.
Orange butter: Mix together ¼ cup softened butter, the grated rind of a small orange and 1 teasp of the juice, salt and pepper to taste. Form into circular pats, chill and serve with broiled steaks.
Sautéd mushrooms: Sauté 8oz button mushrooms in ¼ cup butter until softened. Stir in 1 teasp fresh lemon juice and season to taste.
Provençal garnish: Stir-fry 1 medium onion, peeled and sliced, 1 garlic clove, crushed, and 1 small green or red pepper, de-seeded, blanched and sliced, in a little olive oil for about 2-3 minutes. Add 2 ripe tomatoes, peeled and thickly sliced and 8 black olives (pitted) and cook for another minute. Season with salt and pepper and a pinch of sugar. Spoon the mixture over cooked steaks and serve.

Lamb

Joints for roasting

When buying lamb, look for pale pink flesh and firm white fat; older lamb has darker flesh with yellowish fat, and is more sinewy.

One of the most popular roasting joints is the leg which is sold whole or halved. It makes a flavorful meaty roast which is easy to cook and carve. Shoulder of lamb is also popular but it is best cooked boneless and rolled as a ballotine. The section of rib between the neck and loin is known as the best end of neck and can be prepared as a single 'rack' with the rib bones trimmed at the ends or double as a guard of honor where 2 racks are tied facing each other with the rib bones crossed. A crown roast is formed by 2 racks with rib bones trimmed and cut through at the bases so that they can be tied, back to back, to form a circle. The cavity in the center is usually filled with a savory stuffing.

One of the prime joints of lamb for roasting is the saddle which consists of both the loins and includes the kidneys. This large joint, which usually needs to be specially ordered from a butcher, is ideal for a large party or family celebration. A single loin consists of approximately 6 chops and can be boned, stuffed and rolled for easy serving.

Cuts for broiling

As lamb is young and tender meat, quite a variety of cuts can be quickly cooked.

Roast Rack of Lamb.

Chump chops: These large, meaty chops with little bone are cut from between the loin and the top of the leg.

Loin chops: These are sold singly or as double chops and usually measure about 1in in depth and have a short T-bone.

Cutlets: These slender chops are cut from the rack or best end of neck with a small sweet nugget of meat.

Noisettes: These are prepared from the rack or best end of neck which is boned, rolled and tied and then sliced between the string to form plump rounds of tender meat.

Shoulder cuts: Slices of shoulder meat can be bought for broiling or baking. They are generally lean and flavorful but less tender than chump or loin chops.

Leg steaks: Lamb 'steaks' are slices cut through the leg. These are best baked but can be broiled or fried.

Lamb for broiling should be brushed with oil or melted butter and cooked under high heat. Approximate cooking times for lamb:

Cutlets	5 minutes each side
Chump and loin chops	6-7 minutes each side
Noisettes	8-9 minutes each side
Shoulder cuts and leg steaks	8-9 minutes each side

Carving a leg (illustrated)
Step 1: Lay the leg on the carving dish with the thick side uppermost. Cut ¼in slices down towards the bone, across the grain of the meat.
Step 2: Then ease the knife under the first slice and cut across, parallel to the bone to remove the slices.
Step 3: Continue slicing downwards towards the bone.
Step 4: Turn the joint over and slice across to remove the remaining meat.

Carving a shoulder
Step 1: As this is a very awkward joint to carve, a tip is to loosen the blade bone (on the cut edge of the joint) with a sharp knife *before* cooking.
Step 2: Once the joint is cooked, a little firm twisting of the blade bone will release it completely, giving a good section of the joint to carve in neat slices.
Step 3: Once you reach the bone turn the joint round so that it is at right angles to the previous cut edge and continue carving until you again reach the bone.
Step 4: Continue to carve around the bone until all the meat is removed.

Carving a loin
Step 1: Again, this needs a little attention *before* cooking to facilitate carving. Saw along parallel to the backbone to detach the ribs (or ask your butcher to *chine* it for you).
Step 2: Carve downwards following the line of the bones into neat slices or chops.

Carving best end, crown roast and guard of honor
Again it is best to chine the best end by sawing along the backbone. When cooked simply carve downwards between the ribs. With the crown roast also carve downwards between the ribs to cut single chops or cutlets – 2-3 per portion. Remember to serve the stuffing with the chops. When carving a guard of honor, cut downwards and across the whole joint to cut pairs of cutlets. One point to watch is to calculate carefully the servings from this type of joint or the carver may end up going hungry! As a rough guide, a rack or best end will serve 3-4, a crown roast and guard of honor will serve 6.

Accompaniments for lamb
Serve chops with pats of savory butters (see page 83), roasts with mint sauce (see page 125), mint jelly, redcurrant jelly or creamed horseradish. Try broiling lamb with sprays of fresh rosemary or rub the meat with cut garlic for extra flavor. A squeeze of lemon juice will help to offset the fattiness of lamb. The traditional accompaniment is onion sauce (see page 121).

Flavorings for roast lamb
A prime joint of lamb, plainly roasted is always a pleasure to eat but, for a change, try enhancing it in various ways.

Garlic roast: Cut 1-2 garlic cloves into slices and make fairly deep cuts with a sharp knife in the fleshy parts of leg or shoulder joints. Slide in the slivers of garlic and push them well down towards the bone. This is particularly good for frozen joints which may have lost a little flavor.

Rosemary roast: The flavors of rosemary and lamb marry well and sprigs of rosemary make the joint look interesting. Pierce the skin with a larding needle or skewer as if making tacking stitches and push the fresh sprigs under the skin. Add a glass of white wine to the dish before roasting.

Boning a shoulder of lamb
Allow about 20 minutes to bone the joint. Rolled and tied, it carves beautifully.

Specialist boning knives are available; make sure it is very sharp.

First lay the joint on a chopping board with the inside of the shoulder facing upwards. Along the cut edge on the opposite side to the leg bone you will find the edge of the shoulder blade. Slide the point of the knife down the fleshy side of the bone and separate the meat on one side of the blade bone. Turn the joint over and free the other side of the bone. You will have to be careful here not to slice through the skin. When the blade bone begins to feel loose, reach in with the point of the knife and cut the sinews round the ball and socket joint. You will now be able to remove the blade bone. Next, begin to cut away the meat from the leg bone, holding the bone upright and slicing downwards until you reach the equivalent of the elbow joint. Cut through the sinews and release the upper leg bone. Holding the next bone upright you can then release this quickly with firm downward cuts. Trim off excess fat. You can use the bones for stock, provided that you have time to allow it to cool in order to skim off the fat.

You now have a flattish piece of meat with a pocket left by the bones which can be stuffed before rolling and tying the joint. When roasting, remember to allow extra cooking time because the joint is now denser and lacks the conductivity of the bones.

Ballotine of Lamb with Onion and Thyme Stuffing

1 whole shoulder of lamb, boneless with the bones reserved for stock	
1 small onion, peeled and quartered	
1 carrot, peeled and sliced	
1 bay leaf	
2-3 sprigs fresh rosemary	

Preparation time: 15 minutes (excluding time for boning)
Cooking time: approx 1½-2 hours

Stuffing:

1 small onion, peeled and finely chopped
2 tbspns butter
5 tbspns fresh breadcrumbs
1 egg, beaten
½ teasp dried thyme
salt and freshly ground black pepper

Place the lamb bones in a pan and cover with cold water. Bring to the boil, skim off any froth or scum which rises, then add the onion, carrot and bay leaf and simmer for about 1 hour. Allow the stock to cool and skim off the fat.

Preheat the oven to 400°F. Soften the onion in the butter in a pan over a gentle heat. Mix the egg with the breadcrumbs in a bowl. Add the onion, thyme and seasoning.

Stuff the mixture into the pocket in the lamb left by the bones. Roll up the joint and tie securely with string. Slip the rosemary under the string.

Roast for 15 minutes at 400°F then turn the oven down to 375°F and continue to cook, allowing 30 minutes per lb. Remove the string and place the joint on a serving dish to keep warm.

To make the gravy: Pour off most of the fat from the roasting dish, leaving the pan juices from the meat. Stir in 1 tbspn flour and mix well. Add about 1¼ cups of the stock made from the bones and stir until the gravy thickens, boiling well. Add ½ a glass of white wine and bring back to the boil. Simmer for 5 minutes before serving. Season to taste with salt, freshly ground pepper and a pinch of sugar. Strain and serve separately.

Pork

When buying pork look out for moist, pale pink flesh and firm white fat. Nowadays pork is sold young and bred to produce more meat and less fat so there should only be about ½-¾in of fat lying under the skin. The skin itself should be thin, soft and smooth with little sign of hair or bristles. Most cuts of pork can be roasted but the following are the most popular:

Tenderloin: This is the most tender, juicy cut of pork taken from the loin, next to the backbone. It is very lean meat and should be barded when plain roasted to prevent it from drying out. Probably the best method of cooking this delicate and delicious cut is to roast it stuffed and wrapped in puff pastry (see Pork en croûte on page 89).

Loin: This is excellent roasted either on the bone or boneless, rolled and stuffed.

Leg: A large prime joint which is normally divided into at least 2 cuts: the tenderloin (top of the leg) and knuckle end. Joints from the leg can be boned and stuffed.

Shoulder or hand and spring: This is the foreleg, a fairly economical joint whch can be roasted whole on the bone, or boneless and rolled. It is often divided into two; the hand or lower part of the shoulder being roasted while the rest of the cut is used for pies and pâtés.

Neck: An inexpensive joint which includes the spare rib and blade cuts. It can also be roasted whole or boneless. The meat is, however, used mostly for sausages, pies and casseroles.

Accompaniments to Roast Pork

Classic apple sauce: Simmer 3 large dessert apples, peeled, cored and thinly sliced with 2-3 tbspns water, and 1 teasp lemon juice, until soft. Beat with a wooden spoon, adding a large knob of butter, heat through and serve. (See also Cranberry and Apple Sauce, page 124).

Fried apple rings: Peel and core 2 large cooking apples. Cut them into thick slices and dip in soft brown sugar. Fry in about 2 tablespoons butter until golden.

Roast Pork.

Sage and onion sauce: Peel and finely chop one large onion. Melt ¼ cup butter and fry the onion until soft. Stir in 1 rounded tablespoon flour and cook for about 1 minute. Take off the heat and stir in 1¼ cups white stock and a teaspoon of chopped fresh sage. Mix well and return to the heat. Cook, stirring constantly until the sauce thickens. Season to taste and simmer gently for 10 minutes, covered.

Raisin sauce: Melt ¼ cup butter and stir in 2 rounded tablespoons flour. Cook until the flour turns a good golden brown. Take off the heat and stir in a scant 1¼ cups brown stock and a glass of red wine. Mix well and return to the heat. Cook, stirring, until the sauce thickens. Add the grated rind of ½ lemon with a little juice and 2oz raisins (washed). Simmer for 10 minutes and add salt and sugar to taste.

Summer Roast Gammon

Serves 4-6

Joint of corner gammon or ham approx 3-3½lb	1 tbspn clear honey
2 tbspns lime marmalade	**Garnish:** 1 lime, sliced; 1 lemon, sliced; salad cress or watercress

Preparation time: Soaking: 12-24 hours
Cooking time: approx 2½ hours

Soak the joint overnight to reduce saltiness. Drain and weigh the gammon and calculate the cooking time at 35 minutes per lb plus an extra 35 minutes. Place in a pan and cover with cold water. Bring to the boil, then drain off.

Foil-wrap the joint, place in a roasting tin and roast at 350°F. Mix the marmalade and honey together.

Forty minutes before the end of the calculated cooking time, remove the gammon from the oven and unwrap the foil. Leave to cool for 5 minutes.

Carefully strip off the rind and, using a sharp knife, score the fat in a diamond pattern.

Spread the marmalade and honey mixture over the gammon fat and return the joint to the oven. Baste frequently for the remainder of the cooking time or until the joint is golden brown. The edges tend to brown more quickly so protect these with foil, if necessary.

Serve the gammon, sliced hot or cold, on a bed of cress and garnished with lime and lemon slices.

Mustard-broiled Pork Chops with Broccoli and Lemon Jacket Potatoes

4 large potatoes	**Lemon-parsley butter:**
salt	½ cup butter, softened
4 loin pork chops	1-2 tbspns fresh parsley, chopped
1-2 tbspns Dijon mustard	2 teasps grated lemon rind
1lb fresh broccoli, washed	

Preparation time: 10 minutes
Cooking time: 1 hour (total)

Scrub the potatoes well and dry them. Prick all over with a fork, rub with salt and bake in the oven for about 1 hour at 400°F.

Twenty minutes before the potatoes are ready, brush the grid of the broiler with oil. Snip the rind of each chop in 3 or 4 places to prevent them from curling, then spread each chop generously with mustard. Broil under medium heat for about 10 minutes. Turn the chops over, spread the

other sides with mustard and broil for a further 6-10 minutes without allowing them to dry up. While the chops are finishing, put the broccoli on to cook in fast-boiling, salted water and prepare the lemon-parsley butter by mixing the rest of the ingredients together. Serve the pork chops garnished with the broccoli.

Split the skins of the potatoes and top with a knob of the lemon-parsley butter.

Pork en Crôute with Apple and Onion Stuffing

2 × 1lb plump pork tenderloin	2 medium eating apples, peeled and finely chopped
16oz puff pastry (prepared weight)	1 thick slice of bread
1 egg, beaten	pinch of dried sage
Stuffing:	salt and freshly ground black pepper
1 large onion, peeled and finely chopped	**Garnish:** watercress sprigs

Preparation time: 30 minutes
Cooking time: 1 hour

To prepare the stuffing: Cook the onion in a little water for about 10 minutes. Add the apple and simmer for a further 5 minutes. Remove the crusts from the bread and coarsely grate into crumbs. Mix the crumbs into the apple and onion mixture, add the sage and seasoning and stir.

To stuff the pork: Slice the tenderloins halfway through lengthways, open the meat out and flatten it. Arrange the stuffing along one tenderloin and cover with the other. Tie up the stuffed tenderloin with string into a good shape and lay on a baking tray. Roast for 40 minutes in a fairly hot oven (400°F) then allow the meat to cool.

Meanwhile roll out the pastry to a rectangle sufficient to wrap up the meat (about 12 × 10in). Lay the cooled meat (with string removed) on the pastry and paint the edges with the beaten egg. Fold the pastry over and seal the edges. Trim surplus pastry from the edge. Reserve the trimmings for making pastry 'leaves.' Dampen each end of the parcel and seal firmly. Roll out the pastry trimmings and cut into leaf shapes. Paint one side of the leaves with egg and use to decorate the top of the parcel in a herringbone pattern. Paint the whole surface of the pastry with egg and pierce 2 or 3 times with a knife.

Bake at 425°F for 25 minutes until the pastry is a delicious golden brown. Turn off the oven and allow the joint another 10-15 minutes cooking time. Serve garnished with bunches of fresh green watercress sprigs.

Serving suggestion: Accompany the pork en crôute with Spicy Tomato Sauce (see page 123), glazed carrots and new potatoes.

Summer Roast Gammon.

Chicken

Nowadays chicken represents very good value as a satisfying main course, especially with the competitive prices offered by supermarkets for frozen poultry. When buying and cooking frozen poultry, however, remember to allow plenty of time for it to thaw fully before cooking. Check in the body cavity to see that there are no ice crystals present, and the legs should be flexible.

The flavor of chicken marries well with a variety of ingredients and is especially delicious when boned and stuffed.

There are now only two basic categories of chicken available for roasting:

Poussin: Baby chickens between 4-6 weeks old weighing approximately 16oz. These can be roasted whole for around 30-40 minutes at 375°F or split and broiled or fried. Allow 1 poussin per serving.

Roasting chickens (New York dressed): Young chickens about 6-12 months old weighing 3-5lb. Joint and broil or roast whole for 20 minutes per lb plus an extra 20 minutes at 375°F.

Roast Spring Chicken with Spinach Stuffing.

Roast Spring Chicken with Spinach Stuffing

1 roasting chicken approx 3½lb in weight	2 cups soft brown breadcrumbs
salt and freshly ground black pepper	2 tbspns chopped parsley
Spinach stuffing:	rind of ½ a lemon, finely grated
½ cup butter	1 egg, beaten
6 scallions, chopped	1 tbspn chopped fresh thyme or marjoram (or 1 teasp of either herb, dried)
1 garlic clove, crushed	
12oz fresh spinach, cooked and chopped	
1 tbspn chopped fresh basil (or 1 teasp dried basil)	

Preparation time: 30 minutes
Cooking time: 1 hour 45 minutes

Season the chicken inside and out with salt and pepper. Preheat the oven to 375°F.

Melt half the butter in a pan. Add the chopped scallions and crushed garlic and cook gently for 3-4 minutes. Remove the pan from the heat and mix with the cooked spinach, half the chopped basil and thyme, the breadcrumbs, parsley, lemon rind and season to taste. Add sufficient beaten egg to bind.

Fill the cavity of the chicken with the prepared stuffing and truss so that the bird keeps a good shape. Mix the remaining butter and herbs together. Stand the chicken in a roasting tin and spread the herb butter all over the bird. Cover with a piece of foil, dull side up.

Roast the chicken for 1 hour, basting occasionally. Remove the foil, baste the chicken and return for about 40 minutes or until the bird is tender and cooked through.

Serve with new potatoes cooked in their skins, fingers of cucumber, lightly poached, and garnish with watercress or fresh herbs.

Boning a chicken for roasting

It is well worth allowing an extra 30 minutes or so to bone a chicken or game bird. This becomes an impressive joint which is easy to carve into neat slices and which combines both light and dark meats. This type of roast will give generous servings, particularly if filled with a savory stuffing. It is equally delicious served hot with an interesting sauce or cold as part of a buffet.

Step 1: Lay the bird on its breast and, with a very sharp small knife, cut off the ends of the wings, leaving the first joint. Use these pieces with the giblets (neck, crop and heart which are often supplied) to make stock.

Step 2: Make an incision down the back towards the tail. Pare away the thin layer of flesh next to the rib cage on both sides until you reach the wings.

Step 3: Cut through the joint and sinews joining the wings to the carcass and turn the wings inside out, pulling the bone upwards and cutting away the flesh to release it.

Step 4: Continue cutting the flesh from the carcass as close to the bones as possible with short, firm strokes until the thigh is reached. Cut through the joints and sinews as with the wings. Holding the end of the thigh bone, pare away the flesh until the next leg bone is reached. Cut through this joint as before and push down on the final bone of each leg, cutting through flesh and sinews to release the drumstick.

Step 5: Still following closely the line of the carcass cut away the breast meat being careful not to cut through the skin as you approach the breast bone. Repeat on the other side to free the carcass.

Step 6: Flatten the chicken out on a board with the flesh side uppermost. Spread with the stuffing of your choice and fold over the flesh and skin of both sides firmly and sew it together with fine string. Then fold the flap of skin from the neck and the skin from the rump end towards each other and secure with 2-3 stitches. Turn the chicken over and mold and push it into a good neat shape. You may prefer to leave the bone in the wing to give a more authentic chicken shape. Tie the chicken round with string if you wish.

Stuffed Boned Chicken with Dubonnet Sauce   Serves 4-6

1 × 4-4½lb roasting chicken, boned	4oz mushrooms, chopped
2 tbspns melted butter	1 egg, beaten
freshly ground black pepper	½ cup soft breadcrumbs
Stuffing:	1oz chopped pistachio nuts
2 tbspns butter	pinch of dried thyme
1 small onion, peeled and finely chopped	salt and freshly ground black pepper
2oz bacon, with rind removed, chopped	

Preparation time: about 35 minutes plus boning time (approx 35 minutes)
Cooking time: 1¾-2 hours

Preheat the oven to 400°F. Melt the butter in a small pan and gently fry the onion, bacon and mushrooms until soft. If there is a lot of liquid present, continue cooking, uncovered, to reduce. Take off the heat and stir in the egg, breadcrumbs, thyme and seasoning and mix well.

Lay the boned chicken out flat, skin side down and spread the stuffing down the center. Fold and sew as described above.

Place the chicken on a grid in a roasting pan, brush with melted butter and sprinkle with pepper. Cover with waxed paper or foil to protect the skin and roast for 15 minutes before turning the heat down to 375°F and cook for a further 1¼-1½ hours. (Note: a boned stuffed chicken will take longer to cook than an unboned bird of similar size). About 15 minutes before the end of the cooking time, remove the waxed paper to allow the bird to brown. Let it stand in a warm place for about 10 minutes to 'set' the joint before carving.

For the Dubonnet sauce: Pour off most of the chicken fat from the roasting tin, leaving the equivalent of about 2 tbspns. Stir in 2 tbspns flour adding a little more chicken fat if necessary to make a smooth roux. Stir in ⅔ cup chicken stock and ½ cup Dubonnet. Cook, stirring until the sauce thickens, then strain into a small pan. Add 1 teasp soy sauce, 1 tbspn redcurrant jelly and simmer for about 10 minutes. Check the seasoning, adding salt and sugar to taste.

Broiled Chicken with Bacon and Cucumber Sauce

4 chicken breasts	1 bay leaf
oil for basting	salt and freshly ground black pepper
Bacon and cucumber sauce:	3in piece of cucumber, peeled and finely chopped
2 tbspns butter	2 tbspns heavy cream
2 slices of smoked bacon, with rind removed and finely chopped	1 teasp chopped or scissored chives
2 tbspns flour	
1¼ cups milk	

Preparation time: 20 minutes
Cooking time: 20 minutes

Wash the chicken joints and pat dry with kitchen paper. Brush them lightly with oil then brush the grid of the broiler with oil to prevent the chicken from sticking. Broil under a moderate heat for about 20 minutes, turning frequently and basting with the fat and juices from the pan. While the chicken is cooking, prepare the sauce.

Melt the butter in a small pan and lightly fry the bacon. Stir in the flour and cook for about 1 minute. Take off the heat and pour in the milk, stirring well to mix thoroughly. Return the pan to the heat and cook, stirring constantly, until the sauce thickens. Add the bay leaf and seasoning (little salt is needed) and simmer very gently for 10 minutes. Add the cucumber and cook for a further 5 minutes. Just before serving, stir in the cream and chives.

Crispy Oven-baked Chicken Joints

Serves 6

6 chicken joints	½ teasp barbecue spice
¼ cup butter, melted	salt and freshly ground black pepper
6oz cornflakes	

Preparation time: 15 minutes
Cooking time: approx 1 hour

Preheat the oven to 350°F. Wash the chicken pieces and pat dry with kitchen paper. Put the cornflakes in a plastic bag and crush finely with a rolling pin. Pour the melted butter into a shallow dish and mix in the barbecue spice, and seasoning. Coat each joint in the melted butter and place in the bag with the cornflakes and shake them together to cover the chicken with crumbs evenly. Repeat with the other joints.

Place the joints on a wire grid in a baking tin and bake for about 1 hour until they are golden brown and juices run clear when the chicken is pricked with a skewer. Serve with Spicy Tomato and Onion Sauce (see page 123).

Crispy Oven-Baked Chicken Joints.

Chicken and Pepper Kebabs.

Chicken and Pepper Kebabs

4 chicken thighs	8 tomatoes, quartered
8 slices of bacon, cut in half and rolled	oil for cooking
1 onion, quartered	**Garnish:** lettuce and watercress
½-1 green pepper, cubed	

Preparation time: 10 minutes
Cooking time: 15 minutes

Cut the flesh of the chicken thighs away from the bone and cut into cubes. Thread the chicken, bacon rolls, onion, pepper and tomatoes alternately on 8 skewers. Brush with a little oil, place under a preheated broiler and cook for about 15 minutes, turning frequently.

Serve on a bed of lettuce and watercress, with crusty rolls.

Duck

Duck makes delicious eating for festive occasions but is a fairly extravagant dish. A 5-6lb bird will only provide 4 reasonable portions. A 3-4lb duckling will have enough meat for 2 servings.

As they are very fatty birds, it is best to roast them and serve a tangy, fruity sauce to complement the richness.

Roast Duck with Black Cherry Sauce

5-6lb roasting duck, dressed	**Black cherry sauce:**
salt and freshly ground black pepper	16oz can black cherries
flour for dusting	½ cup port wine
	2 tbspns flour
	salt and pepper to taste

Preparation time: 25 minutes
Cooking time: about 2 hours (see below)

Preheat the oven to 375°F. Sprinkle the duck with salt and black pepper and place, breast side up, on a grid in a baking pan. Pour in about ½in cold water and place the pan in the center of the oven. Allow 20 minutes per lb and 20 minutes over. After about 25 minutes of cooking time turn the duck over. 30 minutes before the end of cooking time, turn the duck over again (breast side up), sprinkle with flour and turn the oven up to 425°F to crisp the skin.

To make the sauce: While the duck is roasting, drain off the juice from the cherries and mix it with the port. Make the liquid up to a scant 1¼ cups with water if necessary. Remove the pits from the cherries. When the duck is cooked, place it on a serving dish to keep warm and pour off most of the fat from the roasting pan, leaving about a 1-2 tbspns or so. Stir the flour into the pan juices over gentle heat (you can cook this stage in the roasting pan) and, when it is well mixed to a smooth paste, add the cherry juice and port. Mix well then strain into a small saucepan, add the cherries and cook gently for about 5-6 minutes. Season to taste and serve separately with the duck.

Canton Roast Duck with Stir-fried Chinese Leaves

This method of cooking helps to reduce the fattiness of duck. The meat is tender and succulent, enhanced by the delicious honey glaze.

1 roasting duck, approx 5lb, dressed	salt and 1 teasp black peppercorns
1¼ cups dry white wine or dry cider	1 tbspn soy sauce
1 piece fresh ginger root (approx 1in), sliced	3 tbspns clear honey
1 bay leaf	1 tbspn sherry

Preparation time: 10 minutes (duck)
Cooking time: 1 hour 25 minutes

Preheat oven to 400°F. Place the duck in a large pan with the white wine and sufficient cold water to just cover. Add the ginger, bay leaf, salt to taste and the peppercorns. Bring to the boil, turn down the heat and simmer gently for 45 minutes. Remove the duck from the pan and place, breast side up on a grid in a roasting pan. Sprinkle with a little salt and place in the oven for 20 minutes, then turn the oven up to 450°F. Put the soy sauce, honey and sherry into a small pan and heat gently to combine. Take the duck out of the oven and brush the skin liberally with this glaze. Roast for 20 minutes more, basting once with glaze.

Canton Roast Duck with Stir-Fried Chinese Leaves.

Stir-fried Chinese leaves

Mix together 1 tbspn sherry, 4 tbspns good stock; 2 tbspns cornstarch and salt to taste.

Heat 2 tbspns peanut oil or corn oil in a skillet and stir-fry-toss ¼ head of chopped Chinese leaves; 2 chopped stalks of celery; 2-3 chopped scallions; 1 crushed clove of garlic (optional) and the drained slices of ginger from the duck liquid for 1 minute over fairly high heat. Stir in the stock mixture and toss the vegetables until the sauce makes a thick glossy coating. Serve immediately.

To carve roast duck

First cut off the legs and wings. Next, make a downwards cut at right angles to the breastbone at the neck end to remove the wishbone. Then, beginning at the breastbone, and parallel to it, make deep, angled cuts to remove the breast meat in neat slices.

Traditional Festive Turkey

For important celebrations such as Thanksgiving, Christmas and Easter, roast turkey has long been established as the main course dish. The simple method of cooking combined with generous servings, and the adaptability of the cooked meat for use in salads or made-up dishes make turkey very popular. Nowadays turkey is marketed all the year round in a variety of different cuts and joints. Boneless rolled turkey roasts are very good value for family meals.

When cooking a large turkey there are two important points to remember: allow plenty of thawing time if using a frozen bird, and allow enough cooking time. Use the charts below to calculate timings:

Thawing times and approximate servings

Oven-ready weight	Room temperature thawing time	Approx servings
5-8lb	15-18 hours	6-10 servings
8-11lb	18-20 hours	10-15 servings
11-15lb	20-24 hours	15-20 servings
15-20lb	24-30 hours	20-30 servings
20-25lb	30-56 hours	30-40 servings

To check whether the bird is thawed, look in the body cavity – there should be no ice crystals.

Guide to cooking times

Weight	Time 350°F	Time (foil-wrapped) 350°F
5-8lb	2-2½ hours	2½-3½ hours
8-11lb	2½-3¼ hours	3½-4 hours
11-15lb	3¼-3¾ hours	4-5 hours
15-20lb	3¾-4¼ hours	5-5½ hours
20-25lb	4¾-5½ hours	not recommended

Roast Turkey Dinner.

Tips on turkey cooking

The times given above are approximate as oven temperatures vary. At times, when there is a great demand for power, you may find that your electric oven temperature fluctuates, so it is a good idea to buy a cooking thermometer to test the heat inside the bird and, therefore, whether it is done. Test the bird about 30 minutes before your estimated end of cooking time. If you do not have a thermometer, insert a skewer into the thickest part of the drumstick or breast. If the juices run pink then allow at least another 20 minutes cooking time. Allow the turkey to stand for 15 minutes before carving to 'set' the meat.

Cooking in foil

Cooking a turkey in foil has a number of advantages. It helps to prevent the delicate breast from drying out and gives tender succulent meat without the need for frequent basting. Also, using foil helps to keep your oven clean, preventing the fat and juices from splashing the oven walls.

Wrap the bird very loosely in foil after spreading it with softened butter and sprinkling with seasoning. About 30-45 minutes (depending on size) before the end of cooking time, turn up the oven slightly and open up the foil to brown the breast.

Stuffing the Turkey

Turkey and stuffing are inseparable partners, whether you choose the traditional varieties or go for something more unusual. Never stuff the body cavity as it is too big, and you may get a soggy, greasy and possibly undercooked mush. Instead, with your fingers, gently separate the skin from the breast at the neck end to make a pocket. Push the stuffing into this pocket and make a neat round shape. Then tuck the neck skin underneath and secure with a small skewer. Handle the skin very carefully without tearing it. With small birds it is a good idea to use the stuffing to cover the breast meat. The advantage of this is that the stuffing protects and flavors the tender breast during cooking and it can be carved with the meat.

Chestnut and Sausage Stuffing

Sufficient for a 12-14lb turkey

1½lb fresh chestnuts or 1 large can unflavored whole chestnuts
1 medium onion, peeled and finely chopped
2 tbspns butter
1lb sausagemeat
1 large egg, beaten
2 stalks celery, trimmed and finely chopped
1 tbspn fresh parsley, chopped
½ teasp dried thyme
little salt and generous amount of freshly ground black pepper

Preparation time: 25 minutes
Cooking time (prior to stuffing or baking): 40 minutes

Prepare fresh chestnuts well in advance. Cut through the skin on both sides with a sharp knife. Boil for about 5 minutes then drain and cool slightly. You will then be able to peel off the outer and inner skins. Simmer until tender (30-40 minutes) in chicken or vegetable stock. Chop or mince finely. If using canned chestnuts, drain and chop finely.

Fry the onion in the butter until soft. Remove from the heat and mix with the chestnuts and all the other ingredients. Use the mixture to stuff the neck end of the turkey. If any remains, form into small balls and place around the bird to bake. If preferred, you can bake the stuffing separately in a greased cake or loaf tin.

Forcemeat Balls   Serves 4-6

6oz lean pork or veal
2oz bacon
1 large egg, beaten
1 cup soft breadcrumbs
1-2 tbspns fresh parsley, chopped
½ teasp dried thyme or dried mixed herbs
grated rind of ½ lemon
salt and freshly ground black pepper

Preparation time: 20 minutes
Cooking time: 30-35 minutes

Mince the meats finely or work in a food processor. Combine with all the other ingredients until the mixture is of a soft, workable consistency. If dry add a little cold water to moisten; if wet add extra breadcrumbs. Form into small balls with the hands. Bake in a greased roasting tin or place round the turkey or joint for about 30-35 minutes at moderate heat (350°F).

Game cooking guide

While the species of game hunted vary from country to country, broadly speaking the category includes such birds as pheasant, partridge, grouse, ptarmigan, dove, quail, woodcock, snipe, wild duck and goose. Furred game includes wild rabbit, hare and venison.

Most types of game make excellent eating, provided that they are properly hung and correctly cooked. Hanging is essential for most species as it tenderizes the flesh and provides the characteristic flavor. The length of time needed to hang game depends on the type, the weather and how 'high' you wish to eat it. When buying game from a butcher or poulterer, it should already be fully hung and 'dressed' for the table (ie plucked and gutted). If, however, you are given a brace (pair) of game birds, hang them up by their necks in a cool place. Unless the weather is very cold, tie a large paper bag loosely but securely around the birds to keep away any flies. In warm weather, a week may be sufficient hanging for a pheasant or partridge, while in winter 2-3 weeks may be needed. As a rough guide, the skin on the abdomen becomes a greenish color and the tail feathers pull away easily when the birds are ready. If you prefer not to dress them yourself, your butcher or fish seller will probably do it for you for a small charge.

General cooking tips

Game has very little fat so it is important to protect the meat from drying out, particularly when roasting. Do this by barding the breast of birds or exposed surface joints with fat. You can use fat bacon or pork or thin slices of pork fat. These are tied to the birds or joints with string and removed 10 minutes before removing from the oven to allow the meat to brown. Alternatively, spread the breasts or meat with butter and cover with foil or greaseproof paper. Baste the meat with the melted butter from time to time. Remove the paper 10 minutes before the end of the cooking time to allow browning.

Put a knob of butter inside the body cavity before roasting to help keep the flesh moist. A peeled onion or apple is also effective and adds extra flavor.

Make sure that the game is suitable for roasting – only young, properly hung game should be cooked in this way. If you have any doubts about age, pot-roast slowly or cook in a casserole.

Pheasant

This is one of the most popular and readily available game birds. The breast meat is white and well textured and has a delicious nutty flavor – enjoyable to most palates – and is not excessively gamey. A good-sized cock bird will serve 3-4 portions.

Pheasants should be hung for 2-3 weeks, depending on the weather. Young roasting hens have soft flexible skin on their feet while young cocks can be identified by their spurs which are short and fairly blunt.

To roast: Bard with bacon or pork fat and place a small peeled onion in the body cavity. Roast in a hot oven (400°F) for 15 minutes, reduce the oven to 375°F and continue cooking for a further 40-50 minutes, depending on size. Test with a skewer in a fleshy part – the juices should run clear when the bird is cooked. Do not overcook or it will become dry.

Serve roast pheasant with gravy and/or Bread Sauce (see page 121), breadcrumbs fried in butter, bacon rolls, redcurrant or rowan jelly and garnish with watercress.

Partridge

These are smaller than pheasant and more delicately flavored. They are more plentiful at the beginning of the season. Young birds should be hung for only a short time –

4-6 days depending on the weather. One plump young partridge will serve 2 portions and can be roasted, or split and broiled.

To roast: Insert a good knob of butter and half a lemon into the body cavity. Bard with bacon or pork fat and roast in a hot oven (425°F) for about 30-40 minutes depending on size. Serve with bigarade sauce (see page 122) or a clear gravy, fried breadcrumbs and bacon rolls and garnish with orange or lemon wedges.

Grouse and ptarmigan
Grouse is regarded as one of the finest game birds for the table. It has a fairly strong, almost musky flavor and dense, dark-textured breast meat. Unlike most game, grouse should be eaten reasonably fresh as they tend to get 'high' quickly, especially early in the season when the weather is still warm. Young birds are normally roasted and it is best to allow one bird per person. To identify a young grouse hold the bird by the lower mandible which should feel flexible. Also the third feather of the extended wing is short in a young bird.

To roast: Knead a large knob of butter with a little lemon juice, grated lemon rind and seasoning and place it in the body cavity. Bard the breast with bacon or pork fat and roast at 425°F for about 35 minutes. Serve with fried bread-crumbs, thin gravy and lemon slices. If allowing half a grouse per person serve with bacon rolls or slices of boiled ham or bacon.

Ptarmigan are related to grouse but are smaller and more subtle in flavor. Roast in a hot oven (as for grouse) for about 25 minutes.

Dove
This is an inexpensive but flavorful game bird. Only the very young birds should be roasted or split and broiled. Older birds are best pot-roasted or casseroled. These birds should not be hung but eaten fresh. The best way to prepare them is simply to slice off the breasts while still feathered and skin them. Young birds will be smaller and have a little flexibility in the breast bone.

To roast dove breasts: Make sure that the whole of the breast is well covered with fat bacon or pork fat and roast on a grid in a pan in a hot oven (425°F) for about 20 minutes, with a little water in the bottom of the pan. Remove the fat and brown swiftly under the broil and serve on croûtons of fried bread with Espagnole Sauce (see page 122).

To broil: Spread with plenty of softened butter and broil for 15-20 minutes, basting and turning frequently.

Quail
Although classified as a game bird, most quail on sale are reared on farms. Allow 2 quail per person unless serving as an appetizer. Roast whole, undrawn.

To roast: Spread the breast of each bird with softened butter and cover well with fat bacon. If canned vine leaves are available, wrap the birds with these and secure with string or a skewer. If the vine leaves are very salty, soak then first. Roast at 425°F for about 20 minutes. Serve on croûtons of fried bread with the usual game accompaniments as given for pheasant.

To broil: Quail can be split and broiled, well basted with butter for 6-7 minutes on each side.

Woodcock and snipe
Regarded as the 'hunter's prize,' these are well-flavored birds which are usually hung until quite high. As with quail the birds are cooked undrawn and, traditionally, the head should be left on (skinned) so that the long beaks can be used as a skewer to secure the legs to the body. Roast

Woodcock as for quail (omitting the vine leaves) and roast snipe for 6 or 7 minutes less. Serve on croûtons.

Wild duck and goose
Although not strictly classified as game birds, wildfowl make excellent eating and cannot be overlooked. The term 'wild duck' includes such species as widgeon, teal and black duck but the most commonly available species is the mallard. They are hung for a very short time (3-4 days at the most) and are drawn for roasting as for pheasants. One duck will give 2 servings. It is usual to serve duck slightly undercooked – the flesh is succulent and delicate and is easily spoiled by overcooking.

To roast: Spread the breasts of the duck with softened butter and pour over a glass each of red wine and fresh orange juice. Roast at 425°F for about 35 minutes, basting frequently with the juices from the pan. Serve with slices of fresh orange and Bigarade Sauce (see page 122), or make a gravy from the pan juices and stock slightly thickened with all-purpose flour mixed with a little water.

Wild goose is quite similar to domestic goose in flavor but is less oily. Place a peeled apple in the body cavity and add a little red wine to the roasting tin. Cover loosely with foil and roast at 350°F allowing 25 minutes per lb and baste fairly frequently.

Rabbit and hare
Rabbits are usually drawn immediately and hung for no longer than 1-2 days. Young ones can be roasted whole stuffed with forcemeat (see page 97) but they must be well barded with fat and basted or the flesh will be dry. Roast for about 1 hour in a hot oven (425°F).

Hares are usually hung for 1-2 weeks before being skinned and drawn. A whole young hare or leveret can be stuffed and roasted whole, well barded with fat bacon and covered loosely with foil, at 375°F for 1½-2 hours depending on size. A whole leveret will serve 4-6 portions while a fully grown hare will serve as many as 8 portions. Serve with a rich brown sauce and redcurrant jelly.

Venison
The haunch is the prime cut of venison to choose for roasting. This delicious, gamey, fine-textured meat benefits from being steeped in a marinade before cooking. For the marinade use a proportion of half oil (olive oil is best) to red wine with a medium onion, peeled and sliced; a carrot, peeled and sliced; a trimmed, chopped celery stalk; 2-3 parsley stalks; a bay leaf; 6 crushed juniper berries and a teaspoon of black peppercorns. Bring all the ingredients to the boil then allow to cool. Pour the cool liquid over the meat (in a non-metallic dish) and leave to marinate for at least 24 hours. The traditional method of roasting venison was to coat it with a stiff paste of flour and water to seal in the flavor and juices, but you can bard it with fat, as described previously, and cover it loosely with foil. Roast at 375°F for 30 minutes per lb, basting frequently. Approximately 10-15 minutes before the end of roasting time, remove any fat. Baste and sprinkle the meat with a little flour and finish cooking.

Make gravy by stirring about a tablespoonful of flour into the juices in the roasting pan and cooking until brown. Then add ⅔ cup of red wine and the same quantity of brown stock and stir until the sauce thickens. Season and flavor with a teaspoon of grated lemon rind and a tablespoon of redcurrant jelly. Garnish with decorative croûtons and watercress and serve redcurrant jelly separately.

Barbecues

Cooking on a barbecue

Make sure that most of the food to be cooked and salad or other accompaniments are prepared before you start.

First, line your firebowl with foil. This helps to reflect heat and also keeps the bowl clean. Spread a single layer of charcoal across the bowl then pile it up in a heap over 1-2 firelighter blocks cut into quarters. Light the firelighters and keep an eye on it to make sure it ignites properly. Once you are satisfied that the charcoal is burning well, leave it for about 30 minutes or until there is a light coating of grayish-white ash over all the coals. Rake the charcoal back into a flat, even layer and you are now ready to begin cooking. Before putting the grid over the firebowl brush it with oil to prevent the food sticking.

Tips:

✩ When cooking meats such as pork and chicken which need to be well done, try using the indirect cooking method: rake the burning coals into two sections leaving a clear center section on to which you place a rectangular foil freezer container to catch drips. Place the food directly over the charcoal for a few minutes to seal and brown each side then move it to the center over the drip-tray. Food cooked this way will need longer cooking than the direct method but it will cook through satisfactorily without being scorched on the outside and raw in the middle!

✩ Do not try to cook too much food at once or it will cook unevenly with much flaming and smoke and give poor results.

✩ Use tongs to turn the food frequently to ensure even cooking and keep basting or brushing with oil. Do not leave the barbecue unattended and be careful to ajust the height of the grid above the coals to prevent scorching.

Marinading

Try marinading meat for 2-3 hours beforehand. This will help to tenderize the meat and enhance the flavor. Use the marinade for basting, too.

For a simple beef marinade: Combine ⅔ cup red wine; 3 tbspns olive or corn oil; 1 teasp Worcestershire sauce; 1 crushed clove of garlic; 1 teasp dried mixed herbs; 1 teasp sugar; salt and freshly ground black pepper.

For pork, lamb and chicken (especially kebabs): Combine ⅔ cup white wine; 3 tbspns olive or corn oil; 1 small onion, sliced; 1 tbspn chopped fresh parsley; grated rind of 1 lemon and 1 teasp of dried thyme; salt and freshly ground black pepper.

Accompaniments to barbecue meals

Jacket potatoes: Scrub large, even-sized potatoes, brush with oil and cut a cross in one side. Wrap each one in foil and bake over the grid for 45-60 minutes, turning from time to time. It is best to half-cook them in the conventional oven and finish them off on the barbecue, opening up the foil for 5 minutes to crisp the skins.

Whole kernel corn: Spread with butter and season with salt and pepper. Wrap each ear in foil

and cook over the barbecue for 25-35 minutes, turning occasionally.

Garlic or herb bread: Combine ½ cup of softened butter with 1-2 crushed or finely-chopped garlic cloves or 1 tablespoon chopped fresh parsley and 1 teaspoon dried mixed herbs. Make diagonal cuts about 1in apart almost through the loaf. Spread the flavored butter down in between the slices. Wrap the loaf in foil and place on the grid to heat through for at least 15-20 minutes.

Barbecuing fish

Always choose firm fish when barbecuing cutlets, such as monkfish, halibut or salmon. If you intend to barbecue fish regularly then it is a good idea to buy one of the flat, hinged wire holders which help to keep steaks and whole fish intact.

When barbecuing whole fish such as trout, red mullet or snapper, try marinading them for an hour or two (in a non-metallic dish) in the following mixture: 3 tbspns olive or corn oil; 1 tbspn lemon juice; 1 tbspn soy sauce; 1 tbspn sherry.

Cook the fish over direct heat for 6-7 minutes each side (turning only once) depending on the size, basting from time to time with the marinade.

You can also cook fish by wrapping it in foil with a spoonful or two of the marinade. This method requires a longer cooking time and you should open up the parcel to allow the smoke from the barbecue to flavor the fish. An alternative method is to line a thick foil container with foil to make a shallow pan and lay the fish in this, well basted with marinade or melted butter.

For a special treat try barbecuing uncooked lobster tails (buy them frozen from freezer centers or supermarkets) or jumbo shrimp. For lobster, cut away the membrane on the underside with scissors then bend the tail backwards until it cracks to prevent it curling up. Brush with melted butter and place, shell-side down, over direct heat and cook for 6-10 minutes, depending on the degree of heat. Turn over and brush the underside with more butter and broil for another 6-10 minutes. Serve with lemon wedges and more melted butter (and finger bowls). For the shrimp, cook these whole brushed with melted butter or oil for 3-4 minutes each side.

Quick Barbecue Sauce

2 tbspns tomato catsup
1 tbspn mushroom catsup
1 tbspn Worcestershire sauce
1 tbspn soy sauce
1 tbspn Hoisin sauce
dash of tabasco (to taste – use sparingly)

Preparation time: 3 minutes
Cooking time: 5 minutes

Combine all the ingredients in a small saucepan and heat gently, mixing well. Use this sauce to baste foods, particularly chicken, during cooking and for serving separately.

VEGETABLE COOKERY

Artichoke Vinaigrette

Choose fat, fresh-looking artichokes (one per person) free from brown spots or shrivelled leaves. Cutt off the stems level with the bases and neatly level the tops with a sharp knife. Using scissors, snip off the prickly points of the lower leaves. Wash well and cook in boiling salted water for about 30 minutes, depending on the size. They are cooked when you can pull away one of the outer leaves easily. Drain upside down and allow to cool. Serve with side bowls of vinaigrette dressing (see page 130).
To eat: Pull off the outer leaves, dip the bases in the dressing and nibble off the soft edible part. Discard the rest of the leaves. Working inwards round the artichoke you will

eventually reach a pointed circle of tiny leaves – these will lift off together revealing the hairy 'choke.' Using a spoon, scrape off the hairy bit to reveal the dish-shaped 'heart' which is delicious.
Variation: Artichokes can also be served cold with mayonnaise (see page 130) or warm with hollandaise sauce (see page 125). For a special occasion, try removing the chokes and stuffing with your favorite ingredients such as shrimp or crabmeat mixed with spicy mayonnaise; chopped button mushrooms and fresh tomatoes sautéd in a little butter; chopped liver or ham mixed with herb-flavored breadcrumbs or rice bound with a little melted butter and baked for about 20 minutes in a moderate oven. Remember to give your guests finger bowls with these.

Variations
Leeks: Take about 1½lb young leeks, and cut off the green tops and roots. Slice the stems almost through to the base, open out the layers and wash well. Boil in salted water for about 10 minutes until they are tender. Drain well and allow to cool. Serve with a sharp vinaigrette dressing (see page 130).
Carrots: Scrub about 1-1½lb young carrots and boil whole in salted water, with a good pinch of sugar, for about 10-15 minutes. Drain and allow to cool. Serve with vinaigrette dressing (see page 130) and thinly sliced onion rings.
Green Beans Greek-style: Wash, top and tail about 1lb French beans and cook in salted boiling water for between 5 and 10 minutes according to taste (they should retain plenty of 'bite') and drain. To a basic vinaigrette dressing, (see page 130) add a finely chopped or crushed garlic clove and a pinch of cayenne pepper. Pour this over the beans while they are still warm and marinate for at least 2 hours in the refrigerator.

Artichoke Vinaigrette.

Tomato-Mushroom Filo

A savory strudel-like pastry made with wide, paper-thin sheets of filo pastry – obtainable at many delicatessens and large supermarkets.

4 large, ripe tomatoes, peeled, de-seeded and chopped	⅓ cup butter
1 medium onion, peeled, and finely chopped	½ cup fresh breadcrumbs
1 stalk celery, trimmed and finely chopped	pinch of basil
2 slices bacon, de-rinded and finely chopped (optional)	salt and pepper
½ cup button mushrooms, finely sliced	6-7 sheets filo pastry (approx 4oz)

Preparation time: 25 minutes
Cooking time: 55 minutes

Gently 'sweat' the tomatoes, onion, celery, bacon and mushrooms in 2 tbspns butter for 5-6 minutes. Take off the heat and stir in the breadcrumbs, basil and salt and pepper to taste.

Melt the remaining butter. Open out the pastry and lay a sheet on a clean dry surface. Brush with melted butter and lay another sheet of pastry over and brush this with butter. Continue until all the pastry is used up.

Preheat the oven to 350°F. Spread the filling evenly over the center section of the layered pastry sheets. Fold one third of the pastry over the filling. Brush with butter and fold the outside edges over towards each other like an envelope. Fold the third section over the top and tuck in the edges. Brush with melted butter and bake for about 50 minutes until the pastry is golden.

Cut into 4 and serve as an unusual hot starter or as a lunch dish with salad. It is equally good warm or cold.
Tip: While preparing each sheet of pastry keep the rest covered with plastic wrap to prevent it drying.

Greek-style Mushrooms

3 tbspns olive oil	2 teasps tomato paste
1½lb fresh button mushrooms, sliced (leave whole if tiny)	1 teasp sugar
1 celery stalk, trimmed and sliced	bouquet garni (see page 126)
1 medium onion, peeled and coarsely chopped	salt and freshly ground black pepper
3 ripe tomatoes, peeled and sliced	**Garnish:** Chopped fresh parsley
⅔ cup red wine	

Preparation time: 10 minutes
Cooking time: 25 minutes

Heat the oil in a heavy-based saucepan and add the mushrooms, celery and onion, cover and cook for 2-3 minutes. Add the rest of the ingredients and simmer, covered, for a further 15-20 minutes. Remove the bouquet garni, drain, chill well and serve as a starter with lots of crusty bread or as part of a salad course.
Variations: Leeks, zucchini, eggplant, carrots, cauliflower, and baby onions are also good cooked in this way.

Cauliflower and Egg Bake

1 medium head of cauliflower	1¼ cups milk
1 medium onion peeled and sliced	¾ cup cheddar cheese, finely grated
2 slices smoked bacon, de-rinded and chopped	½ teasp mustard powder
¼ cup butter	2 eggs, beaten
2 tbspns flour	salt and freshly ground black pepper
	2 large ripe tomatoes, peeled and sliced (optional)
	¼ cup walnuts, chopped
	1 tbspn dried breadcrumbs

Preparation time: 20 minutes
Cooking time: 50-55 minutes

Wash the cauliflower and divide into small florets. Bring a pan of salted water to the boil, add the cauliflower and cook for 5-6 minutes. Drain and lay the florets in an ovenproof casserole and keep warm.

Stir-fry the onion and bacon in the butter for 2-3 minutes. Add the flour and cook for a further minute. Take off the heat and gradually stir in the milk. Cook until the sauce thickens, stirring continuously. Add ½ cup of the cheese, the mustard powder and seasoning and cook until the cheese has melted. Take off the heat and allow to cool slightly then whisk in the eggs. Preheat the oven to 350°F.

Lay the peeled, sliced tomatoes over the cauliflower and pour over the sauce. Sprinkle the top with the rest of the cheese mixed with the walnuts and breadcrumbs. Bake for about 35-40 minutes or until the egg mixture has set. Serve with warm crusty wholewheat rolls.

Lentil-stuffed Eggplant

2 large eggplants	1 cup button mushrooms, sliced
Stuffing	2 tbspns chopped parsley
½ cup brown lentils	salt and freshly ground black pepper
1 leek, trimmed and finely chopped	**Topping:**
2 garlic cloves, crushed	½ cup wholewheat breadcrumbs
3 tbspns olive oil	¼ cup grated cheese

Preparation time: 20 minutes
Cooking time: 1 hour 35 minutes

Place the lentils in a pan, cover with cold water and simmer until tender (about 45 minutes).

Cut the eggplants in half lengthways and scoop out the flesh from each half, leaving a ¼in thick shell. Place the skins in a lightly greased, shallow ovenproof dish.

Fry the leek and garlic in oil for 4-5 minutes; add the chopped flesh of the eggplants and mushrooms and cook for a further 5 minutes. Add the lentils, parsley and seasoning and pile this stuffing into the shells. Mix together the breadcrumbs and cheese and sprinkle this over the eggplant. Bake at 350°F for 35-40 minutes.

Serve with natural yogurt or Spicy Tomato-Sauce (see page 123).

Ratatouille.

Ratatouille

A tasty vegetable casserole which is equally delicious served hot or cold

1 large eggplant	6 tbspns olive oil
4 large ripe tomatoes	2 fat garlic cloves, crushed
2-3 medium zucchini	large pinch of oregano
1 large onion	1 teasp sugar
1 large carrot	salt and freshly ground black pepper
1 green or red sweet pepper	**Garnish:** chopped fresh parsley

Preparation time: 40-70 minutes
Cooking time: 30-40 minutes

Cut the eggplant into thick slices and quarter them. Place these chunks in a strainer on a plate or in the sink. Sprinkle them with salt and place a heavy pan on top of them. Leave for about 30 minutes.

Pour boiling water on to the tomatoes and leave for 2-3 minutes. Wash and cut the zucchini into thick slices and set aside. Peel, quarter, and de-seed the tomatoes and set aside. Peel and roughly chop the onion. Peel and cut the carrot into slices. Wash, de-seed and cut the pepper into squares.

Heat the oil in a heavy-based pan and gently sauté the garlic and onion for 3-4 minutes. Add the carrot, pepper and zucchini. Drain the egg-plant and pat dry with kitchen paper and add to the pan. Finally stir in the tomatoes, oregano, sugar and seasoning. Put on the lid and simmer gently for 30-40 minutes. Garnish with chopped parsley.

Tip: This dish is best cooked the day before it is needed and reheated or chilled before serving.

Stuffed Peppers

6 medium green or red sweet peppers

Stuffing:

1 medium onion, peeled and finely chopped

1 stalk celery, trimmed and finely chopped

¾ cup button mushrooms, finely chopped

¼ cup butter

2 ripe tomatoes, peeled, de-seeded and chopped

1 heaped tbspn pine kernels

¼ cup chopped ham (optional)

large pinch dried oregano

2 tbspns chopped fresh parsley

scant cup long grain rice, cooked

grated cheese or breadcrumbs for topping

salt and freshly ground black pepper

Preparation time: 35 minutes
Cooking time: 35-40 minutes

Soften the onion, celery and mushrooms in the butter for 2-3 minutes. Remove from the heat and stir in all the other ingredients (except for the breadcrumbs) mixing well.

Cut the bases off the peppers, scoop out the cores and seeds, taking care not to split the sides. Blanch the peppers by placing in fast-boiling salted water. Return the water to the boil and cook the peppers for 2 minutes. Refresh in cold water and drain.

Preheat the oven to 350°F. Fill the peppers with the stuffing, sprinkle with a small amount of breadcrumbs or grated cheese and sit them in a greased ovenproof dish. Add two spoonfuls of water to the dish and bake the peppers in the oven for about 40 minutes. Test for softness with the point of a sharp knife. Do not let them overcook or they will shrivel.

This makes a very substantial hot or cold starter — ideal to precede a salad meal.

Variations:
Stuffed tomatoes: for 6 people select 12 large, ripe even-sized tomaoes. Cut off the rounded end and take out the cores and seeds. Fill with the stuffing given, omitting the tomatoes and adding a pinch of sugar. Cover with foil and bake for about 15-20 minutes at 375°F.
Stuffed zucchini: for 6 people choose 6 fairly large (fat) zucchini. Parboil whole for 5 minutes in fast-boiling salted water. Allow to cool and slice in half, lengthways. Scoop out the centers and add them to the filling. Pile the stuffing into the zucchini halves and sprinkle each one with grated cheddar cheese. Bake for about 35-40 minutes at 350°F. Serve hot.

Rice-stuffed peppers (left); Spinach and Cheese Terrine.

Vegetable and Walnut Pâté

An unusual low-calorie vegetable and nut savory pâté which makes an interesting first course or a vegetable accompaniment.

¼ cup butter	pinch of dried thyme
1 medium onion, peeled and finely chopped	pinch of ground mace
3 celery stalks, trimmed and finely chopped	salt and freshly ground black pepper
8oz carrots, peeled and grated or shredded	
2-3 zucchini peeled and thinly sliced	
2 eggs, beaten	
½ cup chopped walnuts	
1½ cups soft wholewheat breadcrumbs	

Preparation time: 30 minutes (less with a food processor)
Cooking time: About 1 hour

Melt the butter in a large skillet or a wok and stir-fry the onion, celery, carrots and zucchini for 4-5 minutes until soft. (All these vegetables can be quickly and easily prepared in a food processor.) Transfer the vegetables into a mixing bowl and stir in the eggs and the rest of the ingredients. Mix well and turn into a greased 1lb loaf tin and bake at 325°F for 50-60 minutes until golden brown and firm. Allow it to stand for 5-10 minutes if serving hot, otherwise unmold and allow the pâté to cool.

Serve the pâté hot with Spicy Tomato Sauce or a Cheese or Mushroom Sauce (see page 120) followed by roast chicken or boiled ham. Or try it cold with brown toast or crackers garnished with sliced tomatoes and watercress.

Spinach and Cheese Terrine

1lb fresh leaf spinach	dash of Worcestershire sauce
1 medium onion, peeled and finely chopped	salt and pepper
2 tbspns butter	2 eggs, hard-boiled
⅔ cup cream cheese	
2 eggs, beaten	

Preparation time: 15 minutes
Cooking time: 50-60 minutes

Wash the spinach well and remove any coarse stalks. Drain well and cook without any water for 4-5 minutes with a pinch of salt and 1 teasp of sugar. Cool and squeeze out the juice through a sieve.

Fry the onion in the butter until just soft.

Beat the cheese with the eggs, onion and Worcestershire sauce and seasoning until smooth. Slice the eggs.

Pre-heat the oven to 350°F. Grease a 1½ cups terrine and cover the base with a layer of spinach (open out the leaves). Follow with a layer of egg then with a layer of the cheese and onion mixture. Repeat these layers until all the ingredients are used up, finishing with spinach. Cover with a double sheet of waxed paper and put on the lid. Place the terrine in a baking tin and pour in about ¾in water. Bake for about 50-60 minutes or until the mixture has just set. Press with a heavy weight and allow to cool before turning out.

Baked Red Cabbage with Apples

1 1½-2lb head of red cabbage	2 teasps brown sugar
2 large dessert apples, peeled, cored and sliced	⅛ teasp ground cinnamon
1 medium onion, peeled and sliced	pinch of grated nutmeg
1 tbspn melted butter	salt and freshly ground black pepper
3 tbspns wine vinegar	

Preparation time: 15 minutes
Cooking time: approx. 1 hour

Pre-heat the oven to 375°F. Slice the cabbage fairly finely removing any tough outer leaves and coarse stalks. Blanch for 3 minutes in a pan of fast-boiling salted water with 1 tbspn of the vinegar. Place in a greased baking dish with the apples and onion.

Pour over the melted butter, the rest of the wine vinegar and 2 tbspns water. Stir in the sugar, cinnamon, nutmeg and seasoning. Cover closely with buttered foil and bake for about 1 hour. This is delicious served as an accompaniment with gammon, pork, poultry or game.

Baked Red Cabbage with Apples.

Celeriac, Carrot and Corn bake

¼ cup butter *or*
  2 tbspns corn oil

12oz celeriac, peeled and grated or shredded

8oz carrots, peeled and grated or shredded

1 onion, peeled and finely chopped

8½oz can whole kernel corn, drained

⅛ teasp garam masala

salt and pepper

1¼ cups Béchamel sauce (see page 120)

½ cup grated cheddar cheese

1 egg, beaten

1 tbspn dried breadcrumbs

Preparation time: 25 minutes
Cooking time: 50 minutes

Heat the butter or oil in a large skillet or a wok. Add the celeriac, carrot and onion and stir-fry for 3-4 minutes or until the vegetables have softened. Spoon into a greased ovenproof casserole or gratin dish, mix in the whole kernel corn and season to taste.

Add the cheese to the sauce and heat until the cheese has melted. Allow to cool slightly and beat in the egg. Pour this mixture over the vegetables and sprinkle with breadcrumbs.

Bake for about 45 minutes at 350°F until the topping has risen slightly and has turned golden.
Tip: If you have a food processor, it will make light work of preparing this dish.

Herby Leeks and Carrots

12oz young leeks

12oz medium carrots

1 teasp sugar

¼ cup butter

1 teasp chopped fresh tarragon or good pinch of dried tarragon

freshly ground black pepper

Preparation time: 10 minutes
Cooking time: 15 minutes

Trim the coarse green part from the leeks and cut off the roots. Slice into rings and wash well. Scrub or peel the carrots and trim off the tops and tips. With a sharp knife, cut V-shaped slivers down the length of each carrot all the way round – 8 or 9 cuts. Then cut into thin slices and you will have pretty notched circles.

Plunge the leeks and carrots into salted boiling water, add the sugar and cook for 5 or 10 minutes, according to taste – ideally they should be quite crisp. Drain (keeping the liquid for use as vegetable stock). Toss the vegetables in the butter, tarragon and pepper until well mixed and serve.

Stuffed Squash

1 medium squash (2-3lb))

1 tbspn oil

8oz ground meat (bacon, pork or beef)

1 medium onion, peeled and finely chopped

scant cup cooked rice

½ teasp dried mixed herbs

1 egg, beaten

1 stalk celery, trimmed and finely chopped

½ tbspn tomato paste

salt and freshly ground black pepper

Preparation time: 25 minutes
Cooking time: approx. 1 hour

Cut the stalk end off the squash and scoop out the fleshy pith and seeds. Fry the meat and onion in the oil. Spoon into a bowl with a slotted spoon, add all the other ingredients and mix well. Use this mixture to stuff the squash and wrap it in foil. Bake in a moderate oven (350°F) for 40 minutes to 1 hour depending on size. Serve with Spicy Tomato Sauce (see page 123).

Braised Cabbage and Celery with Crumble Topping

2-3 slices bacon, with rind removed and chopped (optional)	1¼ cups Béchamel sauce (see page 120)
1½lb white cabbage, sliced	**Topping:**
1 small head of celery, trimmed and sliced	¼ cup lard or vegetable shortening
2 carrots, peeled and thinly sliced	1 cup wholewheat flour
1 small onion, peeled and thinly sliced	1½ cups finely grated Cheddar cheese
salt and freshly ground black pepper	

Preparation time: 15 minutes
Cooking time: 1 hour 20 minutes

Pre-heat the oven to 350°F. Fry the bacon (if using) in its own fat for 1-2 minutes. Fill a greased ovenproof casserole (7 cups) with alternate layers of cabbage, celery, carrot and lightly seasoned onion. Sprinkle with bacon and pour over the sauce. Bake uncovered in the oven for 35 minutes.
Topping: Rub the fat into the flour until the mixture resembles fine breadcrumbs. Stir in the cheese. Take the casserole out of the oven and sprinkle an even layer of the topping over the casserole. Increase the oven temperature to 400°F.

Bake for a further 35-40 minutes or until the topping is crisp and golden.

Kashmiri Vegetables

3 tbspns peanut or corn oil	3 cups potatoes, peeled and cut into small dice
½ teasp ground ginger	2 cups carrots, peeled and cut into small dice
1 teasp ground coriander	2-3 stalks celery, trimmed and sliced
½ teasp cardamom	1lb diced mixed vegetables (eg peas, French beans, cauliflowers, zucchini, okra, green or red peppers, eggplant, celeriac or parsnips)
¾ teasp cumin	
⅛ teasp cayenne pepper	
¼ teasp cinnamon	1 teasp sugar
1 tbspn wholewheat flour	salt to taste
⅔ cup vegetable stock or water	1 cup natural yogurt
1 teasp whole fennel seeds	**Garnish:** slices of red or green pepper; fresh coriander leaves
6 cloves	
pinch of grated nutmeg	

Preparation time: 15 minutes
Cooking time: 35 minutes

Heat the oil in a deep skillet or shallow flameproof casserole. Add the spices and stir-fry for 2-3 minutes then add the flour and cook, stirring, for another minute. Take off the heat and add the stock or water, stirring well until mixed. Return to moderate heat and cook, stirring, until it thickens. Add the fennel, cloves and nutmeg and firm-textured (root) vegetables and cook, covered, over very low heat for about 5 minutes. Add the remaining vegetables with a pinch of salt and the sugar and simmer gently for a further 15-20 minutes.

Beat the yoghurt until smooth and add a spoonful at a time, stirring well until it is all used up. Keep stirring for a few more minutes until it is heated through. Adjust the seasoning, adding more salt and cayenne if preferred, and serve garnished with sweet pepper and coriander leaves.

Boston Baked Beans

1⅔ cups dried navy beans	1 teasp made mustard
1 bay leaf	2 tbspns brown sugar
8oz salt belly pork or bacon in the piece	1 tbspn tomato catsup
1 medium onion, peeled and sliced	2 cups unseasoned vegetable or chicken stock
2 tbspns molasses	salt and freshly ground black pepper

Preparation time: 15 minutes
Soaking time: approx 12 hours
Cooking time: 7-8 hours

Rinse the beans, cover with cold water and leave overnight to soak. Drain and rinse the beans, cover with cold water and simmer with the bay leaf for about 1 hour. Drain and place in a deep, ovenproof casserole.

Cut the pork into fork-sized cubes and add to the beans with the onion. Mix the rest of the ingredients together and add to the casserole.

Add a little more stock or water if necessary to cover. Put on the lid and cook in a low oven (300°F) for 6-7 hours. Check from time to time while it is cooking, adding more liquid if necessary. Uncover the pot for the last 40 minutes to let the top brown.

Kashmiri Vegetables.

Hashed Brown Potatoes

1½-2lb old potatoes, boiled in their skins or baked in their jackets and peeled

1 medium onion, peeled and finely chopped

3 tbspns corn oil

3 tbspns beef drippings or bacon fat (or use all corn oil)

salt and freshly ground black pepper

Preparation time: 25 minutes
Cooking time: 15 minutes

Grate, shred or dice the potatoes into a bowl. Add the onion, season to taste. Heat the oil or oil and fat in a skillet and spoon the potatoes into the pan, pressing them into a cake.

Fry gently until golden brown underneath (use a non-stick pan or shake from time to time to prevent sticking). Invert onto a serving dish, brown side up.

Potatoes Dauphinoise

1½lb potatoes, peeled and thinly sliced

3oz Gruyère or Cheddar cheese, grated

1 small onion, peeled and sliced

⅔ cup light cream

1 garlic clove, finely chopped (optional)

salt and freshly ground black pepper

Preparation time: 20 minutes
Cooking time: 40-45 minutes

Preheat the oven to 375°F. Place a layer of potatoes in a buttered gratin dish, add a layer of onion, a little garlic (if using), a sprinkle of cheese and season lightly. Repeat these layers until all the ingredients are used up, ending with a layer of cheese on top. Pour over the cream, cover with foil and bake in the center of the oven for 40 minutes or until the potatoes are tender. Brown under a hot broiler.

Herbed Potato Cakes

2lb potatoes

1 small onion, peeled and chopped

1 tbspn butter

1-2 tbspns fresh parsley, chopped

2 teasps chopped fresh thyme or good pinch dried thyme

freshly ground black pepper

1 egg, beaten

flour for dusting

oil for frying

Preparation time: 10 minutes
Cooking time: about 25 minutes

Peel the potatoes and cook with the onion in salted water until tender (15-20 minutes).

Drain and mash the potatoes and onion with

the butter, herbs and pepper. Beat in the egg and shape into 8 cakes. Dust with flour and shallow fry for 2-3 minutes each side until golden brown.

Baked potatoes in their jackets
Always a favorite, jacket potatoes make a meal on their own if you flavor them with interesting toppings and stuffings. Choose old potatoes of a good shape and size (8oz-1lb depending on whether they are to be an accompaniment or a

snack meal). Scrub them well and if you like a crispy skin, brush them with oil. Prick the skins all over with a fork and bake for about 1 hour in a fairly hot oven 375-400°F. A good tip to make them cook quicker and more evenly is to insert a long steel skewer through the potato, length-

Stuffed Baked Potatoes.

ways. Squeeze the potatoes (with oven-gloves on) to test if they are cooked. When done, cut a cross in the top or halve them and top with one of the following: a big knob of butter or margarine; large spoonful of soured cream and a sprinkle of fresh chives; cottage or grated cheddar cheese; baked beans; avocado creamed with vinaigrette dressing or Guacomole; or chile con carne.

Based on 4 medium-sized potatoes.

Cheese and bacon: ¾ cup grated Cheddar cheese; 2 slices of bacon, chopped and fried until deliciously crisp.

Egg, onion and mayo: 2 large eggs, hard-boiled and chopped; 1 small onion, peeled and finely chopped and softened in butter or oil; 2-3 tbspns mayonnaise; 1 tbspn chopped fresh parsley.

Tuna and tomato: 4oz canned tuna, drained and flaked; 4 small-medium tomatoes, peeled, de-seeded and quartered; 2 tbspns mayonnaise or natural yoghurt.

Stir-frying vegetables

With the growing popularity of Chinese-style cooking using a wok, stir-frying has now become a well-accepted cookery technique in Western kitchens. The appeal of stir-frying is due partly to its speed, once the ingredients are prepared, and partly due to the fine flavor of vegetables cooked in this way.

The Wok
Stir-frying can be done in any large skillet but the best results are to be achieved by using the traditional Chinese wok. This utensil is made of thin carbon steel, although stainless steel, non-stick and electric versions are now available. The traditional carbon steel wok is the type most commonly and cheaply available but it needs to be carefully looked after as it tends to go rusty with lack of use. After a fair amount of use, the interior will blacken, providing its own semi-nonstick finish. Always wipe over the surface with oil before storing.

Stir-frying technique
The principle of stir-frying is to cook rapidly thinly sliced foods in a little oil over high heat by stirring and tossing so that the food is not scorched. This sounds simple but there are a number of points to be considered in order to get the best results:
The right oil to use: Oil is a better medium than animal fat as it reaches higher temperatures without smoking, especially the modern brands designed for deep-frying use. Avoid using stale oil or highly flavored types such as olive oil. Peanut and pure corn oil are probably the best types to use.
Preparing the ingredients: It is very important to have *all* the ingredients ready-prepared and close at hand. Once you start stir-frying, cooking takes place quickly and you will have no time to measure out items or stop and chop up a few more vegetables. Vegetable (and meat) ingredients should be finely shredded or sliced to a uniform size and shape so that they cook evenly. It is worth taking extra care

over this preparation for it is the key to successful stir-frying.
The correct heat: This knowledge really comes from practice as there is no effective way of measuring the heat of an ordinary wok as there is with deep-frying. The main thing is to watch it carefully, checking for heat-haze and darkening of the oil — if it becomes dark and smells strong it is too hot and may taint the vegetables. If you are unsure of the correct heat, practice with a little cubed bread first.

What vegetables can you stir fry?
Almost all vegetables can be cooked in this way. Some, however, benefit from being blanched or parboiled for 2-3 minutes before being stir-fried. These include: carrots, turnips, rutabega, French beans, asparagus, broccoli, cauliflower and green peas.

Stir-fried mixed vegetables
For 1lb prepared mixed vegetables, heat approximately 2 tbspns peanut or corn oil in the wok on high. Test the temperature by dropping in a piece of vegetable – if it sizzles immediately and begins to brown then start to add the rest, little by little. The best technique is to combine stirring with tossing to keep the ingredients on the move so that they do not scorch. As one batch cooks, push it to one side (up the side of the wok) before adding the next batch. Do not add too many vegetables at once otherwise the temperature of the oil will drop and they will not cook evenly and quickly.
    Add the harder, denser-textured or stalky vegetables first so that they cook for a little longer than the soft vegetables. As a guide, 3 minutes will probably be sufficient for most finely chopped and/or blanched vegetables but test for yourself as you cook. Ideally, stir-fried vegetables should be crisp, crunchy and tasty with a good color.
Seasonings and flavorings: Add about ½ teasp of salt and a good pinch of sugar to this quantity. Many other flavorings

can be used also; try some of the following: finely chopped or shredded fresh ginger root; finely chopped or crushed garlic; finely chopped scallions; blanched and slivered almonds; chopped or grated hazelnuts or walnuts; chopped fresh herbs; spices such as coriander, cumin, cardamom, mace, or cinnamon.

Sauces: If you prefer to serve stir-fried vegetables in a sauce, try mixing a teaspoonful of cornstarch with about 4-5 tbspns stock or water and adding a little soy sauce, Hoisin sauce and sherry for a deliciously Oriental touch. See also the Black Bean Sauce on page 42.

Other methods of frying vegetables

Frying often tends to be disapproved of as a cooking technique, being associated with smoking pans of hot fat in which foods high in calories and low in flavor and nutrition are cooked. Now the technique of sautéing, the French frying method, is popular – vegetables are tossed in a little butter and herbs to enhance their natural taste.

With the introduction of good-quality cooking oils with a high heat-tolerance it is possible to deep-fry so quickly and effectively that the flavor of food is cooked in, and the texture remains crisp yet succulent.

Shallow-frying or sautéing vegetables

Like stir-frying, most vegetables can be sautéd, especially if the coarser textured varieties are parboiled for 2-3 minutes and dried beforehand. Eggplant and zucchini can be sautéd without parboiling but they should be degorged first – a process whereby excess juice and any bitterness is drawn out by slicing the vegetables and sprinkling them with salt and covering them with a heavy weight for 30-40 minutes.

For the best results use butter, corn or peanut oil or, for a stronger flavor, olive oil, as the cooking medium. Do not use too much – the ideal is to quickly brown and seal the surfaces. A mixture of half butter and half corn oil is good. If using all butter, do not allow it to overheat or it will burn and spoil the food. Once the butter and oil is hot, add the vegetables, cut into slices, and stir them briskly until one side is browned, then cook the other sides.

Glazed carrots: Scrape 1lb young carrots, and boil in salted

Stir-fried Vegetables.

water until just tender. Drain well and sauté in 2-3 tbspns melted butter and 1 tbspn honey for 2-3 minutes.

Zucchini with garlic: Cut 1lb zucchini into fairly thick slices. Heat approximately 2 tbspns olive oil with 2 garlic cloves. Add the zucchini and sauté for 6-7 minutes or until tender. Remove the garlic and serve.

Deep-frying vegetables

Apart from perhaps potatoes and parsley, most foods benefit from some sort of coating to seal in the flavor before being deep fried. You can simply use flour or dip the pieces in batter (see Tempura batter on page 33) or beaten egg then breadcrumbs to give a good crispy coating. One advantage of deep-frying is that you do not need to pre-cook. The key point to watch for is the temperature of the oil. A satisfactory heat for most foods is somewhere around 375°F (except for potatoes which are first fried at a lower temperature and then refried to crisp up). Cooking thermometers will help you gauge this correctly but if you do not have one use a cube of stale bread – if it turns brown in 1 minute then the oil is ready. Do not try to deep-fry too much at once or the oil temperature will drop, leading to soggy food.

If you are frying smooth-textured food such as mushrooms, dust them with flour and shake off the excess before dipping them into the batter. This ensures that the batter coating sticks to the food being fried. If you are cooking a large amount of food, fry each batch until it is just golden (between 2-4 minutes depending on the size and texture of each piece), drain on kitchen paper and keep warm. Just before serving return all the fried vegetables to the oil (after checking that the temperature is correct) and fry to crisp up for a few moments.

Tempura

This exciting Japanese cook-at-table specialty is similar in concept to the Western-style fondu bourgnignonne. However, instead of cooking uncoated meat in hot oil, the Japanese dip tiny morsels of fresh seafood and vegetables into a smooth coating batter and deep-fry for a few minutes until they are crisp, golden and delicious. Piquant sauces are prepared in individual bowls for dipping.

Quick Reference Guide To Cooking Fresh Vegetables

Artichokes, globe
Preparation and cooking Cut off stems and coarse outer leaves. Wash well. Boil in salted water for 30-40 minutes. Drain upside down until cool.
Serving suggestions Best served cold with a sharp vinaigrette dressing or mayonnaise. Can also be served hot with melted butter and lemon juice. See page 104 for detailed recipes and cooking method.

Artichokes, Jerusalem
Preparation and cooking Wash well and peel (they can be cooked in their skins and peeled afterwards or par-boiled to soften the skin as they are very fiddly to peel fresh). If required to stand before cooking, place in water with a good dash of vinegar or lemon juice added to stop discoloration. Cook in boiling salted water for about 20 minutes or par-boil and sauté.
Serving suggestions Serve boiled with melted butter or a white sauce. Sprinkle sautéd artichokes with chopped fresh thyme. Can be mashed or puréed with butter or cream and pepper. Makes excellent soup.

Asparagus
Preparation and cooking Trim the bottoms and scrape the white part of the stems. Tie into bundles and, if you have a deep enough pan, stand the bundles upright. Boil for 15-20 minutes in salted water. Do not overcook or the tips will drop off.
Serving suggestions Serve hot with plenty of melted butter or a Hollandaise sauce or cold with vinaigrette dressing made with lemon juice or a well-flavored mayonnaise.

Beans, Broad (Fava)
Preparation and cooking Choose either tiny, immature pods which can be cooked whole (topped and tailed) or medium-sized mature pods containing smallish, tender beans. Do not buy or pick very large pods – the beans will have a bitter skin. Boil in salted water for about 10-15 minutes.
Serving suggestions Serve whole beans hot with butter and chopped parsley. Serve shelled beans with a cream or parsley sauce.

Beans, Green (French, wax, pole or runner)
Preparation and cooking Wash, top and tail and remove 'string' if necessary. If small, leave whole; slice larger beans diagonally. Cook in boiling salted water for 5-10 minutes.
Serving suggestions Drain and toss in butter with chopped herbs or crushed garlic if liked. Serve cold with a vinaigrette dressing spiced up with a little tomato paste and chilli powder.

Bean Sprouts (Alfalfa and mung beans)
Preparation and cooking Wash, drain and use in salad dishes or stir-fry for 1-2 minutes. Do not overcook, they should be crunchy.
Serving suggestions Add other vegetables, finely sliced with water chestnuts and sliced bamboo shoots and stir-fry to accompany a Chinese-style meal. Also good as a salad dish with a yoghurt dressing.

Beets
Preparation and cooking Select young beets. Wash well, handling carefully to avoid damaging the skins. Cut off the leaves and tapering root but do not peel. Cook whole for about 1 hour in salted water. Rub off the skins before serving.
Serving suggestions Slice thickly and serve hot with heated cream or a white sauce. Serve cold pickled in vinegar to accompany cold meats. Very good with cheese.

Broccoli
Preparation and cooking Wash well and cut off the coarse outer leaves and stalks. Slice through any thick stems lengthways. Cook uncovered in boiling salted water for 10-15 minutes depending on the size of the florets. Do not overcook; drain and serve immediately.
Serving suggestions Serve with a good cream sauce, or Hollandaise or Bernaise Sauce.

Brussels Sprouts
Preparation and cooking Remove any discolored leaves and cut a cross into the base of the stems. Cook in boiling salted water for about 10 minutes depending on size. Drain well and toss in the pan with butter before serving. Do not overcook or sprouts will turn yellow.
Serving suggestions Serve hot sprinkled with flaked almonds or chopped walnuts. Serve raw, thinly sliced, as an unusual winter salad vegetable.

Cabbage, Green or Savoy
Preparation and cooking Remove outer leaves and cut into quarters. Cut out the tough core and then slice the rest fairly finely so that it cooks quickly. Drop it into a pan of salted boiling water and cook fast for 6-8 minutes. Drain well, pressing down to extract the water. Toss the cabbage in the pan with butter.
Serving suggestions Serve buttered with plenty of freshly ground black pepper.

Cabbage, Red
Preparation and cooking Discard outer leaves and quarter. Cut out the core and slice finely. Place in a large pan with a large knob of butter, 2 tbspns each of wine vinegar and brown sugar, about 1⅔ cups of stock and seasoning. Cover tightly, bring to the boil, and reduce heat. Simmer very gently for 40 minutes-1 hour until the liquid has evaporated and the cabbage is very tender.
Serving suggestions Serve with roast meats and poultry. Particularly good with pork, bacon or sausages. A good winter salad vegetable.

Cabbage, White
Preparation and cooking Prepare as for green cabbage above but cook for slightly longer. Drain well and toss in the pan with butter.
Serving suggestions Serve very hot, buttered with tiny snippets of crisply fried bacon and lots of black pepper. Try scalloped cabbage: par-boil it, drain well and lay it in a greased gratin dish. Mask with a white sauce and sprinkle with breadcrumbs before baking in a moderate oven for about 25 minutes. Delicious raw in coleslaw with a tangy yoghurt dressing.

Carrots
Preparation and cooking Trim off the tops and tips and scrub if young, otherwise scrape or peel if old. Cook baby carrots whole, slice older ones. Cook in salted boiling water for between 10 and 20 minutes depending on size.
Serving suggestions After draining, heat equal amounts of butter and sugar in the pan until the sugar has dissolved. Reheat the carrots in this glaze and sprinkle with chopped parsley or tarragon. Older carrots are good mashed or puréed with butter and a sprinkle of freshly grated nutmeg.

Cauliflower
Preparation and cooking Wash well and remove outer leaves and coarse stems. Cook whole or divide into florets. If cooking whole, slice through the center of the stems. Cook for 15-20 minutes for a whole head or 10-15 minutes for florets in salted water with a dash of lemon juice.
Serving suggestions Serve with melted butter and chopped nuts or grated cheese. Mask with a cream or cheese sauce. Individual florets can be par-boiled and deep-fried in batter.

Celeriac
Preparation and cooking Wash, peel and slice, cut into julienne strips or grate. Boil in salted water for 20-30 minutes or braise as for celery. Delicious cooked with sliced carrots (see page 109).
Serving suggestions Serve with grated cheese or a cheese sauce.

Celery
Preparation and cooking Cut off the root, leaves and any discolored stalks. Separate the stalks and scrub well, trimming off any stringy fibers. Cut into neat lengths and cook for 20 minutes in fast-boiling salted water. Can be braised slowly in the oven in a little stock with sliced onion for 1-1½ hours.
Serving suggestions Serve hot as for celeriac. Try serving raw stuffed with cream cheese or taramasalata.

Chicory
Preparation and cooking Generally served raw in salads but also good braised in a little well-flavored stock. Cut away the base and stem before cooking.
Serving suggestions Thicken the cooking liquid before serving with a little cornstarch. Good with pork or veal.

Chinese leaves
Preparation and cooking Remove outer leaves and chop finely. Stir-fry for 1-2 minutes in oil. Serve raw in salads.
Serving suggestions Delicious served lightly seasoned with soy sauce and black pepper. Serve raw with a sharp vinaigrette dressing.

Corn-on-the-cob
Preparation and cooking Remove the outer husks and silky threads. Cook very young corn in unsalted water with a little sugar added for 5-6 minutes. Do not overcook it or it will become tough. Corn can also be wrapped in foil and roasted in a hot oven or over a barbecue for about 30 minutes.
Serving suggestions Serve with plenty of melted butter, sea salt and black pepper.

Cucumber

Preparation and cooking Mostly served raw in salads but also good sautéd or stir-fried.
Serving suggestions Makes an interesting flavoring in a white sauce for fish or a tangy cold dip with yoghurt and garlic. Delicious puréed raw for a cold soup.

Eggplant

Preparation and cooking Wash and peel (if preferred) slice and *degorge* by sprinkling with salt and leaving to stand, pressed with a plate. Drain off liquid and pat dry. Fry, coated in batter or seasoned flour. Can be halved and baked in a moderate oven.
Serving suggestions Serve with broiled meats, pasta or rice dishes. At its best stuffed (see recipe page 104) and baked or cooked in vegetable or meat casseroles.

Fennel

Preparation and cooking Cut off the leafy stems and root. Soak in cold water, wash well and cook as for celery.
Serving suggestions Serve raw, thinly sliced as a salad vegetable or boiled and coated in a white sauce to accompany fish.

Kale

Preparation and cooking Strip the green parts of the leaves off the stem and cook as for green cabbage with a little longer cooking time.
Serving suggestions Serve very well drained with plenty of butter.

Kohl Rabi

Preparation and cooking An interesting vegetable related to the cabbage. Cook as for celeriac.
Serving suggestions Good grated raw in salads.

Leeks

Preparation and cooking Cut off the green tops and roots. Slice through the white part of the stem towards the base but not quite through. Can be cut into halves or short lengths or rings. Boil in salted water for 10-15 minutes or braise slowly in stock in the oven for 40 minutes to 1 hour.
Serving suggestions Should be very well drained after cooking. Delicious served au gratin masked with a white sauce, sprinkled with crumbs and browned. Serve cold with a vinaigrette dressing.

Onions

Preparation and cooking Trim off the roots and papery skin. Cook baby onions whole in salted boiling water for 10-15 minutes. Large onions are good sliced and dipped in seasoned flour and shallow or deep-fried. Scallions are good stir-fried with other vegetables.
Serving suggestions Serve baby onions glazed as for carrots. Also good in a white sauce. Crisply fried onion rings make a good garnish for broiled meats or savory rice dishes.

Parsnips

Preparation and cooking Cut off the tops and tails and peel. If young, bake whole or par-boil in salted water and sauté. If fairly old, cut out the woody core and slice.
Serving suggestions Toss boiled parsnips in butter, black pepper and chopped parsley. Mash with butter, pepper and a pinch of cinnamon.

Peas, Garden or Green

Preparation and cooking Shell and boil in salted water with a spoonful of sugar and 1-2 sprigs of fresh mint for between 5 and 15 minutes depending on age and size. Drain well.
Serving suggestions Serve well buttered and garnished with fresh mint, snippets of cooked bacon or ham. Older peas can be served as a purée swirled with cream.

Peas, Snow, Sugar or Mange tout

Preparation and cooking Wash, top and tail. Fast boil for 2-3 minutes. Drain and season with salt and pepper.
Serving suggestions Serve with melted butter. Delicious stir-fried with carrots and cauliflower.

Peppers, Sweet or Capsicums

Preparation and cooking Wash and cut off the tops, deseed and slice; fry or stew. If stuffing, leave whole and blanch in boiling water before cooking in a moderate oven for 30-35 minutes.
Serving suggestions Serve stuffed with savory rice, breadcrumbs and nuts or a minced meat mixture. Use as part of a vegetable stew or raw in salads.

Potatoes

Preparation and cooking Cook by boiling, steaming, baking or frying. See page 127 for detailed cooking methods.

Pumpkin
Preparation and cooking Peel and cut into thin slices or cubes. Steam for 30-40 minutes or par-boil and sauté.
Serving suggestions Use puréed pumpkin in soups or as an accompanying vegetable or sweeten for use as a pie or tart filling.

Rutabega
Preparation and cooking Trim off leaf top and tapering root and peel thickly. Cut into small dice and boil in salted water for 25-30 minutes. Drain well, return to the pan and shake over heat to dry thoroughly.
Serving suggestions Serve diced with butter, grated nutmeg and plenty of black pepper or mashed. Makes a delicious soup with potatoes, carrots and onions.

Salsify or Oyster plant (White or black skinned)
Preparation and cooking Trim, wash and peel and cut into short lengths. If required to stand, cover with cold water containing a little lemon juice. Boil, steam or par-boil before sautéing in butter.
Serving suggestions The delicate earthy flavor is enhanced by a creamy sauce. Goes well in stews and mixed vegetable dishes.

Seakale
Preparation and cooking Wash well and tie into bunches. Boil in salted water for 20-25 minutes. Drain well.
Serving suggestions Serve with plenty of butter, seasoning or a white sauce.

Spinach
Preparation and cooking Wash thoroughly in plenty of water. Remove any yellowed leaves and coarse stems. Sprinkle with salt and a little sugar and boil without adding extra water for 7-8 minutes. Drain and press out excess water.
Serving suggestions Serve with butter or a Hollandaise sauce or finely chopped with soured cream.

Squash
Preparation and cooking Peel and remove the pithy core and seeds. Slice and par-boil before sautéing in butter and garlic for 5-6 minutes. Par-boil unpeeled whole or halved, stuff and bake for about 1 hour in a moderate oven wrapped in foil.
Serving suggestions Serve with chopped fresh herbs or a rich tomato sauce.

Sweet Potatoes
Preparation and cooking Scrub well, prick and boil in the skins for about 30 minutes. Or prick and bake in their skins in a moderate oven for about 1 hour. Can also be par-boiled and fried in slices.
Serving suggestions Split the skins and serve with plenty of butter and seasoning.

Swiss Chard
Preparation and cooking Wash well and separate the green leaves from the fleshy white stems. Boil the leaves in a small amount of salted water for about 10 minutes and simmer the stems in stock for 25-30 minutes.
Serving suggestions Thicken the liquid used to braise the stems to make a sauce and serve the leaves with butter and a squeeze of lemon juice.

Tomatoes
Preparation and cooking Cut in half, brush skins with oil and broil, or bake whole for 15-20 minutes in a moderate oven. Purée by peeling (plunge into boiling water for 2 minutes), deseeding and 'sweating' in a very little butter or oil.
Serving suggestions Serve raw, sliced with fresh basil, tarragon or onion rings. Bake stuffed with herbs, grated cheese, breadcrumbs or rice.

Turnips
Preparation and cooking Prepare as for parsnips. Boil in salted water for 20-30 minutes. Roast in the pan with a meat joint.
Serving suggestions Serve with butter or parsley sauce or as part of a mixed vegetable or meat casserole.

Zucchini
Preparation and cooking Wash, top and tail and leave whole if tiny or half-peel and cut into slices or strips if older. Blanch in boiling water for 2-3 minutes then drain and sauté in butter.
Serving suggestions Serve sprinkled with chopped fresh tarragon, parsley or thyme. Very good tossed in butter with garlic. Excellent par-boiled and stuffed with cheese, chopped tomatoes and breadcrumbs, then baked.

SUCCESSFUL SAUCES

As sauces form the basis and provide the finish for so many dishes, it is well worthwhile mastering basic sauce-making techniques. When you can quickly stir ingredients together into a sauce with litle effort it becomes an easy matter to turn an otherwise ordinary cut of meat or fish into a memorable meal.

Saucemaking is by no means as difficult as many people think, in fact, like most things it is just a matter of practice. The following classic white sauce recipe is a good basis for many sauces and if you follow the measurements and method carefully, a perfect white sauce is virtually guaranteed.

Béchamel Sauce

(makes about 1¼ cups)

1¼ cups milk	6 peppercorns
2-3 slices of onion	2 tbspns butter
1 small carrot, peeled and sliced	¼ cup flour
1 fresh parsley sprig	salt and pepper
1 bay leaf	

Preparation time: 5 minutes
Cooking time: 20 minutes

Heat the milk gently with the onion, carrot, parsley, bay leaf and peppercorns for about 10 minutes. Take off the heat and strain.

Heat the butter over moderate heat until foaming, but do not let it brown. Sprinkle in the flour and stir this 'roux' for a minute or two. Let it foam without browning. Take the pan off the heat and add the milk gradually, stirring to mix in all the roux well before returning to the heat. Cook, stirring constantly, until it thickens, then simmer gently for at least 5 minutes to ensure that the flour is properly cooked. Season to taste.

Time saving tip: Make the sauce with warmed but unflavored milk. Make up the flavorings into a bouquet garni in cheesecloth (or perforated kitchen cloth material) and add to the sauce while it is cooking. Remove before serving.

Note: It is important that your measurement of flour is accurate – the roux should have the consistency of melted honey *not* instant porridge. If you think that you have used too much add a little more butter and more milk.

The following variations can be made using the basic Béchamel sauce:

Cheese sauce (Sauce Mornay – a classic sauce for coating fish, eggs and vegetables. See also Coquilles St Jacques, page 53). Add to the sauce ½ cup grated Cheddar cheese or for a stronger flavor try ¼ cup Gruyère and ¼ cup Parmesan. Cook gently until the cheese melts.

Mustard sauce (especially good with broiled mackerel). Add to the sauce about ½-1 tbspn dry mustard powder (according to taste), a dash of Worcestershire sauce and a good pinch of sugar.

Mushroom sauce (good with fish, pork or chicken). Add to the sauce ½ cup fresh button mushrooms, wiped and sliced and cook for 10-15 minutes, stirring from time to time.

White wine and mushroom cream sauce (an easy touch of luxury for a special occasion). Make a basic Béchamel with ⅔ cup milk and ½ cup dry white wine. Once the sauce has thickened, add ½ cup fresh button mushrooms, wiped and sliced and cook for 10-15 minutes. Just before serving, stir in 1-2 tbspns heavy cream and heat through without boiling.

Methods of thickening sauces

A sauce, soup or liquid in a casserole can be thickened in various ways. You can stir into the hot liquid a small quantity of cornstarch, arrowroot or all-purpose flour which has been well mixed with a little water. The quantity used can be adjusted according to the amount of liquid and the desired consistency.

A useful way of thickening the juices of a stew when you don't want to stir it around too much, is to use **beurre manie**, a liaison of 2 parts butter to 1 part all-purpose flour. Mix together the 2 ingredients with a palette knife on a plate. Form it into small knobs and drop them onto the surface of the hot casserole. Shake and swirl it around to mix in. Keep adding beurre manie until the desired consistency is reached.

Egg yolks beaten with heavy cream will slightly thicken and enrich a sauce or stew.

Watch Points

☆ *Lumpy sauces* should be beaten vigorously. If still lumpy, pass through a strainer or whizz in a liquidizer and then simmer for a further 5-10 minutes to ensure that the flour is cooked.
☆ *Runny sauces* should be gently cooked to reduce the liquid by evaporation or thickened with beurre manie (see above).
☆ *Thick sauces* should be thinned with a little of the base liquid and the seasoning adjusted accordingly.
☆ *Salty sauces*, where the stock was too salty, can be helped by adding slices of peeled raw potato which will absorb some of the salt. Add a little sugar.
☆ *If a sauce has to stand* before using, cover the surface with greased waxed paper to prevent a skin forming.

Velouté Sauce

Another classic white sauce which is made with well-flavored white stock instead of milk. Using the same quantities of butter and flour as given for Béchamel sauce (above) follow the same method and blend 1¼ cups of good stock (chicken, veal or fish) into the roux with a squeeze of lemon juice. For extra creamy-richness stir in a beaten egg yolk and a spoonful of heavy cream. Season to taste. A velouté can be enhanced with a number of flavorings including chopped fresh parsley, or other fresh herbs, chopped egg or shellfish.

Onion Sauce

Peel and finely chop 2 medium onions and cook in about ½ cup of salted water until soft. Strain the onions, reserving the liquid which you make up to 1¼ cups with milk. Make the white sauce by the method described under Béchamel sauce (see above). Add the softened onions when the sauce has thickened. Cook for about 10 minutes. Add a spoonful of cream before serving if liked.

Bread Sauce

1¼ cups creamy milk	1 tbspn butter
1 small onion, peeled and stuck with 2 or 3 cloves	salt and pepper
1 cup fresh white breadcrumbs	

Preparation time: 10 minutes
Cooking time: 40 minutes

Heat the milk with the onion to boiling point. Take off the heat and allow to stand for about 20 minutes so that the onion and cloves flavor the milk. Take out the onion. Stir the breadcrumbs into the milk and cook over low heat for 15-20 minutes until the sauce is thick and creamy. Stir in the butter and season to taste. This is a good accompaniment for roast chicken and turkey.

Brown Sauces

These are based on a brown roux which is achieved by cooking the flour and butter together gently until it is light brown in color. The following recipe is a basic brown sauce which can be adapted in various ways. It is a good idea to make up a fairly large quantity for freezing in batches, or it can be stored in the refrigerator for several days.

Sauce Espagnole

(makes approx 2½ cups)

⅓ cup butter	2 tbspns tomato paste
2oz bacon, with rind removed and chopped	2-3 mushrooms or mushroom stalks, wiped and chopped
1 medium onion, peeled and finely chopped	1 bouquet garni (see page 126)
2 medium carrots, peeled and finely chopped	½ cup brown sherry
1 celery stalk, trimmed and chopped	pinch of ground coriander
½ cup flour	salt and freshly ground black pepper
3¾ cups good brown stock	

Preparation time: 10 minutes
Cooking time: 1¼ hours

Melt 2 tbspns butter in a large pan and fry the bacon and vegetables for 2-3 minutes then remove from the pan with a slotted spoon. Melt the rest of the butter, add the flour and cook gently, stirring, until the roux turns a golden brown, making sure that it does not burn. Take the pan off the heat and stir in the stock, scraping the bottom of the pan well to mix in all the cooked flour. Add the bacon and vegetables. Return to the heat and bring to the boil, stirring well until the sauce has thickened. Add the remaining ingredients and cover the pan. Simmer for about 30 minutes then continue cookng uncovered (to reduce) for a further 30 minutes. If any fat is present on the surface, skim this off and then pass the sauce through a fine strainer. Reheat a serving quantity and allow the rest to cool and freeze in suitable batches.

The following variations can be made using 1¼ cups basic Espagnole Sauce:
Demi-glace: This rich brown sauce is an easy adaptation of the classic 'half-glaze,' which makes an excellent coating for meat cuts. Mix together in a pan equal quantities (eg 1¼ cups) of Espagnole sauce and a good, grease-free brown stock which is unseasoned. Bring to the boil, then lower the heat and simmer, uncovered, for about 30-40 minutes until the quantity has reduced by about half. The sauce should then have a good syrupy, glossy look to it. Season to taste before serving.

Madeira sauce: Add to the sauce ½ cup of Madeira and season to taste.
Red wine or port wine sauce: Add ½ cup of red wine or port wine, 1 tbspn redcurrant jelly to a scant 1¼ cups of Espagnole Sauce, in a pan. Bring to the boil and simmer uncovered for about 10-15 minutes or until reduced to a good coating consistency.
Bigarade sauce: This version of a classic accompaniment to duckling is made with the demiglace (see above). Remove the zest of a small orange in fine strips, squeeze the juice and add these to the sauce with 1 teasp lemon juice and 1 teasp of sugar. Simmer for 5-10 minutes. A dash of Cointreau or Grand Marnier will give a fine finish to this interesting sauce.

Spicy Tomato and Onion Sauce

¼ cup butter	1 tbspn tomato catsup
1 tbspn oil	⅛-¼ teasp chilli powder
1 medium onion, peeled and chopped	1 teasp Worcestershire sauce
2 tbspns flour	1 teasp sugar
1¼ cups stock	salt to taste
16oz can tomatoes	

Preparation time: 15 minutes
Cooking time: 15-20 minutes

Heat the butter and oil in a pan and cook the onion until soft then stir in the flour. Cook gently for about 1 minute and remove from the heat. Pour in the stock and the strained juice from the tomatoes, stirring well. Return to the heat and cook, stirring constantly until the sauce thickens. Add the tomatoes and the rest of the ingredients. Cover and simmer for about 10 minutes. If it appears very thick add a little more stock. Pass the sauce through a strainer and reheat, checking the seasoning.

Bigarade Sauce.

Spiced Sauce for Curries

Rather than just using mixed curry powder, it is more interesting to use individual spices and a more authentic taste will result.

¼ cup butter	1½ teasps ground cumin
1 small onion, peeled and finely chopped	½ teasp turmeric
1-2 fat garlic cloves, peeled and crushed	1 tbspn flour
½ teasp ground ginger	⅛ teasp chilli powder
1 teasp ground coriander	⅔ cup chicken or vegetable stock
½ teasp ground cinnamon	4-5 tbspns natural yoghurt, lightly whipped
½ teasp ground cardamom	salt to taste

Preparation time: 10 minutes
Cooking time: 15 minutes

Melt the butter in a pan and fry the onion and garlic gently for 2-3 minutes. Add the spices and flour and stir-fry for another 2-3 minutes. Take the pan off the heat and gradually stir in the stock until the spices and flour are well mixed in. Return to the heat and cook, stirring well until the sauce thickens. Cook gently for about 5 minutes. Add the yoghurt in spoonfuls, beating in each one. Do not allow the sauce to boil and stir well to avoid curdling. Add salt to taste.

Serving suggestion 1: Add 1½ cups chopped cooked chicken or turkey and ½ cup sultanas to the sauce. Cook for 10 minutes and serve with boiled rice and fruit chutney and garnished with flaked almonds.

Serving suggestion 2: Serve as part of a vegetarian dish – with cauliflower, broccoli, leeks or mixed vegetables or as a coating sauce for halved hard-boiled eggs on a bed of spinach.

Cranberry and Apple Sauce

2 dessert apples, peeled, cored and sliced
2 cups cranberries
4-6 tbspns sugar (according to taste)
⅔ cup water
1 tbspn butter

Preparation time: 10 minutes
Cooking time: 10-15 minutes

Pick over the cranberries, removing any discolored fruit and place in a saucepan with the apples, sugar and water. Bring to the boil, reduce the heat and simmer for 10-15 minutes until soft. Pass through a strainer and reheat, stirring in the butter and checking for sweetness. Serve with roast turkey, pork or game dishes.
Variation: Cranberries are very pretty fruit, keeping their color and shape when cooked. Simmer them on their own with sugar and water and serve separately without puréeing. Baked pastry tartlet cases or halved peaches filled with cranberries make very attractive garnishes for roasts.

Horseradish Dressing

⅔ cup heavy or soured cream
2-3 tbspns horseradish, grated
1 tbspn wine or cider vinegar
pinch of sugar
salt to taste

Preparation time: 1-2 minutes

Beat all the ingredients together until well mixed or combine in a blender. Check the seasoning and serve. This is a delicious accompaniment for smoked fish such as trout and mackerel.

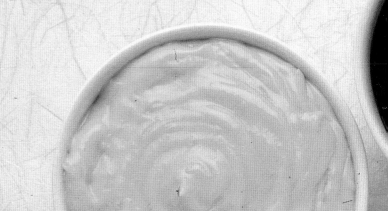

Hollandaise Sauce

2 tbspns lemon juice

2 large fresh egg yolks

4-6 tbspns butter, cut into small pieces

1-2 teasps wine vinegar (to taste)

salt and pepper

Preparation time: 5 minutes
Cooking time: 15-20 minutes

Boil the lemon juice in a small pan until it has reduced by half then allow to cool slightly. Put the egg yolks into a glass or china bowl and sit it over a saucepan containing gently simmering (not boiling) water. The bottom of the bowl should not reach the water level. Whisk in the lemon juice and seasoning. Keep whisking until the eggs begin to go thick and creamy then start to drop in the butter, piece by piece. Make sure that each piece has melted and is well mixed in before adding the next. *Do not overheat the sauce* or it might curdle. If you suspect that the water is getting too hot, take the pan off the heat for a moment or two. For a sharper flavor, add wine vinegar to taste.

If your sauce does begin to curdle, take it straight off the heat and add about a dessert-spoonful of cold water and whisk well. If this fails to restore it, don't panic. Whisk another egg yolk in a bowl and gradually stir it into the sauce until creaminess is regained. Serve with vegetables, fish or chicken dishes.

Variation
Bearnaise sauce: Substitute 2-3 tbspns of wine or tarragon vinegar for the lemon juice and boil with a bay leaf and a slice of onion until reduced to a 1 tbspn. Using the same quantities of egg yolks and butter, follow the method given for Hollandaise sauce adding 1 tbspn chopped fresh tarragon to flavor the sauce.

Mint Sauce

3-4 leafy mint sprigs

2 teasps sugar

2-3 tbspns good (red or white wine or cider) vinegar

Preparation time: 5 minutes
Standing time: about 30 minutes

Wash the mint well and strip the leaves from the stalks. Place the leaves on a chopping board with the sugar and chop finely. Transfer to a small serving bowl and add the vinegar. Stir well then leave to stand for 30 minutes or until the sugar dissolves and the mint flavors the vinegar. Store in a screw-topped jar.

Left-right: Hollandaise, Cranberry and Apple, Mint, and Hollandaise Sauce.

Glossary of Culinary Herbs

Balm *(Melissa officinalis)* Sometimes called lemon balm, balm is a perennial herb belonging to the MINT family. It has a strong, lemony scent and flavor. Its chief use is for flavoring fruit drinks and punches, salads and for herb teas.

Basil, Sweet *(Ocimum basilicum)* An annual herb which has attractive, bright-green leaves and is very aromatic. Basil has a number of culinary uses in salads, sauces, soups and stews but particularly complements tomato and egg dishes. In its own right it makes a delicious *pesto* sauce to accompany pasta, when pounded with garlic and olive oil (see page 165).

Bay, Sweet *(Laurus nobilis)* The edible leaves of this tree, belonging to the laurel family, have a distinctively strong, spicy smell and taste and should be used carefully. One of the ingredients of BOUQUET GARNIS, bay is invaluable for flavoring casseroles, soups and pâtés and is also frequently used in marinades.

Bergamot *(Monarda didyma)* A perennial herb belonging to the mint family, bergamot has attractive red flowers and dark, scented leaves. It is mainly used for flavoring wine cups or herb teas but it can also be used in salads or for garnishing meat dishes.

Borage *(Borage officinalis)* This is a very attractive annual plant with fairly large leaves and bright-blue flowers. An essential ingredient for a good Pimms cup, the subtle cucumber tang of the leaves will enhance the flavor of many summer iced drinks or wine cups. The flowers make a very pretty garnish, either fresh or candied.

Bouquet Garni Traditionally, this is a little bunch of aromatic plants tied together and used for flavoring stocks, soups, stews and other slow-cooked dishes. The advantage of the bouquet garni is that it can be removed from the cooking liquid before blending or serving.

A bouquet garni can be as simple as a few parsley stalks or can contain a number of different herbs. For a well-flavored bouquet garni, select a small celery stalk, 2-3 sprigs of fresh parsley with plenty of stalk, a sprig each of fresh thyme, marjoram and rosemary and a bay leaf. Using the celery stalk as a base, arrange the herbs on it and tie round firmly with strong thread or fine string. If fresh herbs are unavailable make up a bouquet garni using a mixture of dried herbs tied up in a square of cheesecloth; to this you can add a few black peppercorns and a clove for added flavor. When you tie up your bouquet garni leave a long trailing thread which you can fasten to the handle of the pan so that you can remove it easily.

Chervil *Anthriscus cerefolium* A hardy annual with feathery leaves similar in appearance to parsley but with a delicate aniseed flavor. Chervil is one of the *fins herbs* used for flavoring omelettes and is delicious added to sauces, particularly mayonnaise or Hollandaise. The pretty leaves of this herb make an attractive garnish for cooked dishes.

Chives *(Allium schoenoprasum)* A member of the onion family, chives have slender, needle-like leaves with a very delicate onion flavor. Delicious snipped into egg dishes, over salads, cooked vegetables and as a garnish for soups.

Dill *(Anethum graveolens)* An annual herb resembling FENNEL, dill is grown for both its seeds and leaves. The seeds are used for flavoring pickles, particularly cucumbers. The leaves, with their pungent flavor reminiscent of caraway, are known as dill weed and can be used fresh or dried in a variety of dishes including fish.

Fennel *(Foeniculum vulgare)* A tall, stately plant with fine feathery leaves which can be grown as an annual or perennial. The annual variety is grown chiefly for its bulbous base which is eaten as a vegetable. The seeds and leaves of the perennial fennel with their aniseed flavor are used for salads, fish and meat dishes.

Garlic *(Allium sativum)* A member of the onion family, garlic is renowned for its pungent smell and flavor. It consists of a bulb which is divided into 'cloves' which can be broken off, peeled and crushed or finely chopped. Garlic is used extensively in Mediterranean cooking, particularly stews, meat or fish dishes. Raw garlic makes a good flavoring for salad dressings.

Lovage *(Levisticum officinale)* A perennial herb similar in appearance to celery and with a tangy, celery-like flavor. It can be used fresh (sparingly) in salads or cooked in soups and stews.

Marjoram, Pot *Origanum onites)* A strong-growing perennial herb much favored for general culinary use because of its strongly aromatic flavor. It can be used fresh or dried but if dried, less should be added as the flavor is much stronger.

Mint *(Mentha sp.)* A large family of plants with a number of varieties but 3 main culinary types. Spearmint is the type used for mint sauce or for flavoring vegetables. Bowles mint has a furrier leaf than spearmint and a more delicate flavor; it can be used in the same way as spearmint. Applemint has pretty, round variegated leaves with an attractive appley-minty taste; it is very good in mint sauce.

Oregano *(Oreganum vulgare)* This is the wild form of marjoram which grows in the Mediterranean regions and is used extensively in European cookery, particularly for tomato dishes and sauces for pasta.

Parsley *(Petroselinum crispum)* This curly-leaved biennial herb is popular for garnishing and flavoring sauces and salads. It forms one of the main ingredients for BOUQUETS GARNIS where the stalks as well as the leaves should be used to impart the maximum flavor.

Rosemary *(Rosmarinus officinalis)* A decorative perennial herb with a delightfully fragrant flavor. It is excellent used fresh with grilled or barbecued meats or roasts, particularly lamb. It is also good with chicken, fish, sauces and stews.

Sage *(Salvia officinalis)* An attractive greyish-green or purplish leaved plant wth a very pungent, spicy flavor. It is reputed to have properties for aiding digestion which makes it a good stuffing ingredient for rich, fatty meats and poultry.

Savory, Summer *(Satureia hortensis)* An annual herb with slender leaves which have a strong, almost peppery flavor. It is good in stuffings if used sparingly and is excellent freshly chopped and sprinkled over cooked vegetables.

Savory, Winter *(Satureia montana)* A perennial variety of savory with a stronger, more pungent flavor than SUMMER SAVORY.

Sorrel, French *(Rumex scutatus)* This perennial herb grows wild in many countries but the cultivated varieties are better for culinary purposes, being less bitter and acid. French sorrel has a similar taste to spinach and is used for salads, in soup or in sauces.

Tarragon *(Artemesia dracunculus)* A perennial herb with tall stems bearing slender leaves. Its distinctive, aromatic taste is used for many classic French dishes. It is particularly good with chicken, fish or eggs and is used for flavoring wine

vinegar, mustards and sauces. It is strong, particularly when dried, so use sparingly. Freshly chopped tarragon is excellent sprinkled over cooked dishes as a garnish and is included among the *fines herbs*.

Thyme *(Thymus sp.)* There are a number of species of this useful shrubby herb but the best-known types for culinary use are probably the common thyme *(Thymus vulgaris)* and lemon thyme *(Thymus citriodorus)*. Common thyme is one of the important ingredients in BOUQUETS GARNIS and is probably one of the most indispensable herbs for the kitchen, either fresh or dried. Lemon thyme has a definite lemon flavor but should be used sparingly as it is fairly pungent.

Drying and Freezing Herbs

It is well worth growing a few herbs for use in the kitchen as it is often very difficult to buy a good selection of cut herbs and they are usually expensive.

Most herbs are very easy to grow either in a flower bed, a window box or even in a flower pot. For a basic herb garden, buy rooted cuttings of thyme, sage, mint, tarragon, marjoram and rosemary (the latter really needs a border as it grows quickly and becomes quite large) which are perennials and go on year after year. Also buy little pots of basil, parsley and chervil; these are annuals but with care will last through a whole growing season. You can of course grow the annuals from seed and propagate the perennials by taking cuttings yourself if you are really keen. Lastly, do obtain a few bulbs of chive (they grow in clumps which can be easily separated) or grow some from seed, as you will find this indispensable in salads, omelettes and many other dishes.

Drying herbs

Fresh herbs have a better flavor than when dried but if you have obtained a large amount of cut herbs or wish to save some of your own annuals while the leaves are at their best, you can dry them.

Select only the best leaves or sprigs and wash them, shaking off the moisture. After picking off any discolored or insect-chewed leaves, lay the sprigs on trays or tie them in small bundles. Put them to dry in a warm dark, well-ventilated place. Check after 2-3 days to see if they are dry and brittle to the touch. When they are ready, strip the leaves off the stalks or rub them through a strainer and store the dried herbs, correctly labelled, in clean, screw-topped jars. Do not leave dried herbs exposed to sunlight or use for more than a year or you will find that the colors fade and the flavors grow weak or musty. You can also dry herbs in a very slow oven.

Freezing herbs

Most fresh herbs freeze well but it is probably only worth freezing the annual herbs or the soft-leaved varieties. Whole or chopped leaves can be dry-frozen in freezer bags or rigid plastic tubs. Whole sprigs can be open-frozen and then immediately crumbled into bags or tubs, while still hard, to save time on chopping.

Finely chopped herbs such as parsley can be packed into ice-cube trays, topped up with water to cover and frozen; the cubes can be stored in plastic bags and are a convenient way of adding flavoring to sauces, soups and stews.

Spices

Allspice The dried fruit of a tree, *Pimenta officinalis* which grows in the Caribbean. The berries resemble large peppercorns and the flavor suggests a blend of cinnamon, nutmeg and cloves. Use allspice for flavoring pâtés and savory pies, casseroles and sauces, pickles and chutneys, fruit cakes, puddings and pies.

Aniseed Liquorice-tasting seeds from a semi-tropical plant *Pimpinella anisum*. The seeds can be sprinkled lightly over cakes and pastries or can be crushed and combined with other cake or pudding ingredients. The oil is extracted commercially from the seeds and used to flavor liqueurs such as anisette and Pernod.

Caraway seeds A member of the carrot family, the caraway plant *(Carum carvia)* is grown extensively in northern Europe. Caraway seed has a distinctive liquorice flavor and is used for flavoring bread, cakes and various regional dishes. Sprinkle over salads and cooked vegetables to give an unusual tanginess.

Cardamom This exotic, highly aromatic spice is a native to Asia and is an important ingredient in Indian cookery. It is very expensive to buy because the seed pods have to be harvested by hand. You can buy either dried, bleached pods; dried, unbleached (green) pods or the dried, separated seeds whole or ground.

Cardamom can be added to many different savory dishes, soups and sauces for its almost bitter, minty flavor adds extra interest. It can also be used (sparingly) to flavor pastries and cakes.

Cayenne pepper The dried, ground fruit of the chilli, one of the 'hottest' of the Capsicum family. It is a bright orange-red color and firey in flavor and so it should be used very sparingly.

Celery seed The dried seeds of the celery plant are a useful store-cupboard item. They can be added as an ingredient to dishes where celery flavoring is required or sprinkled over cooked dishes. Use sparingly.

Chilli powder This is a commercially made ingredient compounded from ground, dried chillies (Capsicum) and blended with other spices and herbs. Chilli powder is generally less hot than CAYENNE PEPPER or the powders labelled as 'ground chillies.' As with any hot ingredient, use sparingly and add gradually, allowing the spice to be absorbed into the other ingredients before adding more. People's tolerances to hot flavors vary considerably and you will also find that if you use chilli powder regularly in cooking, you will gradually prefer it hotter.

Chillies, dried Dried chillies can be used whole for flavoring chutneys, pickles and sauces. If you prefer less 'heat,' remove the seeds before using.

Cinnamon Cinnamon is the dried bark of a tropical tree belonging to the laurel family. It is sold in pipe-shaped sticks or as a fine powder. Its sweet flavor and scent makes it a delicious flavoring for cakes, biscuits and milk puddings. It is also very good in spiced lamb or chicken dishes or with cooked vegetables. The sticks are used for infusing in liquids and removed afterwards – they are essential for flavoring mulled wines.

Cloves These are the unopened flower buds of the beautiful Indian myrtle tree *(Eugenia aromatica)*. A familiar ingredient in puddings, fruit desserts, cakes and savory spiced dishes, cloves are also indispensable in bread sauce and spiced wine.

Coriander A herb belonging to the carrot family, coriander is used extensively in Indian and Eastern cookery and is sometimes known as Chinese Parsley. The dried seeds have a different flavor to the leaves, more subtle and flowery-orangey in aroma and taste. Coriander seeds are at their best when used freshly ground as ready-ground coriander deteriorates quickly.

Cumin The seeds of the annual plant *Cuminum cyminum* provide the powerful, pungent aroma flavor characteristic of curries. Its earthy-woody taste, when used sparingly, complements meat and poultry dishes and can also attractively flavor rice, vegetables including beans, peas and potatoes. Use dried cumin seeds whole or ground; it keeps best in seed form – grind it as you need it.

Garam Masala A blend of ground aromatic spices and

herbs which often includes CORIANDER, CUMIN, GARLIC, CLOVES, BLACK PEPPERCORNS, CARDAMOM, CINNAMON, BAY LEAVES and NUTMEG. In Indian cookery garam masala is added to dishes for extra flavoring towards the end of the cooking time; it may also be sprinkled over cooked meat and vegetable dishes as a garnish.

Garlic salt This is salt with powdered garlic added for flavoring. It is handy to use when a hint of garlic is required on broiled meats or roasts.

Ginger Ginger can be obtained either in dried and powdered form for use in cakes, biscuits and puddings or as a fresh 'root' (it is actually a rhizome). Fresh ginger adds a refreshingly sharp bite to sauces and stir-fried vegetable, meat and poultry dishes. It is also good with baked whole fish and marinaded fish dishes. The root can be grated and pounded into a paste, sliced or chopped after the coarse skin is peeled off. If you have bought a larger piece of ginger than you need it will keep fairly well in the refrigerator, wrapped in plastic.

Horseradish The peppery-hot root of the perennial *Cochlearia armoracia* is grated and mixed with vinegar or lemon juice, whipped heavy cream and salt. This sauce makes a piquant accompaniment for beef and lamb and also makes a perfect partnership with smoked mackerel or smoked trout.

Juniper The dried round, brown berries of the juniper tree. Half a dozen, lightly crushed with the back of a spoon to release the flavor, are good added to casseroles of game and beef or to marinades. The bitter-sweet, aromatic taste complements strong, gamey flavors.

Mace This is the reddish-brown outer husk of the NUTMEG, which, when dried and ground, has a more subtle and delicate taste than nutmeg. Use to flavor milk puddings, fish stews, vegetable dishes, pickles, marinades and also cakes and desserts.

Mustard English mustard powder is made from the seeds of white mustard *(Brassica alba)* and black mustard, *(Brassica nigra)*, ground finely and mixed together. French mustard is sold ready-mixed in bottles and is flavored with whole seeds and herbs. Dijon mustard is flavored with grape juice while Bordeaux mustard has wine included. American mustard is made with only the seeds of the white mustard plant and is very mild.

Nutmeg This is the seed of the nutmeg tree *(Myristica*

fragrans). The fibrous outer husk is stripped off and dried; this is known as MACE. Nutmeg has a pugently, aromatic smell and taste and should be used sparingly in puddings, cakes, savory stuffings, soups and for flavoring hot wine cups. Nutmeg is always best used freshly grated.

Paprika Another member of the Capsicum family but with 'sweet' rather than 'hot' flavor. Its brilliant red coloring and mild flavor make it an attractive ingredient for many dishes including fish and meat stews (particularly goulash), soups and vegetable dishes. It makes a pretty garnish for savory cooked foods of all types.

Peppercorns The tropical pepper vine *Piper nigrum* provides both white and black pepper. White pepper is prepared by soaking the unripe berries after picking so that the outer skin can be removed; this gives a milder flavor. Black peppercorns are prepared by drying the unripe berries so that the outer skin turns black; this yields a stronger, 'pepperier' flavor. Use white pepper in dishes where a milder flavor is needed and where flecks of black pepper would spoil the appearance. Black pepper should always be used freshly ground for the best results.

Poppy seeds These are the seeds of the opium poppy *(Papaver somniferum)* but are, however, totally free from any narcotic effect. The greyish-blue seeds are sprinkled over various types of breads or used as flavoring for cakes and pastries.

Saffron This highly expensive spice is, in fact, the stigma of the mauve autumn crocus *Crocus sativus*. It provides a very delicate flavor but its chief property is its bright yellow coloring, essential for such dishes as Spanish paellas and French bouillabaisse.

Sesame seeds The seeds of an Asian annual herb which are highly flavored and have a high protein content. Sesame seeds are used for flavoring breads and rolls. Sesame seed oil with its distinctive, nutty taste, is excellent for use in stir-frying.

Turmeric Related to the ginger plant, turmeric gives the characteristic yellow color to curry powder and is frequently used in Indian cookery. Turmeric can be used in place of SAFFRON for coloring savory dishes.

Vanilla The dried fruits of a tropical orchid, vanilla pods are infused in milk for making sweet puddings. The sweetly-aromatic essence obtained from the tiny seeds within the pods is added to many cakes and puddings.

SALADS AND COLD DISHES

Quick Mayonnaise

1 egg	½ teasp sugar
1 tbspn wine or cider vinegar or lemon juice	⅔ cup olive or corn oil
½ teasp dry mustard powder	salt and white pepper to taste

Preparation time: 2-3 minutes

Put the egg, vinegar, mustard powder and sugar in the blender goblet. Work at minimum speed.

Remove the central cap and pour the oil through the aperture in a thin steady stream until the mayonnaise is thick and creamy. Season to taste.

Blue Cheese Dressing

2-3oz blue cheese (such as Roquefort, Danish Blue or Stilton)

½ cup mayonnaise

4 tbspns natural yoghurt

1 tbspn wine vinegar

pinch of sugar

1 tbspn chives, chopped

salt to taste

Preparation time: 2-3 minutes

Crumble or grate the cheese and beat with all the other ingredients or combine in a blender. Check the seasoning and chill before use.

Yoghurt Dressing

1 small carton natural yoghurt

1-2 tbspns tbspns wine vinegar or lemon juice (to taste)

1 garlic clove, crushed (optional)

2 dashes of Worcestershire sauce

¼ teasp sugar

salt and freshly ground pepper

pinch of dried mixed herbs or
   1-2 teasps fresh herbs (such as chives, thyme, parsley, coriander or tarragon)

Preparation time: 1-2 minutes

Beat all the ingredients together until well mixed or combine in a blender. Check the seasoning and serve. A tasty, low-calorie dressing.

Vinaigrette Dressing

3 tbspns olive or corn oil

1 tbspn wine or cider vinegar

1 teasp Dijon mustard

1 teasp sugar

salt and freshly ground black pepper

pinch of dried mixed herbs or
   1-2 teasps fresh herbs

Preparation time: 2-3 minutes

Combine all the ingredients in a screw-topped jar and shake well. Check the seasoning and serve. Alternatively place in a blender and work for 30 seconds to 1 minute.
Variations: Add a sliced clove of garlic; a little tomato paste; pinch of cayenne or chilli powder. Substitute lemon juice for the vinegar.

Waldorf Salad

2 sweet dessert apples, cored and sliced

2 tbspns lemon juice

2-3 tbspns mayonnaise (see page 130) (optional)

4 celery stalks, trimmed and sliced

2 heaped tbspns walnuts, coarsely chopped

1 cup natural yoghurt

salt and pepper to taste

Garnish: lettuce leaves or endive

Preparation time: 10 minutes

Mix together the mayonnaise (or 2 tablespoons of the yoghurt) and lemon juice and use this to coat the apple slices to prevent them from discoloring. Combine the rest of the ingredients thoroughly and chill. Serve attractively arranged on a bed of lettuce or endive.

Salad Niçoise

Serves 4-6

1 crisp lettuce heart

7oz can tuna in brine

6 firm, ripe tomatoes, peeled

4 tbspns vinaigrette dressing flavored with garlic but unsalted (see page 130)

3 eggs, hard boiled

8oz French beans cut in half and cooked until tender but still firm

1 shallot, peeled and thinly sliced

8oz new potatoes boiled in their skins, peeled and cut into small dice

14oz can artichoke hearts, drained and sliced (optional)

12 fat black olives, pitted

2oz can anchovy fillets, drained

Preparation time: 10 minutes

Line a salad bowl or individual bowls with washed leaves from the lettuce. Drain the juice from the can of tuna and mix it with the vinaigrette dressing. Flake the fish into fork-sized pieces and put it into a mixing bowl. Cut the tomatoes (saving any juice) and eggs into quarters and add to the fish. Add the beans, shallot, potatoes, artichoke hearts and olives. Shake up or stir the dressing well and check the seasoning. Pour over the salad ingredients and toss well to coat. Spoon the salad into the prepared bowl and garnish with the anchovy fillets laid across in a lattice pattern.

Red Cabbage Coleslaw

½ medium red cabbage, cored and sliced	1 tbspn chopped nuts (such as walnuts, hazelnuts or almonds)
3-4 large carrots, peeled and coarsely grated	yoghurt dressing (see page 130)
1 small onion, peeled and finely sliced	
2 celery stalks, trimmed and sliced	

Preparation time: 10 minutes

Combine all the ingredients thoroughly and serve.

Variation: This mixture of vegetables is also good tossed in a Vinaigrette Dressing (see page 130).

Caesar Salad

3-4 slices white bread	2 tbspns lemon juice
2 fat garlic cloves	wine vinegar to taste
oil for deep frying	2oz can anchovy fillets, drained and chopped
5 tbspns olive oil	1 egg
1 head crisp lettuce	1 teasp French mustard
1 head endive (curly endive or chicory)	dash of Worcestershire sauce
1 shallot, peeled and finely sliced	pinch of sugar
3 tbspns grated Parmesan	salt and freshly ground black pepper

Preparation time: 30 minutes
Cooking time: 5 minutes

Rub the bread with the cut sides of one of the cloves of garlic. Cut into cubes and deep fry until golden brown, then set aside. Crush the other garlic clove and add to the olive oil in a screw-topped jar. Shake well and, if you have time, allow it to stand. Wash and dry the lettuce and endive, tear into pieces and place in a salad bowl. Remove the garlic and combine with the remaining ingredients. Check the seasoning. Pour over the leaves and toss well. Sprinkle with the croûtons and serve.

Red Bean, Corn and Onion Salad; Crunchy Cauliflower and Carrot Salad.

Crunchy Cauliflower and Carrot Salad

Serves 4-6

1 small cauliflower	1 tbspn chopped fresh parsley
4 large carrots, peeled or scraped and thinly sliced or shredded	1 celery stalk, trimmed and thinly sliced
½ cup roasted peanut halves	4 tbspns vinaigrette dressing (see page 130)

Preparation time: 10 minutes
Cooking time: 2 minutes

Wash the cauliflower well and divide into tiny florets, cutting off the coarse central stem (this can be thinly sliced and used if wished). Bring a pan of salted water to the boil and drop in the cauliflower. Allow the water to return to the boil and blanch by boiling for 2 minutes. Drain and allow it to get cold (refrigerate if necessary).

Put all the ingredients in a bowl and toss well to mix and coat the vegetables with dressing.

Red Bean, Corn and Onion Salad

16oz can red kidney beans, drained	1 Spanish onion, peeled and thinly sliced
7oz can of whole kernel corn, drained	4 tbspns vinaigrette dressing (see page 130)

Preparation time: 4-5 minutes

Combine the beans and corn and mix with the dressing (you can add a little of the liquid from the can if you wish). Lay the onion rings decoratively over the salad.

Chinese Bacon and Avocado Cups

½ head Chinese cabbage, divided into 8 even-sized leaves

squeeze of lemon juice

2 ripe avocados, peeled and diced

2 tbspns olive oil

2 slices bacon with rind removed, chopped

2 medium onions, peeled and sliced into rings

4 medium mushrooms, sliced

whites of 2 hard-boiled eggs, chopped (optional)

Preparation time: 15 minutes
Cooking time: 1-2 minutes

Arrange the leaves end to end to make 4 double 'cups' on a serving dish. Squeeze lemon juice over the avocado and place in the cups. Heat the oil and lightly sauté the bacon, onions and mushrooms for about 1-2 minutes. Spoon this over the avocado, making sure that the mushroom slices are on top. Sprinkle with chopped egg white. Serve straight away.

Luscious Lettuce

Hearty salad
Serves 6 and is only 177 calories per portion

6oz zucchini, sliced

¾-1 cup cooked meat or poultry

2½ corn or salad oil

1½ tbspns white wine vinegar

½ teasp dried onion powder or onion salt

black pepper

1 iceberg or Chinese cabbage

8 large radishes, sliced

4 tbspns whole kernel corn.

Preparation time: 15 minutes
Cooking time: 5 minutes

Cook the sliced zucchini in boiling salted water for 4-5 minutes or until just tender. Drain and refresh in cold water. Put in a shallow dish with the meat or poultry cut into thin strips. Mix the oil, vinegar, onion powder and pepper, and pour over the zucchini and meat. Cover and allow it to marinade for 1-2 hours. Cut the lettuce or Chinese cabbage into halves, lengthways and then across into ¾in strips. Spoon it into a salad bowl or into 6 individual bowls. Add the radishes and corn and top with the meat mixture.

Iceberg Cheese Cups
Serves 8 for starters or 4 for lunch or supper.

8 iceberg lettuce leaves (or other crisp lettuce)

1-1½ cups Cheddar cheese, diced

5oz Gouda cheese, sliced then chopped

4oz Danish Blue cheese

2 tbspns hot water

4 tbspns soured cream

2 tbspns chopped parsley

3 tbspns chopped celery

1 melon (ogen or honeydew), peeled and cubed or scooped into balls

4 tbspns salted peanuts

Preparation time: 20 minutes

Arrange the leaves in 'cups' on a serving dish. Scatter the diced and chopped cheeses into each. Mash the blue cheese with the hot water until creamy. Add the soured cream, parsley and celery and mix well. Divide the melon between the lettuce cups and spoon over the dressing. Chill well and serve garnished with peanuts

Potato Salad

1½lb potatoes, scrubbed, cooked in their skins and peeled (new or waxy potatoes are best for this)

½ onion, peeled and thinly sliced

1 tbspn vinegar (wine or malt)

2 dill pickles, finely chopped

1 tbspn chopped fresh chives

⅔ cup mayonnaise (see page 130)

Garnish: sliced dill pickle

Preparation time: 10 minutes

Dice the potatoes and put in a bowl. Lay the slices of onion in a saucer and pour the vinegar over. Leave for 10-15 minutes. Drain and add the onion to the potatoes with the chopped pickles and chives. Pour the mayonnaise over and mix well. Cut one dill pickle into slices and arrange on top of the salad.

Chinese Bacon and Avocado Cups (above); Pasta Salad (below).

Hot Potato Salad

1½lb potatoes, scrubbed (new or waxy potatoes are best for this)

2 slices bacon (optional)

6-8 tbspns vinaigrette dressing (see page 130) flavored with chopped fresh parsley

Preparation time: 10 minutes
Cooking time: 15 minutes

Boil the potatoes until just tender in salted water. While the potatoes are cooking, fry the bacon until very crisp; drain it on kitchen paper and crumble it. Heat the dressing in a small pan until just warm. Slice the potatoes (skin if preferred) and pour the dressing over. Sprinkle with the bacon and serve immediately.

Pasta Salad

Serves 6

3 cups pasta spirals (or any shortcut pasta)

5 celery stalks, trimmed and chopped

1 medium-sized red pepper, diced and blanched for 2 minutes

1 bunch scallions, washed, trimmed and chopped

12oz can whole kernel corn, drained

4 tbspns vinaigrette dressing (see page 130)

salt and freshly ground black pepper

Garnish: 1 cup button mushrooms, sliced

Preparation time: 10 minutes
Cooking time: 10-15 minutes

Cook the pasta in plenty of boiling salted water until tender or *al dente*. Drain and refresh in cold water.

Place the cold pasta in a bowl and add the chopped celery, red pepper, scallions and sweetcorn. Add the vinaigrette dressing and seasoning and mix well. turn on to a flat dish and decorate with sliced raw mushrooms.

Chicken Royale

Serves 6

4lb roasting chicken	1-2 teasps curry powder (to taste)
1 teasp salt	⅔ cup heavy cream
bouquet garni (see page 126)	⅔ cup mayonnaise
2 tbspns sweet brown pickle or chutney	salt
1 tbspn honey	**Garnish:** flaked almonds

Preparation time: 30 minutes
Cooking time: 1 hour

Place the chicken in a large saucepan, cover with cold water, add the bouquet garni and salt. Bring to the boil then reduce the heat and simmer until tender (about 1 hour). Allow to cool in the cooking liquid (it is a good idea to do this the day before the chicken is needed). Cut the meat from the bones and dice it into fork-sized pieces.

Combine the pickle, honey and curry powder in a pan. Heat until bubbling, stirring from time to time, then remove from the heat and allow to cool. Lightly whip the cream into soft peaks and combine with the mayonnaise. Stir in the pickle mixture. Check the seasoning, adding more curry powder and salt to taste. Coat the chicken pieces with the sauce and chill. If you prepare the dish several hours before it is needed it may discolor slightly but a quick stir with a fork will correct this.

Serve on a bed of crisp lettuce, watercress or chicory sprinkled with flaked almonds. A rice salad goes well with this dish.

Salmon en Gelée

Serves 6-8

16oz can red salmon	**Aspic:**
milk	1 tbspn lemon juice
1 envelope unflavored gelatin	7 tbspns water
1 small onion, peeled and chopped	1 envelope unflavored gleatin
⅔ mayonnaise	12oz can asparagus spears, drained
3 tbspns lemon juice	7oz can shrimp in brine, drained
½ teasp dried dill	**Garnish:** cucumber slices and scallion tassels
salt and pepper	

Preparation time: 10-15 minutes
Chilling time: 2-3 hours

Drain the salmon, reserving the juice. Make the juice up to ⅔ cup with milk, then add the gelatin. Heat gently to dissolve the gelatine. Place the salmon, gelatin, onion, mayonnaise, lemon juice and dill weed in a liquidizer. Blend until smooth and season generously with salt and pepper.

To make the aspic, combine lemon juice with water, add the gelatin and dissolve over gentle heat. Arrange a pattern of shrimp and asparagus spears in the base of a 2lb loaf tin, then carefully pour in enough clear gelatin to cover the pattern and chill until it is set. Pour the salmon mixture into the tin to form a ½in layer and chill again until set. Next, pile the remaining asparagus and shrimp in the center of the tin along its length. If the salmon mixture has begun to set, warm it slightly over a pan of hot water and then pour it on either side of the asparagus until level and chill until set. Finally, cover with a layer of the remaining salmon mixture. Cover and chill until required.

To unmold, dip the tin into boiling water and quickly invert the loaf on to a plate. Serve garnished with cucumber slices and scallion tassels.

Stuffed Rice Salad

2 cups vegetable or chicken stock	**Stuffing:**
scant cup long-grain rice	2 ripe avocados, diced
salt and freshly ground black pepper	4 tbspns lemon juice or wine vinegar
3-4 celery stalks, trimmed and chopped	½ cup Stilton or blue cheese, cut into tiny dice
½ onion, finely chopped	**To serve:**
2 tbspns mayonnaise	mayonnaise
¼ small green pepper, diced	
¼ small red pepper, diced	

Preparation time: 25 minutes
Cooking time: 15 minutes
Chilling time: minimum 3 hours

Bring the stock to the boil, pour in the rice and when it comes to boil again, reduce the heat. Season and cook for about 15 minutes until the rice is cooked and the stock is absorbed. While still hot, stir in the celery, onion and mayonnaise. Place the diced peppers on a base of a 3¾ cup ring mold. Pack rice mixture into mold and chill for at least 3 hours, preferably overnight. When required, turn out on to a serving dish. Do not prepare the avocados until they are needed or they will discolor. Stir the lemon juice or vinegar into the avocado pieces. Pile the avocado into the center of the rice ring and sprinkle with the diced cheese. Serve the mayonnaise separately.

Stuffed Rice Salad.

Dressed Salmon

Although regarded as a luxury food, salmon with its dense texture and rich flavor is very satisfying and only about 4-5oz need be allowed per person when planning a cold buffet. If buying a whole fish, however, remember to allow for the head and tail in the total weight. A whole fish can be cooked by either poaching (the traditional way) or baking (a useful method if you do not have a fish kettle). It can be cooked in a microwave oven too, if it will fit in the oven cavity.

Poaching
Clean the inside of the fish, making sure that the dark blood near the back bone is all scraped off as this can make the flesh near it taste bitter.

Place 2 or 3 slices of lemon inside the cavity and lay the fish in the fish kettle. Then make a court bouillon by almost covering the fish with cold water and then adding 1¼ cups dry white wine, salt to taste, 8 peppercorns and a bouquet garni (see page 126). Bring to the boil and cook for just 5 minutes (for fish up to 7lb). For larger fish, cook for 15 minutes. Take off the heat and allow to cool – the fish will go on cooking in the hot liquid. When cold remove the fish from the kettle. Reserve the cooking liquid as this makes good fish stock. Boil until it has reduced and then freeze it in cubes. Lay the salmon on a board and, with a sharp knife, make a cut through the skin down the length of the back, round the head and across the tail. Peel off the skin. Turn the fish over, then repeat on the other side. Down the

center of the sides of the fish will be some soft, brown-colored flesh – gently scrape this away. Arrange the fish on a serving dish and decorate as shown. Alternatively, arrange slices of cucumber topped with sliced stuffed olives down the center, and half-slices of lemon along the belly edge. Serve with mayonnaise, lemon wedges and a selection of salads.

Baking
This is a very good method of cooking whole fish as all the flavor and natural juices are retained. Prepare the salmon for cooking as given for poaching. Lay the fish on a large sheet of foil on a baking dish or sheet. Fold up the sides to form a dish shape, leaving enough spare foil to make a lid. Place 2 or 3 slices of lemon into the belly cavity with 1 or 2 sprigs of parsley. Pour a glass of dry white wine over and sprinkle with black pepper. Fold the foil over to make a loose parcel. Bake in a preheated oven at 300°F allowing 15 minutes per lb. Allow to cool and dress as for poached salmon.

Cooking in a microwave oven
Prepare the fish as for poaching. Brush the skin with melted butter, sprinkle with black pepper and wrap in plastic wrap. Protect the head and tail with foil. Bake for about 2-3 minutes per lb. It is advisable to check your microwave handbook as cooking times may vary.

Dressed Salmon.

Seafood Salad

Serves 6-8

2lb baby squid, cleaned (see page 48) and dried	1½ cups dried short-cut pasta (spirals, shells or macaroni)
1lb monkfish cut into fork-sized cubes	8 tbspns sharp vinaigrette dressing flavored with garlic (see page 130)
2 tbspns olive oil	
⅔ cup dry white wine	2 tbspns fresh parsley, chopped
2 teasps tomato paste	1 cup peeled shrimp
salt and freshly ground black pepper	2 cups cooked, shelled mussels
1 teasp sugar	**Garnish:** lettuce leaves

Preparation time: 20 minutes
Cooking time: 20 minutes
Chilling time: minimum 1 hour

Sauté the squid and monkfish in the olive oil for 2-5 minutes then add the wine, tomato paste and seasoning. Cover and simmer for 5 minutes or until just tender – do not overcook it or the squid will toughen. Strain the juice from the fish and return the juice to the pan. Boil rapidly, uncovered, to reduce. Chill fish and juice for at least 1 hour.

Cook the pasta in salted, fast-boiling water for about 8-10 minutes. Do not overcook, it should be firm not flabby. Allow to cool.

Drain the juice from the fish and mix it with the vinaigrette dressing and chopped parsley. Put the fish, pasta, shrimp and mussels in a serving dish and pour the dressing over. Mix thoroughly and if you have time, refrigerate the salad so that all the ingredients are well chilled. Garnish with a border of lettuce leaves.

Spiced Beef

3lb rump roast beef in one piece but not rolled and tied	⅛ teasp chilli powder
	½ teasp ground cardamon
Marinade:	1 tbspn whole cloves
1 small onion	½ tbspn whole black peppercorns
2 bay leaves	1¼ cups red wine
1 teasp ground coriander	1 cinnamon stick
1 teasp mustard powder	½ teasp salt
1 teasp ground ginger	water
2 teasps dried allspice	

Preparation time: 10 minutes
Cooking time: 2½-3 hours

Lay the piece of beef in a large earthenware bowl (suitable to fit into the refrigerator). Place all the other ingredients in a saucepan and bring to the boil; simmer for about 5 minutes. Allow this marinade to get quite cold, then pour it over the beef. Turn the meat over in the marinade several times to get it well steeped. Cover the bowl with plastic wrap and place in the refrigerator. Allow the beef to marinate for 3 days turning frequently (2-3 times per day – when you open the refrigerator). The idea is to make sure that the marinade seeps right through the joint.

When you have had the bowl in the refrigerator long enough, take up the joint and roll and tie it securely. Place it, with its juices, in a large pan, add water to cover and bring to the boil. Skim any froth from the surface with a slotted spoon, reduce the heat, cover tightly and simmer slowly for about 3 hours. Allow to cool slightly then lift the meat out of the liquid. Place in a clean bowl, cover with a small chopping board and put a heavy weight on top of it. Leave it for 2-3 hours (preferably overnight) to get completely cold. Serve with chutney and salads.

SAVORY EGG & CHEESE DISHES

Types of eggs

Hens' eggs: All hens' eggs on general sale have been graded and quality tested. They are marketed in different sizes, the largest, size 1, is roughly equal to 2½oz and over, going down to the smallest, size 7, weighing less than 1½oz. They are mostly sold in cartons stating the number of eggs, and have codes which give information about the country of origin and area, the quality, and the week of packing.

Turkey eggs: These can occasionally be obtained from poulterers and fish shops or turkey breeders. They have a similar flavor to hens' eggs but are much larger so you have to be a little careful when using them for baking. They are very good for omelettes and soufflés.

Duck and goose eggs: These have a rich, oily taste and are larger than hens' eggs. They have a very porous shell and they should be well cooked to kill any bacteria which may be present.

Gull and quail eggs: These prettily marked eggs are regarded as a delicacy and are usually served hard-boiled with coarse sea salt. As quails are now farmed, the eggs are more readily obtainable. Try serving fried quails' eggs on toast or on a small quantity of fresh ground steak as an unusual starter.

Quality

Always try to buy fresh eggs as stale eggs have a much poorer flavor and texture. Check the codes on the carton to see what week they were packed. Buy free range eggs when you can – the difference in color, flavor and texture is quite surprising, due to the varied diet of the chickens. An egg has three distinct parts: the yolk, which should be rich yellow, and two layers of white or albumen. A good-quality fresh egg should have a rich yellow yolk and a firm white – if the white

spreads out like water when cracked then the egg is stale. To test for freshness place the egg in cold salted water – if it sinks immediately to the bottom, then it is fresh. If it is stale, it will float, half-suspended, in the water.

Storage

Always store eggs with their pointed end downwards in a cool place or in the top of a refrigerator away from the ice-box or any strong-smelling food which may mar their flavor. Remember to take them out of the refrigerator at least 30 minutes before you wish to use them.

Separating eggs

Method 1: Crack the egg over a bowl without separating the 2 halves of the shell. Allow most of the white to run into the bowl, then carefully separate the pieces of shell trapping the yolk in one half. Most of the remaining white will run off the half-shell but to make sure, tip the yolk into the other half and allow the rest of the white to run into the bowl.

Method 2: Break the egg on to a saucer. Using an egg cup or small coffee cup, trap the yolk, tilt the saucer and allow the white to run off into a bowl.

Boiling eggs

Although boiling an egg is often regarded as the simplest form of cooking it is, in fact, necessary to concentrate hard to achieve the perfect soft-boiled egg.

Method 1: For large to medium-sized eggs, place the eggs in a saucepan half-filled with cold water, turn the heat to medium high and cook for 10 minutes (timed from the moment you place the egg into the water). This is one of the easiest and most consistent methods of achieving an egg with a firm white and a reasonably soft yolk. Also the shells are less likely to crack while cooking (especially if you have forgotten to take them out of the fridge).

Method 2: This is the more traditional method whereby you boil a pan of water, slide the eggs (large/medium) into it gently, bring the water back to the boil and then simmer for 3-4 minutes for a lightly boiled egg and 5-6 minutes for a firmer set.

For hard-boiled eggs place the eggs in a pan of cold water, bring to the boil and cook for 10 minutes. Then plunge the eggs into cold water and tap lightly – this prevents a bluish tinge from occurring round the yolk.

Poaching eggs

Use fresh eggs for poaching, otherwise the white will spread everywhere.

If you have no egg-poacher try the following: Break the eggs separately into a saucer in readiness. Heat water in a small pan about 1½in in depth. When it is simmering, gently slide the eggs into the pan (two at a time) and cook for 2-3 minutes. Remove with a slotted spoon and blot up water with kitchen paper. Serve immediately on hot buttered toast.

Frying eggs

Shallow frying: Use butter, lard, corn or even olive oil according to preference (beef drippings, chicken or bacon fat give good-flavored eggs). Heat about ½in fat or oil in a large skillet. Break the eggs into a saucer and slide them into the pan. Cook fairly gently until set, basting with the hot fat or oil. If you dislike even a hint of runny white, cover the pan for 30 seconds –1 minute to set the tops of the whites.

Deep-frying: Make sure that the eggs are fresh. Choose a small pan and half fill it with oil. Heat the oil to 350-375°F or until a cube of stale bread bubbles when dropped in. Meanwhile break the eggs into separate cups (only cook 1 or 2 eggs at a time) and slide them into the oil when it is ready. Cook for 1-2 minutes, lift out with a slotted spoon and drain on kitchen paper. Serve immediately.

Scrambled or buttered eggs

These should be creamy, light and fairly flaky without any large lumps. Do not add milk or cream to the eggs *before* cooking otherwise you will get a watery curdled result. Allow 2 medium-large eggs per person. Break the eggs into a bowl and beat well with a fork. Melt 2 tbspns butter in a small heavy-based pan over low heat without browning. Pour in the eggs and cook gently, stirring and lifting the cooked flakes of egg from the bottom of the pan. Do not leave the pan unattended. Just as the eggs are almost completely set, stir in a large knob of butter or a large spoonful of cream or milk. Serve immediately on hot toast. Scrambled eggs are ideal as a light, quick meal and very delicious if you add a little extra flavoring such as chopped ham or cooked bacon, tuna, salmon (fresh, canned or smoked), or fresh herbs such as parsley or chives.

Baked or shirred eggs

Individual eggs baked *en cocotte* in a *bain marie* make an ideal first course and are very simple to prepare. Preheat the oven to 350°F. Butter the cocotte dishes and stand them in a baking tin which has been half-filled with warm water. Break the eggs into the dishes and sprinkle with salt and pepper. Drop a generous knob of butter onto each egg and bake for between 7-10 minutes or until the egg whites have just set. There are lots of variations to this basic dish:
Convent eggs: Add 1 tbspn heavy cream to each egg in its dish instead of the knob of butter.
Spanish eggs: Sauté a green or red pepper, de-seeded and chopped, and a small onion, peeled and finely chopped, in butter until soft. Spoon this into the bottom of each dish, break the eggs onto each and sprinkle with grated cheese.

You can also bake eggs on peeled and sliced tomatoes, or chopped ham, shredded cooked chicken, sliced garlic sausage or frankfurters, chopped smoked salmon, flaked smoked haddock with 1 tbspn heavy cream added to each dish or a similar amount of Béchamel or cheese sauce (see page 130). You can even cook eggs in a baked potato. Scoop out the cooked potato, mash it with milk and butter and make a 'nest' for the egg in the skin. All these variations are delicious and if you double the quantities of ingredients (2 eggs per person) and cook the eggs in small gratin dishes, baked eggs make a very popular lunch, supper or children's tea-time meal.

Omelettes

This is one of the most versatile egg dishes. Omelettes can be made in minutes for a quick snack or dressed up for a dinner party.

Omelette pans
It is best to use a heavy-based pan with rounded sides. An 8in pan — measured across the base — will be big enough for a 3-4 egg omelette. Do try to reserve this pan for omelette-cooking alone. New ones should be seasoned with salad oil overnight. Do not wash with detergent but wipe out with a damp cloth sprinkled with salt.

Types of omelette
The most familiar is the French omelette, served plain or with a savory filling and folded in 3. A teaspoonful of water for every egg used should be added to the mixture for a light fluffy result. There is also the Italian-style *frittata* where a mixture of beaten eggs and cooked vegetables is cooked without folding and served in wedges. The light soufflé omelette is generally served with a sweet filling as a dessert but it is also delicious served with a savory stuffing.

Omelette with Herbs

Serves 2

4 large eggs	1 tbspn finely chopped fresh herbs (such as chives or thyme) or a mixture of more than one herb
4 teasps water	**Garnish:** fresh parsley sprigs
salt and pepper to taste	
½oz tbspn butter	

Preparation time: 3-4 minutes
Cooking time: 2-3 minutes

Beat the eggs lightly and add the water, seasoning and mix well. Stir in the herbs.

Place the omelette pan over medium heat for about 20 seconds before adding the butter. As soon as the butter begins to bubble and froth, pour in the egg mixture, cook without stirring for about 1 minute, then, using a spatula, lift one edge of the omelette and tilt the pan to allow the liquid egg to run onto the pan to cook. Cook until the omelette has almost set and then flip over ⅓ of the area into a fold. Tip the omelette out of the pan onto a warmed plate or serving dish so that it finishes folded in 3. Serve immediately.

Frittata.

Fillings
Cheese and watercress omelette: Add 3 tbspns each of grated cheese and chopped watercress to the egg mixture before cooking.
Ham and mushroom: Sauté 2oz chopped or sliced mushrooms in a little butter with 2oz chopped ham. Spread across the middle of the omelette before folding.
Onion and tomato: Sauté 1 small onion, peeled and chopped, in a little butter until soft. Add 2-3 ripe tomatoes, peeled and chopped, and cook until the tomatoes are heated through. Spread across the omelette before folding.
Shrimp and sour cream: Stir-fry ½ cup shelled shrimp in a little butter to warm through. Add 2 tbspns sour cream and 1 teasp chopped chives and spread across the omelette before folding.

Eggs Arnold Bennett

Serves 2-3

⅔ cup light cream	1 tbspn chives, chopped
6oz smoked haddock, cooked and flaked	salt and pepper to taste
4-5 large eggs, separated	2 tbspns butter
2 tbspns Cheddar cheese, grated	

Preparation time: 10 minutes
Cooking time: 5-6 minutes

Heat the cream gently with the haddock in a medium-sized pan. Take the pan off the heat and allow the mixture to cool slightly. Beat in the egg yolks, cheese, chives and seasoning. Whisk the egg whites into glossy peaks and fold into the haddock mixture.

Melt the butter in an omelette pan, pour in the mixture and cook over moderate heat until the base has browned and the omelette has half set. Place under a fairly hot broiler to finish cooking and brown the top. Serve immediately with sliced tomatoes and a crisp salad.

Frittata

Serves 2-3

1 small green or red pepper	5 teasps cold water
2 tbspns olive oil	pinch of dried oregano
1 fat garlic clove, crushed	1 tbspn fresh parsley, chopped
1 small onion, peeled and sliced	salt and pepper
2 medium potatoes, cooked, skinned and diced	
2 large tomatoes, peeled and sliced	
2oz ham or garlic sausage, chopped (optional)	
5 eggs	

Preparation time: 15 minutes
Cooking time: 6-7 minutes

Blanch the pepper in fast-boiling salted water for 2 minutes (after returning to the boil) and slice. Heat the oil in an omelette pan and stir-fry the garlic, and onion until soft. Add the pepper, potatoes, tomatoes and ham or sausage (if using) and cook for another minute or two.

Beat the eggs with the water, herbs and seasoning then pour over the vegetables in the omelette pan. Cook over medium heat. Lift an edge with a spatula and tilt the pan to allow the liquid egg to run onto the pan base. When the omelette is nearly set, put it under a hot broiler to finish. Slide it onto a warm serving dish and serve cut into wedges with a green salad and crusty bread.

Cheese Soufflé Omelette

Serves 2 as a light meal or 4 as a starter

4 eggs, separated	3 heaped tbspns Cheddar cheese, grated
4 teasps water	1 tbspn butter
salt and pepper	

Preparation time: 10 minutes
Cooking time: 4-5 minutes

Beat the egg yolks with the water, seasoning and cheese. Whisk the whites into glossy peaks. Fold the whites into the yolks. Melt the butter in an omelette pan and pour in the egg mixture. Cook over moderate heat until the base has turned a golden brown and the omelette has half-set. Place under a hot broiler to set the top. Fold in half and serve immediately.
Variations: Omit the cheese and fill with the following:
Chicken and ham: Sprinkle 2oz each of cooked chopped chicken and ham over the omelette before broiling.
Seafood: Heat ¾ cup mixed seafood (peeled shrimp, crab or lobster meat, or cooked, shelled mussels) in 2-3 tbspns heavy cream with 1 tbspn chopped fresh parsley. Pour over the omelette before folding.
Tuna and whole kernel corn: Mix 4 tbspns milk with 2 teasps cornstarch and stir in 3oz each of flaked, canned tuna and canned whole kernel corn. Heat for 4-5 minutes until thickened and keep warm until the omelette is ready. Pour over the omelette before folding.

Cheese Soufflé

Serves 4 as a starter or 2 as a lunch or supper dish

⅓ cup butter	1 teasp dry mustard powder
½ cup flour	salt and pepper to taste
1¼ cups milk	4 large eggs, separated
4oz cheese, grated (either Cheddar or a mixture of Cheddar and Parmesan or, for extra flavor, equal quantities of Parmesan and Gruyère)	

Preparation time: 20 minutes
Cooking time: 45 minutes

Preheat the oven to 375°F and butter a 2 pint soufflé dish.

Melt the butter in a pan over gentle heat. Stir in the flour and cook for about 1 minute. Take the pan off the heat and add the milk, stirring well to mix in all the roux (flour and butter). Return the pan to moderate heat and cook, stirring, until the mixture thickens into a stiff *panada*. Continue to cook for 2-3 minutes, still stirring and add the cheese, mustard and seasoning. Cook until the cheese has melted, remove the pan from the heat and allow the *panada* to cool slightly. Beat in the egg yolks thoroughly until smooth.

Whisk the egg whites into stiff peaks which are still slightly glossy (not dry-looking). Stir a good spoonful of the egg white into the *panada* then carefully fold in the remaining egg whites, cutting and lifting the mixture with a metal spoon or palette knife. When the whites look well integrated with the sauce (do *not* stir), pour the mixture into the soufflé dish and level the top.

Position the dish in the center of the oven and bake for about 40 minutes or until the soufflé has risen well (2-3in) and is firm to the touch and an attractive golden brown. It will begin to sink when you take it out of the oven so serve it immediately.
Variations: Using the basic soufflé recipe, replace the cheese with one of the following:
Seafood: Try adding 1 cup prepared crabmeat (for preparation see page 50), or 1 cup peeled shrimp, or chopped lobster meat, or flaked, canned or fresh salmon or flaked smooth haddock.
Chicken and ham: Add 1 cup finely chopped chicken or ham, or a mixture of both.

Ham and Mushroom Roulade

5 eggs, separated

5 teasps cold water

½ cup Cheddar cheese, or half Cheddar and half Parmesan, grated

salt and pepper to taste

2 tbspns finely grated Cheddar or Parmesan cheese

Filling:

2 tbspns butter

1 small onion, peeled and finely chopped

2 tbspns flour

1¼ cups milk

½ cup chopped ham

1 cup button mushrooms, sliced

2 tbspns fresh parsley, chopped

Preparation time: 30 minutes
Cooking time: total 30 minutes

To prepare the filling: Melt the butter in a pan and gently sauté the onion until softened. Stir in the flour and cook for a minute, stirring. Take off the heat and pour in the milk, stirring well. Return to the heat and cook, stirring until the sauce thickens. Add the ham and mushrooms and simmer gently for about 10 minutes. Take off the heat, stir in the parsley, and set to one side.

Line a Swiss roll tin with greased waxed paper and preheat the oven to 400°F.

To prepare the soufflé mixture: Beat together the egg yolks, water and ½ cup grated cheese until well mixed. Whisk the egg whites until stiff and snowy and gently fold into the egg yolk mixture with a metal spoon. Using a palette knife, spread the mixture out evenly on the waxed paper in the tin in a neat rectangle. Bake for about 12-15 minutes or until the mixture has risen and is firm to touch. Meanwhile sprinkle the remaining dry cheese over a fresh piece of waxed paper and invert the soufflé onto it. Remove the top piece of paper and spread the filling over. Trim the edges neatly and roll up the roulade by folding over one end and lifting up the edge of the paper beneath it so that the roulade rolls itself up. Serve immediately, cut into slices.

Cheese Soufflé.

Pancakes

Makes 8

1 cup flour	1 tbspn oil
pinch of salt	oil for frying
1 large egg	
⅔ cup milk mixed with ⅔ cup water	

Preparation time: 10 minutes plus 30 minutes standing time
Cooking time: about 20 minutes

Sift the flour into a medium-sized bowl with the salt. Make a well in the middle and break the egg into it. Add about a third of the liquid and draw in the flour until it is mixed in smoothly. Beat well with a wooden spoon. Stir in the rest of the milk and water. Allow the batter to stand for at least half an hour before using. When you are ready to start cooking, stir in the oil and pour the batter into a jug.

Using a heavy skillet with a 7in base (for small pancakes) pour in a very little oil, just enough to coat the pan base, and place over fairly high heat. When the oil is shimmering hot, pour in enough batter to coat the base of the pan thinly, swirling the pan to spread it out evenly. Cook for a minute or so shaking the pan from time to time to loosen the batter. When the base of the pancake is brown, flip it over with a spatula, or toss it, and cook the other side.

Variation: For richer pancakes use 2 eggs and melted butter instead of oil in the mixture.

Savory stuffed pancakes

Pancakes can be stored for several days wrapped in plastic wrap in the refrigrator. They also freeze well layered with plastic or waxed paper and then wrapped in foil. So why not double the ingredients and cook up a big batch. It's good practice too – you will be surprised how slick you become! With the addition of savory fillings you can produce an attractive and satisfying meal very easily.

Fillings

The following fillings will be sufficient to stuff about 8 pancakes and are each based on a basic white sauce made with 3 tbspns butter, 3 tbspns flour and 1½ cups milk.

Pheasant, bacon and mushroom: Fry a small onion, peeled and finely chopped in a little butter and add 1 cup cooked pheasant or other left-over game meat, chicken, duck or turkey; ½ cup chopped bacon or ham and 2oz chopped mushrooms and one celery stalk, trimmed and chopped. Add to the white sauce, season and simmer for about 10-15 minutes. Allow to cool slightly before dividing the sauce between the pancakes. Roll the

pancakes up and place in a greased ovenproof dish. Sprinkle with grated cheese and bake in a preheated oven (375°F) for 30 minutes.

Tuna and tomato: Stir about 7oz canned tuna, drained and flaked and 4 medium-sized tomatoes, peeled and chopped into the white sauce. Season with salt, pepper and a dash of Worcestershire sauce. Proceed as for pheasant, bacon and mushroom pancakes.

Curried chicken: Add 8oz cooked, chopped chicken and 4oz cooked peas or whole kernel corn to the white sauce flavored with 2 teasps mild curry powder. Proceed as above.

Mixed vegetables: Add 8-10oz cooked, diced vegetables and some chopped parsley to the basic white sauce seasoned and enriched with heavy cream. Proceed as above.

Seafood: Add 8-10oz mixed seafood (lobster or crabmeat, mussels, clams, shrimp or flaked fish) to a white sauce seasoned and flavored with a little tomato paste.

Egg and Bacon Florentine

1lb fresh leaf spinach (or 1×12oz pack of frozen spinach)	2oz Cheddar cheese, grated
salt	salt and freshly ground black pepper to taste
1 teasp sugar	4 large slices of bacon with rinds removed
¼ cup butter	2 slices white bread with crusts removed
2 tbspns flour	oil for frying croûtons
1¼ cups milk	4 large, fresh eggs

Preparation time: 30 minutes
Cooking time: 35 minutes

Preheat the oven to 400°F. Remove any coarse stalks and yellowed leaves from the spinach and wash well. Place in a pan with a pinch of salt and the sugar. Cook just in the water clinging to the leaves for about 6-7 minutes over medium heat shaking the pan occasionally. If using frozen spinach follow the directions on the pack. Drain well by pressing in a strainer then chop coarsely.

Melt the butter in a small pan and stir in the flour. Cook for about a minute, stirring, then take off the heat. Pour in the milk and stir well to mix in the roux (flour and butter mixture). Return the pan to the heat and cook, stirring, until the sauce thickens. Add half the cheese, season and cook gently for 10 minutes, stirring occasionally.

Cut the bacon into small squares and fry in their own fat until crisp, then drain.

Lay the spinach in a fairly large, ovenproof gratin dish. Sprinkle over the bacon and then make 4 hollows in the spinach with the back of a serving spoon. Break an egg into each 'nest' and then pour or spoon the sauce over. Sprinkle with the remaining cheese and bake for 12-15 minutes.

Scrambled Egg and Smoked Salmon Baskets

8 slices white toasting bread, with crusts removed	⅓ cup butter
softened butter or magarine	8 stuffed olives, sliced
6 large eggs	**Garnish:** lettuce or watercress
freshly ground black pepper	
2oz smoked salmon, chopped	

Preparation time: 10 minutes
Cooking time: 25-35 minutes

Preheat the oven to 350°F. Spread both sides of the bread thinly with butter or margarine and press each slice into heatproof ramekins, Yorkshire pudding tins or custard cups. Bake for 25 minutes until crisp and golden.

Beat the eggs with the pepper (the salmon should provide enough salt) and smoked salmon.

Melt ¼ cup of the butter in a heavy-based pan, stir in the egg mixture and cook gently, stirring and lifting the cooked egg from the bottom of the pan. When the mixture has almost set, stir in the rest of the butter. Spoon the eggs into the toast 'basket,' decorate with olive slices and serve garnished with lettuce or watercress.

Cheese Dishes

Cheese is one of the most nutritious and versatile foods available. There are dozens of different types and it is worth experimenting with new varieties. When purchasing cheese, try not to buy too much at once as lengthy storage will spoil the flavor and texture. Cheese does not freeze well in the piece but surplus hard cheeses can be grated and frozen for use in cooking.

Buy cheese from good-quality retailers whenever possible and avoid the packaged pre-wrapped blocks as these tend to taste soapy and sweaty, especially the hard varieties. Cheeses such as French Camembert and Brie should be reasonably ripe and soft (though some people do prefer these cheeses firm) with a fairly strong aroma. Blue-veined cheeses, on the other hand, should be reasonably firm with a crumbly texture and should not smell particularly strong. A hard cheese such as Cheddar should look smooth and dry without any oiliness or cracks in the cut surface.

Most cheeses can be stored in the refrigerator but they must be well wrapped in foil or plastic wrap to prevent them from drying and to protect them from absorbing odors from other foods. The ideal temperature range is between 40°F and 50°F which corresponds with the average domestic refrigerator setting for the main compartment. Allow cheese, particularly the soft types, to stand in room temperature for at least 30 minutes before serving.

Greek Salad

Serves 4-6

4-6oz fetta cheese	2 scallions, trimmed and sliced
4 large tomatoes, ripe but firm	4 tbspns Vinaigrette dressing, flavored with oregano and garlic (see page 130)
12 black olives, stoned and halved	
1 head of crisp lettuce, washed and torn into pieces	

Preparation time: 10-15 minutes

Cut the fetta into small cubes. Slice the tomatoes or cut them into quarters if preferred; save any juice to add to the dressing. Combine all the ingredients and toss well to coat with dressing.

Welsh Rarebit

This traditional savory course is much better suited for a quick snack lunch than an after-dinner taster.

1 cup hard cheese (such as Cheddar or Lancashire)	dash Worcestershire sauce
1 tbspn butter	freshly ground black pepper
2 tbspns beer or milk	4 thick slices of crusty bread
½ teasp mustard powder	

Preparation time: 5 minutes
Cooking time: 5-7 minutes

Place all the ingredients except the bread into a small heavy-based saucepan and stir over heat until the mixture is smooth and creamy. Check the seasoning. Toast the bread on one side only and spread the cheese mixture on the other side. Place under a hot broiler until the top is brown and bubbling. Serve immediately with sliced tomatoes.

Swiss Cheese Fondue

This hot dip of creamy cheese dunked wih crusty bread, one of Switzerland's most exciting national dishes, is ideal for an informal lunch or supper party. For equipment you will need a set of narrow, long-handled fondue forks, a pot, usually made of earthenware (wider and shallower than the pot used for the beef fondue cooked in oil), and a spirit burner which can be placed on the table.

1 fat garlic clove	1 teasp fresh lemon juice
8oz Emmenthal cheese, grated	freshly ground black pepper
8oz Gruyère cheese, grated	pinch of nutmeg
3 teasps cornstarch	2 tbspns kirsch or brandy
1¼ cups dry white wine	loaf of French bread cut into 1in cubes

Preparation time: 10 minutes

Rub the fondue pot well with cut garlic and add the cheese, flour, wine and lemon juice. Heat gently, stirring, until the cheese melts and the mixture is smooth and creamy. Add the kirsch or brandy, stir well and invite your guests to spear pieces of bread on their forks and dunk them in the melted cheese.

Tip: If the mixture begins to curdle or is rather thin, add a little more cornstarch mixed to a smooth paste with cold water. Do not allow the fondue to become too hot. If it thickens too much, add a little more wine.

QUICK AND EASY DISHES

Throughout this book there are dishes featured which are quick to prepare and cook – such as Spaghetti Carbonara in the chapter on pasta, and a number of fish and egg recipes. This chapter, however, is devoted to a collection of favorite quick meals which can be prepared and cooked within 30-40 minutes – some even less!

Many of these dishes make use of store-cupboard items and frozen foods and are designed to be useful when time is short or shopping is difficult. It is a good idea to stock up your store-cupboard with items such as canned soups, particularly the condensed varieties which can form a speedy basic flavoring for casseroles; canned meats, fish and vegetables which can quickly be turned into sauces, pies and curried dishes. Stocks of pasta and rice are extremely useful. If you have a freezer, then quick and easy cooking is even simpler as you can freeze whole meals, sauces or ready-prepared ingredients such as pastry for pies and ready-chopped vegetables for casseroles (see page 216 for freezing hints).

Open sandwiches

The Scandinavians have excelled at open sandwiches for decades. Fairly simple foods are combined in such an attractive way that they look almost too good to eat! Experiment with different types of bread such as rye, pumpernickel, whole-wheat and even breads and rolls flavored with ingredients such as onion, caraway seeds, nuts or cheese. Or, as most slimmers know, the ordinary crispbreads can be dressed up to make a delicious lunch or snack. Try some of the following combinations as toppings:

Cottage cheese mixed with chopped cucumber and peeled shrimp or canned salmon and spooned on to a crisp lettuce leaf. Garnish with unshelled shrimp or cucumber slices.

Open Sandwiches.

Egg mayonnaise with chopped stuffed olives included in the sauce, and garnished with olive slices and sprigs of watercress.

Cold or hot buttered egg with chopped smoked salmon or ham, garnished with thin slices of tomato and parsley sprigs.

Cream cheese mixed with finely chopped celery and garnished with lettuce and orange segments.

Cream cheese pounded with crushed garlic and fresh herbs and piped into attractive rosettes on thin slices of tomato.

Rolls of thin beef, ham, salami or garlic sausage garnished with chicory or endive and radish roses.

Slices of hard-boiled eggs, dressed with mayonnaise and black olives, and garnished with a little grated carrot or lattice-strips of anchovy.

Smoked mackerel or pickled herring on lettuce garnished with dill pickles cut into fans.

Rolls of smoked salmon arranged on a bed of shredded lettuce or watercress sprigs, garnished with spoonfuls of creamed horse-radish.

Chicken liver pâté on lettuce garnished with sliced button mushrooms and chopped chives.

Toasted sandwiches
Toasted sandwiches make very popular lunches and snacks. Electric sandwich toasters are excellent and if you buy one you will also receive a list of suggestions for fillings – not that Gorgonzola and chopped dates; banana, cucumber and beef; cooked lamb, prunes and onion rings are to everyone's taste! There are, however, endless combinations of really tasty fillings which can make toasted sandwiches into a substantial meal: try ham, tomato and grated cheese; mashed sardines and tomato; tuna, mayonnaise and cucumber; mushrooms, garlic sausage and onion rings; liver pâté and sliced tomatoes or sliced dill pickles; shrimp, cottage cheese and pineapple; left-over dishes such as chile con carne, Bolognese sauce or curry.

If you do not want to go to the expense of buying an electric sandwich toaster, buy an inexpensive gadget which consists of two hinged metal plates with handles that fit together like a clam shell. Place the sandwich (with the outsides buttered as with the electric type) between the two plates, squeeze the handles together and cook both sides over a hotplate on the stove.

If you prefer simply to use the broiler, follow this method: toast 2 pieces of bread on one side (buttered or plain). Place the filling on the toasted side of one of the pieces of bread; place the other piece on top with the untoasted side facing outwards and broil both untoasted sides until golden brown.

Fried sandwiches
This is an excellent way of using up left-over sandwiches (provided that they are still fresh) particularly if they contain cold meats. Brush the outsides of the sandwiches with melted butter or oil and fry over moderate heat until crisp. Alternatively you can brush them with an egg beaten with a little milk before frying.

Croque Monsieur

This is the classic French hot sandwich with a lovely gooey filling, suitable for a starter or snack.

8 thin slices of white bread (semi-stale ready-cut bread is ideal)	2 eggs, beaten
1 cup Gruyère cheese, grated	¼ cup butter
4 slices cooked ham	2 tbspns corn oil
Dijon mustard to taste	**Garnish:** sliced tomatoes and thin onion rings or scissored chives

Preparation time: 5 minutes
Cooking time: approx. 8 minutes

Cut the crusts from the bread. Divide the cheese between four slices of bread and lay a slice of ham on each. Spread with mustard and press the other 4 slices of bread down firmly on top to make 4 sandwiches. Cut each sandwich into 2 triangles. pour the eggs on to a flat dish and dip both sides of 4 triangles into the egg to coat well.

Heat half the butter and oil in a large skillet and fry the 4 triangles for about 2 minutes on each side over medium heat until crisp and golden brown. Place on a serving dish to keep warm. Dip the other 4 sandwiches in the egg and, using the remaining butter and oil, fry until crisp and brown. Serve immediately, garnished with sliced tomatoes and thin onion rings or chives.

Quick Seafood Curry

¼ cup butter

1 small onion, peeled and sliced

1 garlic clove, crushed (optional)

1 tbspn mild curry powder

½ teasp ground ginger

½ tbspn flour

½ tbspn ground almonds

⅔ cup natural yogurt

1 tbspn lemon juice

1lb firm white fish (for instance monkfish, halibut, cod)

1¼ cups peeled shrimp

½ teasp sugar

salt to taste

Garnish: coriander leaves

Preparation time: 15 minutes
Cooking time: 15-20 minutes

Melt the butter in a pan and stir-fry the onion, garlic (if using) and spices for 2-3 minutes. Stir in the flour and almonds and cook gently for a few moments. Add the yogurt and lemon juice and cook very gently, stirring for 3-4 minutes then add the fish and continue cooking for a further 5 minutes. Stir in the shrimp, sugar and salt to taste and, when heated through, serve immediately, garnished with coriander leaves.

Serve on a bed of boiled rice with side dishes of buttered spinach and crisply fried onion rings.

Variations: Quick Chicken Curry: replace the shrimp and fish with 4 chicken breasts, boned and cut into thin strips or small cubes. Sauté the chicken in the butter until cooked through before adding the onion, garlic and spices.

Devilled Mackerel

A tasty fish dish which takes only about 10 minutes to cook and is equally good with herrings.

4 mackerel, cleaned

4 tbspns French mustard

4 tbspns white breadcrumbs

¼ teasp cayenne pepper

salt and pepper

2 tbspns melted butter

Garnish: 4 lemon wedges

Preparation time: 5 minutes
Cooking time: 8-10 minutes

Preheat the broiler to medium-low. Score the mackerel on both sides with 3 or 4 cuts with a sharp knife and spread them with the mustard. Mix the breadcrumbs and seasonings together and roll the fish in them until well coated. Lay them on an oiled grid and spoon over half the butter. Broil for 4-5 minutes, turn and spoon over the remaining butter and broil for a further 4-5 minutes. Serve with lemon wedges and a crisp salad.

Tuna-Mushroom Sauce

This is a very quick and delicious sauce for pasta or rice which can be whisked together, mostly using ingredients from the store-cupboard.

| 16oz can tomatoes, chopped |
| 2 celery stalks, trimmed and finely chopped |
| 2 cups fresh or canned button mushrooms |
| 7oz can tuna in brine |
| 1 garlic clove, crushed |
| ½ teasp dried basil or mixed herbs |
| salt and freshly ground black pepper |

Preparation time: 3-5 minutes
Cooking time: 15 minutes

Place the tomatoes, with their juice, and celery in a pan and bring to the boil. Cover and simmer for 5 minutes on reduced heat. Add the mushrooms, tuna (flaked into large pieces), garlic, herbs, a little salt and plenty of pepper. Simmer for a further 10 minutes and serve with noodles, spaghetti or rice.

Savory Fish Cakes

A quick and easy family favorite – ideal for a light lunch. This dish is economical and also freezes very well.

12oz inexpensive white fish fillets, skinned	1 tbspn chopped fresh thyme or marjoram or a good pinch of dried thyme or marjoram
1 bay leaf	
2-3 slices of onion	1 tbspn tomato catsup
1 teasp black peppercorns	salt and freshly ground black pepper
1lb potatoes, boiled and mashed	seasoned flour for coating
1 small egg, beaten	oil for shallow frying
2 tbspns chopped fresh parsley	**Garnish:** parsley sprigs

Preparation time: 15-20 minutes
Cooking time: 15-20 minutes (total)

Poach the fish fillets in water with the bay leaf, onion and peppercorns for about 10 minutes or until the fish flakes easily. Lift it out of the cooking liquid and mash it up well with the potato. Add the egg, herbs, catsup and seasoning and mix well. Shape the mixture into 8 cakes and dust them with seasoned flour.

Shallow-fry the fish cakes for 2-3 minutes on each side until golden brown.
Variation: Left-over cooked fresh salmon, canned salmon or tuna in place of white fish make these fish cakes extra-specially good.

Sautéd Kidneys with Mushrooms.

Sautéd Kidneys with Mushrooms

8 lambs' kidneys	3 tbspns sherry
¼ cup butter	4 tbspns light cream or chicken stock
1 small onion, peeled and sliced	salt and freshly ground black pepper
2 cups button mushrooms, wiped	**Garnish:** triangles of fried bread; chopped fresh parsley
1 tbspn flour	
good pinch of dried rosemary	

Preparation time: 20 minutes
Cooking time: 15-20 minutes

Wash the kidneys and pat dry with kitchen paper. Slice them lengthways, remove the skins and cut out the white inner cores. If large, slice the halves into smaller, fork-sized pieces.

Melt the butter in a skillet and sauté the kidneys and onion for about 5 minutes. Add the mushrooms and cook for a further 2-3 minutes. Remove the kidneys, onion and mushrooms from the pan with a slotted spoon to a serving dish and keep warm. Stir the flour and rosemary into the pan juices and cook for about a minute. Add the sherry, stirring well, bring to the boil then stir in the cream or stock and cook until you have a smooth sauce. Season to taste and pour over the kidneys.

Sautéd kidneys are extremely good with boiled egg noodles or rice. Serve with fresh garden peas, French beans or a crisp salad.

Sautéd Liver and Bacon

1lb calves' or lambs' liver cut in thin
  slices

8 slices bacon, with the rind removed

1 medium onion, peeled and sliced

2 tbspns corn oil

1 tbspn flour

1¼ cups unseasoned chicken or beef stock

1 tbspn white or red wine or vermouth (optional)

½ teasp sugar

salt and freshly ground black pepper

Preparation time: 5 minutes
Cooking time: 10 minutes

Wash the liver and pat dry with kitchen paper; cut away any tubes remaining. Fry the liver gently for 4-5 minutes until cooked but still very slightly pink inside. Remove from the pan and keep warm in a serving dish. Fry the bacon and onion for 2-3 minutes until the bacon is cooked through and the onion is just soft. Add to the liver in the serving dish. Stir the flour into the pan and cook for about 1 minute. Add the stock and wine (if using) and stir until the sauce thickens. Add the sugar and seasoning to taste and cook for 2-3 minutes. Strain the sauce over the liver and bacon or serve separately.

Mid-week Chicken

4 roasting chicken quarters

2 tbspns oil

16oz can tomatoes

1 medium onion, peeled and sliced

1 green or red sweet pepper, de-seeded and sliced

1 cup button mushrooms, trimmed and wiped

½ teasp oregano

salt and freshly ground black pepper

Preparation time: 10 minutes
Cooking time: 30-40 minutes

Fry the chicken in the oil in a flame-proof casserole until the pieces are brown all over. Stir in all the remaining ingredients, cover and simmer on reduced heat until the chicken is tender.

Danish Floddies

1 large potato

1 medium onion, peeled

1 large egg, beaten

¼ cup self-rising flour

6oz bacon, with the rind removed and chopped
  finely

pinch of dried mixed herbs

very little salt and freshly ground black pepper

oil for frying

Preparation time: 10 minutes
Cooking time: 10 minutes

Peel and grate the potato and onion into a bowl. Add the egg, flour, bacon, herbs and seasoning and mix well.

Heat a little oil in a skillet and drop in large spoonfuls of the mixture. Fry all over until golden and serve with broiled tomatoes and fried eggs.

Quick Pork Cassoulet

1lb lean pork (such as tenderloin, or spare rib)

1 tbspn corn oil

2-3 celery stalks, trimmed and chopped

1 medium onion, peeled and sliced or chopped

1 fat garlic clove (optional)

4oz garlic sausage, sliced

large pinch dried thyme or mixed herbs

16oz cans of baked beans in tomato sauce

salt and pepper

1-2 tbspns dried breadcrumbs

2 tbspns butter

Preparation time: 10 minutes
Cooking time: 40 minutes

Preheat the oven to 400°F. Cut the pork into fork-sized cubes and fry in the oil until golden. Re-

move with a slotted spoon and place in an oven-proof casserole. Fry the celery, onion, and garlic until the onion is soft then transfer the mixture to the casserole. Add a spoonful or two of water to the pan, stir and cook for a moment or two, then pour the juices over the meat and vegetables. Stir in the garlic sausage, herbs and baked beans, season to taste and sprinkle over a light layer of breadcrumbs. Dot with butter and bake for about 30 minutes until the casserole is bubbling and the top is golden.

Gammon Steaks with Orange Butter.

Pork Stroganoff

1½lb pork tenderloin

¼ cup butter

1 large onion, peeled and thinly sliced

2 cups fresh button mushrooms, wiped and sliced

1¼ cups soured cream

¼ teasp ground nutmeg

salt and freshly ground black pepper

Preparation time: 5-10 minutes
Cooking time: 15-20 minutes

Trim the fat and thin membrane from the pork and cut into thin strips. Melt the butter in a large skillet and stir-fry the pork over fairly high heat until just cooked through. Remove with a slotted spoon and keep warm. Stir-fry the onion and mushrooms until the onions are soft. Return the pork to the pan and stir in the soured cream, nutmeg and seasoning. Cook until the cream has heated through without allowing it to boil. Serve immediately on a bed of boiled rice or fresh pasta accompanied by a green salad.

Gammon or Pork Steaks with Orange Butter   Serves 2

2 large gammon steaks, pork chops

1 orange

3 tbspns butter

Garnish: 1 large orange peeled and cut into slices, parsley sprigs

Preparation time: 10 minutes
Cooking time: 10 minutes

Cut the rinds off the steaks or chops and snip the fat at intervals to prevent them curling up. Grate the rind from the orange and mix well with the butter. Form into 2 pats and chill.

Cook the steaks under a moderate broiler for about 5 minutes each side. Serve with the orange butter and garnished with slices of fresh orange and parsley.

A salad of par-boiled zucchini, peeled and quartered fresh tomatoes and sliced onions goes well with this dish.

Nasi Goreng

This version of the Indonesian rice dish is a speedy way of using cooked meats and rice to make a very tasty meal.

3 tbspns corn oil
3 large eggs, beaten
salt and pepper
1 large garlic clove, crushed
1 large onion, peeled and sliced
1 red or green sweet pepper, de-seeded and sliced
4 cups cooked long-grain rice or   1 cup plus 2 tbspns raw long-grain rice, cooked

1 cup shreddded or chopped cooked meat (chicken,   turkey, duck, pork or ham)
1 cup peeled shrimp
⅛ teasp chilli powder
2 tbspns soy sauce

Preparation time: 10 minutes
Cooking time: 15-20 minutes

Heat 1 tbspn oil in a large skillet. Season the eggs and pour them into the pan. Cook fairly gently until brown underneath then cook the other side. Turn this omelette on to a plate and cut into narrow strips and keep warm.

Heat the remaining oil in the pan and stir-fry the garlic, onions and pepper until soft. Add the rest of the ingredients and stir-fry-toss until they are all well mixed and heated through.

Serve garnished with the strips of cooked egg and accompanied by plenty of sliced tomatoes and green salad. Green Beans Greek-style (see page 102) also go well with this dish.

Steak Special.

Steak Special

4 portions tender steak
¼ cup butter
1 cup button mushrooms, sliced
⅔ cup soured cream
1 dessertspoon chopped fresh chives
3oz blue cheese, grated or crumbled
salt and pepper

Preparation time: 5 minutes
Cooking time: 10-15 minutes

Fry the steaks in the butter on both sides until cooked to your preference. Remove and place on a serving dish to keep warm. Fry the mushrooms in the pan juices until lightly cooked, and stir in the remaining ingredients. Cook, stirring, until the cheese has melted and pour the sauce over the steaks to serve.
Variation: Try this sauce with fried slices of pork tenderloin or broiled pork chops.

Chinese Gingered Beef

A deliciously different way to serve beefsteak, either as a classy supper dish with Chinese noodles or fried rice and a simple vegetable or as part of a wider range of Chinese dishes.

1lb tender beefsteak
salt and freshly ground black pepper
1 teasp ground ginger
3 tbspns corn or peanut oil
approx. 1in piece fresh root ginger, finely chopped
⅔ cup dry sherry
2 teasps cornstarch
⅔ cup natural yoghurt
2 tbspns chopped scallions
Garnish: scallion tassels

Preparation time: 5-6 minutes
Cooking time: 7-10 minutes

Cut the beef into thin strips. Put them in a bowl with the seasoning and ground ginger.

Heat the oil in a frying-pan or wok, add the chopped ginger and stir-fry for 1 minute. Add the beef strips and stir-fry for 2-3 minutes until they are just cooked. Blend the sherry and cornstarch together and add to the meat; stir until the liquid has thickened and then add the yoghurt. When heated through, serve immediately sprinkled with the chopped onion.

Bobotie

Serves 4-6

⅔ cup milk	juice and grated rind of 1 large lemon
1 cup soft breadcrumbs	½ teasp grated nutmeg
1½lb lean ground beef or lamb	3 tbspns sultanas (optional)
1 large onion, peeled and thinly sliced	salt and freshly ground black pepper
1 tbspn mild curry powder	2 large eggs, beaten
1 tbspn chopped almonds	

Preparation time: 10 minutes
Cooking time: 40-45 minutes

Preheat the oven to 350°F. Pour the milk over the breadcrumbs in a bowl.

Cook the beef in its own fat in a large saucepan until browned and separated. Add the onions and cook until soft. Stir in all the rest of the ingredients, including the bread and milk but reserving the eggs. When all these additions are well mixed into the beef, turn the mixture into a large, greased casserole or pie dish and press down. Pour the eggs over and bake for about 30 minutes until the eggs have set and the top is crusty.

This popular South African dish makes a substantial main course served with rice, thinly sliced tomatoes and onions and chutney.

Tip: This dish can be left in a low oven to keep warm for about an hour if necessary. The basic meat mixture freezes successfully; to cook: defrost fully, pour over the eggs and cook as given above.

PASTA

Pasta has become the modern favorite for family meals. It is filling and nutritious and yet surprisingly low in calories – only about 200 calories to every 2oz of dry pasta. Pasta is so versatile that it can become a simple but satisfying spaghetti bolognese for a family supper, or dressed up with a delightful pesto sauce as an exciting dinner-party first course and even served cold with vegetables and a piquant dressing as a salad (see page 135). Cooked pasta dishes freeze very well and make perfect standby meals.

Good quality pasta is usually made from durum wheat, either refined or whole-wheat. Dried pasta comes in five main types: long pasta such as macaroni and spaghetti; short pasta such as cut macaroni, rings, wheels (*ruote*) or shells (*conchiglie*); folded pasta such as ribbon noodles (*tagliatelle* or *fettuccine*); sheet pasta such as lasagne; and pasta for soup such as tiny shells (*conchigliette*) and grains (*pastine*).

Fresh pasta is usually made with fresh eggs and can be flavored with such ingredients as spinach, mushrooms and tomatoes.

Cooking pasta

Dried or fresh pasta should always be cooked in plenty of fast-boiling water – allow about 15 cups of water to every 1lb of pasta. Add about 1 tbspn oil to the water to help to prevent the pasta from sticking together.

Feed long pasta into the water gradually and return the water to the boil. Do not boil too rapidly and stir from time to time during cooking to keep the pasta separated.

The cooking time depends on the size of the pasta and whether it is fresh or dried. Dried long pasta takes from 10-15 minutes to cook while the short-cut dried shapes take from 6-15 minutes. Fresh pasta can take as little as 2-3 minutes for spaghetti and tagliatelle and 7-8 minutes for lasagne. Check the cooking instructions on the pack and cook for the minimum time recommended; then test by tasting. Pasta is best served *al dente*, that is it should be firm with a little 'bite'

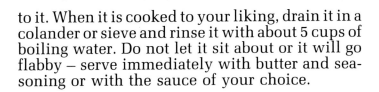

to it. When it is cooked to your liking, drain it in a colander or sieve and rinse it with about 5 cups of boiling water. Do not let it sit about or it will go flabby – serve immediately with butter and seasoning or with the sauce of your choice.

Using a Pasta machine

Follow the instructions for making the dough as above, but there is no need to knead it, the machine does this for you. Place the dough on the machine and put it on its widest setting. Feed it through by turning the handle. This will give you a strip of dough about 1in wide. Turn the setting down one notch and repeat the operation. Feed the dough through the machine several times, decreasing the width each time. When the dough is the width you want it, put it through the machine to give the shape of spaghetti you require.

Basic Pasta Dough

4 cups flour	1 teasp salt
4 medium eggs, beaten	cold water to mix
½ tbspn melted butter	

Preparation time: approx 20 minutes
Drying time: 1½-2 hours

Sift the flour with the salt into a glass or china mixing bowl. Make a 'well' in the center of the flour and pour in the eggs. Using a fork, draw the flour into the eggs and mix well. Add a teaspoon of water until you have a smooth elastic dough which you can form into a ball.

Knead the dough on a floured surface for 5-10 minutes and divide into 4. Roll out one piece evenly to a paper-thin sheet. Dust well with flour then leave to dry for about an hour. Roll up the dough, and using a sharp knife, cut it into noodle or lasagne widths. Repeat with the other 3 pieces of dough. Separate the strips of pasta and spread out to dry on a floured tray. Leave for 1½-2 hours to dry. Homemade pasta can be frozen or stored for several days in the refrigerator.

Cheesy Pasta Scallops

6oz pasta shells, macaroni or any short-cut pasta	¼ cup flour
1 tbspn corn oil	1¼ cups milk
6 slices bacon	salt and freshly ground black pepper
2 eggs, hard-boiled	¾ cup Cheddar cheese, grated
2 tbspns butter	**Garnish:** crisp bacon and parsley sprigs

Preparation time: 10 minutes
Cooking time: 15-20 minutes

Cook the pasta in plenty of boiling salted water with the oil until just tender. Drain well.

While the pasta is cooking, de-rind the bacon and grill until crisp. Cut or snip into small pieces. Shell the hard-boiled eggs and chop. Mix the eggs, bacon and pasta together, reserving a little bacon for garnishing. Spoon the mixture into 4 scallop shells.

Melt the butter in a pan and stir in the flour, cook for about 1 minute then remove from the heat. Gradually stir in the milk until well mixed then return to the heat. Cook, stirring constantly until the sauce thickens. Season and add 2oz of the cheese and cook until the cheese melts.

Spoon the sauce over the pasta mixture in the shells and top with the remaining cheese. Brown under a broiler and serve garnished with the remaining bacon and parsley sprigs.

Variation: Replace the bacon with 6oz cooked, flaked, smoked haddock or peeled shrimp for a luxury touch.

Chicken and Pasta Pan Fry

Serves 6

14oz pasta wheels or any other small pasta shape	⅔ cup sherry or white wine
1 tbspn corn oil	⅔ cup unseasoned chicken stock
4 chicken breasts or large chicken quarters	8oz can tomatoes
2 tbspns flour	1 tbspn chopped fresh tarragon or thyme
¼ cup butter	salt and freshly ground black pepper
8oz bacon with rind removed, chopped	
1 medium onion, peeled and chopped	
2 cups mushrooms, sliced	

Preparation time: 25 minutes
Cooking time: approx 25 minutes

Cook the pasta in plenty of boiling salted water with the oil until barely tender. Rinse under cold running water and drain well.

Cut the chicken into fork-sized pieces and roll in the flour. Melt the butter in a large skillet and brown the chicken. Add the chopped bacon and onion and fry for a minute or two. Add the sliced mushrooms and stir-fry until softened, then pour on the sherry or wine, stock and tomatoes (chopped if preferred). Add the chosen herb, and seasoning and boil until the liquid has reduced. Stir in the cooked pasta and heat through. Serve immediately.

Cheesy Pasta Scallops.

Chicken and Corn Macaroni

¼ cup butter	pinch of dried thyme
1 tbspn oil	1 tbspn chopped fresh parsley *or* 1 tbspn dried parsley
1 small onion, peeled and chopped	
2 tbspns flour	salt and pepper
2½ cups milk	2 cups dried macaroni
8oz cooked chicken, chopped	1 tbspn oil
¾ cup frozen or canned whole kernel corn, drained	½ cup Cheddar cheese, grated
	Garnish: 2-3 tomatoes, sliced

Preparation time: 20-30 minutes
Cooking time: 25-30 minutes

Melt the butter with the oil and cook the onion until it has softened. Stir in the flour and cook over a moderate heat for about a minute. Remove from the heat and stir in the milk until it is well mixed. Return to the heat and cook, stirring continuously until the sauce has thickened. Add the chicken, sweetcorn, herbs and seasoning and simmer for 10 minutes. Remove from the heat. Cook the macaroni in a large pan of fast-boiling water with the oil until tender (about 12-15 mi-nutes). Drain the macaroni and place in a heated, flameproof dish and keep warm.

Return the sauce to the heat, until it begins to bubble. Mix the sauce with the macaroni, sprinkle the top with the cheese and cook under a moderate broiler until the cheese browns. Serve immediately, garnished with tomato slices and accompanied by a side salad — celery goes well with this dish.

Spaghetti Bolognese

A variation of this classic pasta sauce served slightly thickened and flavored with sweet pepper.

1lb lean ground beef	⅔ cup beef stock
2 slices of bacon with rind removed, chopped	1 green or red sweet pepper, de-seeded and sliced
1 small onion, peeled and finely chopped	pinch of oregano
1 fat garlic clove, crushed	1 teasp sugar
1 carrot, peeled and finely chopped	salt and pepper
1 celery stalk, trimmed and sliced	1 tbspn oil
1 tbspn flour	1lb spaghetti
16oz can tomatoes	

Preparation time: 30 minutes
Cooking time: 45-60 minutes

To prepare the sauce: Brown the ground beef in its own fat in a heavy-based pan. Add the bacon, onion, garlic, carrot and celery and cook for 3-4 minutes. Sprinkle the flour over and stir-fry for another minute. Coarsely chop the tomatoes and add these, with their juice, to the sauce. Stir in the rest of the ingredients and simmer gently for about 45 minutes. Alternatively, cook in a slow oven (325°F) for about 1 hour.

To cook the spaghetti: Bring a large pan of salted water to the boil. Add the oil and spaghetti. Cook until tender (about 15 minutes).

Spaghetti alla Carbonara

Serves 4 as a main course or 6-8 as a starter

16oz dried spaghetti	1 cup fresh button mushrooms, sliced
1 tbspn corn oil	2 eggs
salt to taste	¼ cup Ricotta or cream cheese
2 tbspns butter	⅔ cup light cream
1 small onion, peeled and finely chopped	generous amount of freshly ground black pepper
8oz cooked ham, finely sliced	**Garnish:** chopped fresh parsley

Preparation time: 15 minutes
Cooking time: 15-20 minutes

Cook the spaghetti in plenty of salted boiling water with the oil until tender.

Fry the onion in the butter until softened. Add the ham and mushrooms and stir-fry for 1-2 minutes. Beat the eggs with the cheese until smooth and stir in the cream.

Drain the pasta and rinse with boiling water and drain again carefully. Rinse out the pan and return the spaghetti to it with the onion, ham and mushroom. Heat gently, stirring, until the spaghetti has heated through, add the egg mixture and pepper, and stir until the sauce begins to coat the spaghetti, then serve at once.

Tip: The egg mixture needs very little cooking otherwise it may separate.

Spaghetti alla Carbonara.

Tagliatelle with Pesto Sauce

12oz dried tagliatelle

1 tbspn corn or olive oil

1oz fresh basil leaves

2 garlic cloves

½ cup pine kernels

½ cup Parmesan cheese, freshly grated

6 tbspns olive oil

salt and freshly ground black pepper

Preparation time: 10 minutes (or less)
Cooking time: 10-12 minutes

Cook the tagliatelle in plenty of boiling salted water with the oil until just tender. Drain well. While the pasta is cooking prepare the pesto sauce.

Chop the basil finely and chop or crush the garlic and pine kernels, by hand or in a food processor or blender. Add the cheese and when the mixture resembles a thick purée, add the oil, a little at a time. Season to taste and serve with the tagliatelle.

Lasagne alla Marinara

Serves 4-6

8oz baby squid

8oz monkfish, cod, haddock or any other firm
  white fish

16oz can tomatoes

6-8oz dried lasagne

1 tbspn corn oil

salt to taste

¼ cup butter

1 medium onion, peeled and chopped

1 garlic clove, crushed

2½ tbspns flour

½ cup dry white wine

1 teasp sugar

large pinch of dried dill

1 tbspn chopped fresh parsley

salt and freshly ground black pepper

½ cup peeled shrimp

2 cups Béchamel Sauce (see page 120) made with 3
  tbspns butter; 4 tbspns flour; 2 cups milk

½-¾ cup grated Cheddar cheese

Preparation time: 1 hour
Cooking time: 1 hour

Prepare the squid as described on page 48. Skin and cut the fish into small cubes.

Push the tomatoes through a sieve or strainer with their juice to remove the pips.

Cook the lasagne in plenty of salted water with the oil for 15-20 minutes until tender. While the pasta is cooking, prepare the sauce.

Melt the butter in a pan and gently fry the onion and garlic without browning. Stir in the flour and cook for a few moments. Take the pan off the heat and stir in the tomatoes, wine, sugar, dill, parsley, salt and pepper, and cook gently for 10 minutes. Add the squid, fish and shrimp and cook for another 5 minutes.

Drain the pasta. Line a greased, ovenproof dish with a layer of lasagne. Spoon over the seafood sauce and cover with a single layer of lasagne. Repeat until the sauce and pasta is used up. Cover with béchamel sauce and sprinkle with the grated cheese. Bake in a moderate oven (375°F) for about 35-40 minutes. Serve with a crisp green salad, tossed with a sharp vinaigrette dressing.
Tip: This dish can be kept warm without spoiling in a low oven. It freezes well.

**Lasagne
al Forno.**

Lasagne al Forno

Serves 4-6

6-8oz dried lasagne	⅔ cup brown stock or red wine
1 tbspn corn oil	salt and pepper
salt	**White sauce:**
Beef and tomato sauce:	3 tbspns butter
1lb ground beef	4 tbspns flour
1 large onion, peeled and finely chopped	2 cups milk
16oz can tomatoes	salt and pepper
2 tbspns Worcestershire sauce	**Topping:**
1 tbspn tomato paste	¾ cup grated Cheddar cheese
1 teasp dried mixed herbs	

Preparation time: 1 hour
Cooking time: 50-60 minutes

Cook lasagne in plenty of salted boiling water with the oil until just tender. Drain well.

To make the meat sauce: Fry the beef in its own fat in a heavy-based pan until browned and separated. Pour off any surplus fat, add the onion and cook until soft. Then add the tomatoes, coarsely chopped, with their juice and the rest of the sauce ingredients. Cover and simmer gently for 20-30 minutes, stirring occasionally.

To make the white sauce: Melt the butter in a pan, add the flour and cook for 1 minute. Remove the pan from the heat and stir in the milk. Return to the heat and cook gently, stirring continuously until the sauce thickens. Season to taste.

Line a greased ovenproof dish with a layer of lasagne. Spread with a thin layer of meat sauce followed by a thin layer of white sauce. Continue these layers until all the ingredients are used up, ending with a layer of white sauce on top. Sprinkle with the grated cheese and bake for about 35-40 minutes in a moderate oven (375°F).

A salad of sliced tomatoes and cucumber goes well with this dish.

Tip: This dish can be prepared well in advance. It also freezes very well.

Fish and Pasta Creole

A delicious supper dish, with an interesting mixture of tastes and textures, which is very simple and quick to cook.

2 tbspns butter	1 bay leaf
1 garlic clove, crushed	1 cup frozen or drained canned whole kernel corn
2-3 celery stalks	1½lb firm white fish (monkfish, cod, haddock or coley), skinned and cubed
16oz can tomatoes	
1¼ cups fish, vegetable or chicken stock	salt and freshly ground black pepper
8oz short-cut pasta (such as macaroni, twists, or shells)	**Garnish:** chopped fresh parsley

Preparation time: 15 minutes
Cooking time: 15-20 minutes

Melt the butter in a large pan and gently fry the garlic and celery. Add the tomatoes with their juice, the stock, pasta and bay leaf. Cover and simmer for 5-6 minutes. Add the whole kernel corn and fish and continue to simmer very gently for a further 5-6 minutes, adding a little more stock or water if necessary. Season to taste. Serve when the pasta is tender, garnished with chopped parsley.

SAVORY RICE DISHES

Perfect rice can elude the most talented cooks at times but, provided that you choose the right type for the dish which you intend to cook and follow one particular cooking method carefully, perfection is not too hard to achieve. There are quite a number of different varieties, including the processed easy-cook brands for which directions for cooking are usually supplied on the pack and these should be carefully adhered to.

Long-grain white rice
This is the patna or American rice, traditionally used for accompanying savory dishes, particularly Eastern specialities. There are 3 basic methods of cooking long-grain rice:

Method 1: For 4 servings, wash 1 cup plus 2 tbspns regular long-grain rice (to remove any flour left after the polishing process) and pick out any dark grains. In a large pan, bring about 3-4 pints salted water to the boil. Add the rice with 1 teasp lemon juice, bring back to the boil, stir and cook for 8-10 minutes. Check to see if the rice is tender by tasting or squeezing a grain between finger and thumb – if there is still a gritty core then cook for a minute or two longer. Drain the rice and rinse with boiling water to remove any starch. Turn out in a warm serving dish, cover with foil and place in a low oven (300°F) for 10-15 minutes to dry. One advantage of this method is

that provided the rice has not been overcooked and is not overheated, it will not suffer if kept standing for 30 minutes or so. Just before serving, fluff up the grains with a fork and add a knob of butter.

Method 2: It is best to measure the ingredients for this method by volume rather than weight, so for 4 servings measure out a level cup of rice to 2 cups of water. Salt the water and bring it to the boil. Wash the rice and add it slowly. Stir once and bring it back to the boil then turn the heat down to low. Cover tightly and simmer for about 20 minutes or until all the water has been absorbed. Add a knob of butter, fork over the grains to separate them and serve. One advantage of using this method is that less nutrients are lost from the rice than when it is cooked in a large volume of water. During the cooking time all the water should be absorbed. The rice more or less steam-cooks, giving fluffy separate grains. Success depends on the quality of the rice and the degree of heat used (ie some stoves have a much lower simmering heat than others). With this method, therefore, a certain amount of practice is needed. If you find that the rice is cooking too quickly on a low setting, try using a wire diffuser on the stove to lower the simmering heat.

Method 3 Following the quantities given for Method 2, boil the correct quantity of salted water. Wash the rice and place it in an ovenproof dish. Pour the boiled water over, cover tightly with a lid or foil and cook in a medium oven (350°F) for 30-35 minutes or until all the water has been absorbed and the rice is tender.

Brown rice
This is unprocessed long-grain rice with only the husks removed. It is high in nutritional value and has a pleasant, nutty flavor. It can be cooked in the same way as Method 1 for white long-grain rice but takes longer (25-30 minutes).

Basmati rice
Originating in the foothills of the Himalayas, this fine white rice with its slender grains is highly regarded in India. When cooked it is deliciously light and tender and possesses a delicate flavor and fragrance. It does require careful cooking but the resulting dish is well worth the trouble. For 4 servings wash well 1 cup plus 2 tbspns basmati grains. Place the rice in a pan with 2 cups cold water and salt. Bring to the boil, stir once and cover tightly. Reduce the heat to very low and simmer for about 12-15 minutes without stirring again. Check the pan – if there is still some water left, replace the lid and cook until all the water is absorbed. Serve with a knob of butter.

Italian rice
This is a short-grain rice used mainly for risottos as it absorbs a lot of liquid and gives a pleasant creamy texture to the dish.

Wild rice
This is not a true rice but the seeds of a wild lakeside grass which grows in the United States. It is harvested by hand and is therefore an expensive grain to buy but it has an interesting flavor and texture. Like brown rice, it requires a long cooking time.

Spiced Rice

¼ cup butter	½ teasp ground cumin
1 small onion, peeled and finely chopped	½ teasp ground cinnamon
1 fat garlic clove, crushed	½ teasp cardamom, crushed
1¼ cups long-grain rice	2-3 cloves
3 cups hot stock (chicken or vegetable)	pinch of chilli powder
½ teasp ground coriander	salt to taste
	pinch of dried dill

Preparation time: 10 minutes
Cooking time: 35 minutes

Melt the butter and fry the onion and garlic gently for 2-3 minutes in a large, heavy-based pan (with lid). Add the rice and stir-fry until it looks transparent – do not allow it to brown. Stir in the stock slowly, add the spices and seasoning and bring to the boil. Stir, then turn down the heat to low, cover and simmer gently for 15-20 minutes or until the rice is tender and the stock is all absorbed. Transfer to a heated serving dish and allow the rice to dry in a low oven (300°F) for 10-15 minutes. Stir in a knob of butter and serve.

Chinese Egg Fried Rice

1 cup long-grain rice, cooked (about 3 cups cooked quantity – preferably cooked the day before)	½ cup sliced button mushrooms
4 tbspns peanut or corn oil	½-¾ cup shredded mixed cooked meats (such as chicken, ham, or pork)
1 teasp sesame oil	⅓ cup peeled shrimp (optional)
1 garlic clove, crushed	2 eggs, beaten
4 small scallions, trimmed and sliced	1 tbspn soy sauce

Preparation time: 10 minutes
Cooking time: 5 minutes

Mix the oils together and heat in a heavy-based skillet. Add the rice and stir-fry for 1-2 minutes, separating the grains. Add the garlic, scallions and mushrooms and stir-fry for another minute before adding the meat and shrimp. Heat through, turning the rice over well. Move the mixture to one side of the pan and pour in the eggs. Cook for about a minute without stirring until the eggs are almost set then stir them into the rest of the mixture (it should have the appearance of fine strands). Add the soy sauce and toss the rice well using 2 spoons to ensure that all the ingredients are well mixed.

Paella Valencia

Serves 6-8

5 cups fresh mussels	2 small sweet peppers (1 green, 1 red), sliced or cut into squares
⅔ cup dry white wine	4 fresh tomatoes, peeled and quartered
1 bay leaf	1 tbspn chopped fresh parsley
1 roasting chicken (approx 3½lb) or 12-16 frozen chicken thighs or drumsticks, defrosted	pinch of dried basil
5-6 tbspns olive oil	4oz sliced chorizos, or garlic sausage, or Polish paprika sausage
1 large Spanish or Bermuda onion, sliced	1 cup peeled shrimp
2 fat garlic cloves, crushed	**Garnish:** ¼ cup stuffed olives, sliced; 6-8 lemon wedges; 6-8 jumbo shrimp
1lb risotto or long-grain rice	
3 cups good chicken stock	
large pinch of powdered saffron	

Preparation time: 40 minutes
Cooking time: 45-60 minutes

Prepare and cook the mussels as given on page 18 using the wine, and bay leaf. Strain off the liquid and reserve and keep the mussels warm.

Cut the chicken into 12-16 pieces. Heat the oil in a large paella pan or skillet and fry the chicken until it is well browned. Remove the chicken from the pan and keep warm.

Add the sliced onion and garlic to the pan (and a little more oil if necessary) and fry gently for 1-2 minutes. Add the rice and stir-fry gently until the rice just begins to color. Stir in the chicken stock, mussel liquid and saffron. Add the peppers, tomatoes, parsley, basil and chopped sausage and return the chicken to the pan. Stir well and cook very slowly, uncovered until the liquid is absorbed and the rice is tender.

Finally, stir in the peeled shrimp and cook until they are heated through. Arrange the mussels, in their shells, round the pan and garnish with the olives, lemon wedges and whole shrimp. Serve with crusty bread and lots of Rioja.
Variation: For a special occasion add the meat of a cooked lobster with the shrimp.

Kedgeree

¼ cup butter	salt and freshly ground black pepper
1 medium onion, peeled and sliced	⅔ cup single cream
1lb smoked haddock, cooked and flaked	3 hard-boiled eggs, quartered or chopped
1¾ cups long-grain rice, cooked	**Garnish:** chopped fresh parsley
1 teasp mild curry powder	

Preparation time: 20 minutes
Cooking time: about 15 minutes on top of the stove or 35 minutes in the oven.

Melt the butter in a heavy-based pan and fry the onion for 2-3 minutes. Add the haddock, rice, curry powder and seasoning and stir-fry-toss for 3-4 minutes. Add the cream and stir well with a fork until the mixture has reheated and is creamy. Add the eggs and cook for a moment or two longer. Serve very hot garnished with chopped parsley.

Tip: Use an ovenproof pan and, after frying the onions, add all the other ingredients, cover and cook in a low oven (325°F) for about 30 minutes.

Kedgeree.

Chicken Risotto

Serves 4-6

2 tbspns butter

1 medium onion, peeled and chopped

1¾ cups risotto or long-grain rice

1 tbspn mild curry powder

1 tbspn fresh parsley, chopped

salt and freshly ground black pepper

pinch of garlic salt

2 cups cooked chicken, chopped

4 fresh tomatoes, peeled and quartered

3¾ cups well-flavored stock

¾ cup cooked peas

1oz stuffed olives, sliced

Preparation time: 20 minutes
Cooking time: 30-40 minutes

Melt the butter in a large skillet and fry the onion until soft. Add the rice and stir-fry for about 7 minutes. Add the curry powder, parsley, a little seasoning and garlic salt. Cook for a further 2-3 minutes. Add the chicken, tomatoes and stock. Mix well, bring to the boil, cover and cook very slowly for 20-30 minutes or until the rice is tender and all the liquid has been absorbed. Stir in the peas and sliced olives and serve.

Variation: For ham and mushroom risotto, substitute 8oz of cooked chopped ham and 4oz of mushrooms (fried with the onion) instead of the chicken.

Shrimp and Mushroom Pilaf

½ cup butter

1 large onion, peeled and chopped

1 garlic clove, crushed

8oz button mushrooms

1¾ cups long-grain rice

3¾ cups chicken stock

2 cups peeled shrimp

4 fresh tomatoes, peeled and quartered

1 teasp turmeric

salt and freshly ground black pepper

Garnish: slices of cucumber cut half through and arranged in twists

Preparation time: 20 minutes
Cooking time: 30 minutes

Preheat the oven to 350°F. Melt the butter in a large, ovenproof pan with a lid. Add the onion, garlic and mushrooms and fry gently for 2-3 minutes. Add the rice and stir-fry for another minute or two.

Add the stock to the pan and bring to the boil.

Stir in the remaining ingredients and the seasoning. Cover the pan and cook in the oven for 20-30 minutes or until the stock is all absorbed and the rice is tender. Serve garnished with twists of cucumber.

Spiced Lamb Casserole with Orange Almond Rice

Serves 4-6

3lb leg of lamb, boneless and diced	
½ teasp ground ginger	
3 tbspns corn or peanut oil	
3 medium onions, peeled and sliced	
1 tbspn ground coriander	
2 tbspns garam masala	
2 teasps ground cumin	
salt and pepper	
finely grated rind and juice of 1 lemon	
finely grated rind and juice of 1 orange	
1½ tbspns flour	
1¼ cups chicken stock	
16oz can tomatoes	

Orange almond rice:

1 tbspn oil
2 cups rice
4 cups chicken stock
1 teasp turmeric
salt and pepper
grated rind of 1 orange and the flesh cut into segments
2 tbspns almonds, roasted
1 tbspn fresh parsley, chopped

Preparation time: 10 minutes
Cooking time: 20-25 minutes

Preparation time: 35 minutes
Cooking time: 1 hour 40 minutes (total)

For the spiced lamb casserole: Sprinkle the meat with ginger. Heat the oil in a large, flameproof casserole and brown the meat evenly over fairly high heat. Remove the lamb with a slotted spoon and set aside. Fry the onions until they begin to brown. Return the meat to the pan, stir in the spices, seasoning, lemon and orange rind and flour. Stir-fry for about 2 minutes. Gradually stir in the fruit juices and stock and add the tomatoes, coarsely chopped with their juice. Bring to the boil, cover and simmer very gently for about 1½ hours.

For the orange and almond rice: Heat the oil and add the rice. Stir-fry for a minute or so until the rice is well coated with oil. Add the stock and bring to the boil. Stir in the turmeric, salt and pepper. Cover and simmer very gently for about 20 minutes or until all the liquid has been absorbed. Gently stir in the remaining ingredients and serve hot with the lamb casserole.

Avgolemono Soup

Serves 6

A deliciously fresh yet satisfying rice-based soup based on a recipe from the Greek island of Corfu.

6¼ cups well-flavored, unseasoned chicken stock (see page 14)	2 eggs, beaten
½ cup long-grain rice	salt and pepper
juice of 1 large lemon	**Garnish:** chopped fresh parsley

Preparation time: 5 minutes
Cooking time: 25 minutes

Boil the stock in a large pan. Add the rice and cook until it is tender (15-20 minutes). Stir in the lemon juice. Whisk a little of the hot stock into the eggs and then pour this mixture into the soup. Season to taste and heat gently for about a minute and serve sprinkled with chopped parsley.

DESSERTS

Ice Cream

Before you begin to make ice-cream, ensure all the implements are chilled. Remember that on freezing, ice cream loses color, sweetness and taste so compensate for this as you make the ice cream. If you have a food processor, the ice cream can be completely frozen, whisked in the machine then returned to the freezer to harden again. Remember to make in small enough quantities to fit the processor bowl. Lastly, always remove the finished ice from the freezer to the refrigerator about 30 minutes before it is to be eaten, or it will be too hard.

Flavorings
Chocolate: For custard-based ice cream, melt 4 squares semi-sweet chocolate with the cream and vanilla. Omit the vanilla if preferred. For mousse-based ice cream, cool the melted chocolate before adding.

Fruit purées: You will need about 9-12oz fruit purée for each 2½ cups ice cream. Some milder tasting fruits like strawberries may need an increased amount to give adequate flavor. Likewise, add more sugar to tart fruits like gooseberries and blackcurrants.
Coffee: For custard-based ice cream, add about 2 tbspns instant coffee to the cream and vanilla, omitting vanilla if preferred. For a mousse-based ice cream, dissolve the coffee in 3 tbspns hot water and leave to cool before adding.
Nuts: Add about ¼ cup finely chopped or ground walnuts, almonds, pistachio nuts or hazelnuts.
Praline: Smash ¼ cup chopped or ground walnuts, almonds, pistachio nuts or hazelnuts.
Toffee: Smash about ¼ cup toffee into tiny pieces inside a plastic bag.

Mousse-based Ice Cream

Makes 2½ cups

½ cup water	⅔ cup heavy cream, stiffly whipped
⅓ cup sugar	
3 egg yolks	

Preparation and cooking time: 25 minutes
Freezing time: 3 hours

Put the water and sugar into a heavy-based pan and boil without stirring until the syrup reaches 230°F on a sugar thermometer. Remove from the heat.

Whisk the yolks in a bowl and gradually pour on the boiling syrup. If some of the syrup sets on the whisk, heat it in the saucepan with 1 tbspn water until liquid again. Whisk until the mixture shows a ribbon trail when the whisk is lifted. Whisk until cool.

Add the chosen flavoring, then fold in the cream. Pour into a container and freeze until firm – about 3 hours.

Custard-based Ice Cream

Makes 2½ cups

2½ cups heavy cream	½ cup superfine sugar
1 vanilla pod	1 teasp cornstarch
4 egg yolks	

Preparation and cooking time: 30 minutes
Cooling and freezing time: 2½ hours

Heat half the cream with the vanilla pod in a pan over low heat until the cream just begins to bubble around the edges. Remove the pan from the heat and leave to infuse for 15 minutes.

Whisk the egg yolks, sugar and cornstarch together in a bowl until pale. Strain the warm cream onto the egg yolk mixture, stirring constantly. Place the bowl over a pan of simmering water and cook until thick and smooth, stirring constantly. Leave to become cold.

Lightly whip the remaining cream and fold thoroughly into the cold custard, with any chosen flavoring. Pour into a shallow container and freeze until just frozen around the edges – this takes about 2 hours. Pour the ice cream into a chilled bowl and beat until smooth. Return to the container for 40 minutes and beat again. Freeze until firm. Remember to take out of the freezer about 30 minutes before serving.

Left to right, Strawberry, Vanilla and Chocolate Ice Cream.

Pear Sorbet

Serves 6

1½lb pears, peeled and cored	¾ cup superfine sugar
thickly pared rind and juice of 1 lemon	2 cups water

Preparation and cooking time: 20 minutes
Cooling and freezing time: 2½ hours

Put the pear flesh and lemon juice into a blender or food processor and blend to a purée. Put the sugar and water in a heavy-based pan and stir over low heat until the sugar has dissolved. Add the lemon rind and boil for 5 minutes without stirring. Remove the lemon rind, then stir in the pear purée. Leave to cool.

Pour the mixture into a container and freeze for 30 minutes. Turn into a chilled bowl and whisk well to break up the ice crystals. Return to the container and freeze for a further 40 minutes or until almost solid.

Turn into the chilled bowl again and whisk until smooth. Tip the ice back into the container and freeze until firm – about 1 hour.

Tips: You will need about ¾lb of pear purée – about 5 average-sized pears. If the sorbet is not smooth enough, repeat the whisking and freezing process once more.

Orange Sorbet in Chocolate Boxes

Serves 6

¾ cup sugar	8 squares semi-sweet chocolate
2 cups water	**Decoration:**
thickly pared rind of 2 oranges	6 orange segments, membrane and pith removed
juice of 6 large oranges – about 2½ cups	6 mint leaves

Preparation time: 1 hour
Freezing time: about 2 hours plus cooling

Put the sugar and water in a heavy-based pan and stir over low heat until the sugar has dissolved. Add the orange rind and boil for 5 minutes without stirring. Remove the rind, then stir in the orange juice. Leave to cool.

Pour the mixture into a container and freeze for 30 minutes. Turn into a chilled bowl and whisk well to break up the ice crystals. Return to the container, and freeze for a further 40 minutes or until almost solid. Turn into the chilled bowl again and whisk until smooth. Pack the ice into a 2in deep 6in square container and freeze until firm – about 1 hour.

Meanwhile, melt the chocolate, then spread thinly on to a cool, smooth surface – marble is ideal, but waxed paper will do. When cold and firm, cut into 30×2in squares.

When ready to serve, cut the sorbet into 6×2in cubes. Place a cube of sorbet on a square of chocolate. Place 4 chocolate squares on each side of the cubes of sorbet. Decorate with orange segments and mint leaves.

Orange Sorbet in Chocolate Boxes.

Crème Brûlée

Serves 6

4 egg yolks	1 vanilla pod *or* 1 teasp vanilla essence
1 tbspn superfine sugar	
2½ cups heavy cream	6 tbspns brown sugar

Preparation and cooling time: 35 minutes
Cooking time: 40 minutes
Chilling time: 8 hours or overnight plus 30 minute

Whisk the egg yolks with the superfine sugar until smooth. Put the cream and vanilla pod into a pan and heat gently until bubbles begin to appear around the edges. Remove from the heat and leave to infuse for 15 minutes.

Remove the vanilla pod and gradually stir the cream into the egg yolks. Place the bowl over a pan of simmering water and cook gently, stirring all the time, until the custard coats the back of a spoon. Add the vanilla essence if using. Pour the custard into 6 ramekin dishes and chill overnight in the refrigerator.

Preheat the broiler to high. Sprinkle the tops of the custards with the sugar. Place as close to the broiler as possible and broil until the sugar caramelizes. Cool, then chill in the refrigerator until the caramel is hard.

Crème Brulée.

Lemon Cream

Serves 6

1¼ cups heavy cream	1 tbspn superfine sugar
grated rind and juice of 1 large lemon	**Decoration:**
2 tbspns sweet sherry	pared lemon rind cut into thin strips

Preparation time: 10 minutes

Whip the cream until thick, then gradually stir in the lemon rind and juice, sherry and sugar.

Spoon into individual dishes and decorate with the pared lemon rind.

Chocolate Mousse

Serves 6

4 squares semi-sweet chocolate, broken into pieces	⅔ cup heavy cream, whipped until soft
3 eggs, separated	**Decoration:**
2 tbspns sherry, orange liqueur or orange juice	Extra whipped cream
grated rind of 1 orange	Chocolate coffee beans or chocolate curls

Preparation and cooking time: 10 minutes
Setting time: 2 hours

Melt the chocolate in a bowl set over a pan of hot water. Stir in the egg yolks and sherry and mix well. Fold in the cream. Stiffly beat the egg whites to a firm snow and fold into the chocolate mixture. Spoon into 6 ramekin dishes and place in the refrigerator to set. Decorate with whipped cream and chocolate coffee beans or chocolate curls.

Raspberry Soufflé

Serves 6

1lb raspberries	4 tbspns hot white wine
4 eggs, separated	1¼ cups heavy cream, stiffly whipped
⅔ cup superfine sugar	**Decoration:** whole raspberries; raspberry leaves
2 tbspns unflavored gelatin	

Preparation time: 25 minutes
Cooking time: 5 minutes
Chilling time: 3-4 hours

Tie a double strip of waxed paper around the outside of a 6-7in soufflé dish, to come 2in above the rim.

Rub the raspberries through a fine sieve. Whisk the egg yolks and sugar together in a bowl placed over simmering water until pale and fluffy. Whisk off the heat for 5 minutes. Dissolve the gelatin in the hot wine. Stir the raspberry purée, gelatin and cream into the egg mixture. Stiffly beat the egg whites and fold in. Spoon into the dish and chill until set – about 3-4 hours.

Remove the paper and serve decorated with raspberries and leaves.

Apricot Refrigerator Cake (left); Raspberry Soufflé (right).

Neapolitan Cheesecake

Serves 6-8

Pastry:

1½ cups flour

pinch salt

¼ cup superfine sugar

¼ cup unsalted butter, softened

grated rind of ½ lemon

1 egg yolk

Filling:

1½ cups ricotta, curd or quark cheese

⅓ cup superfine sugar

2 eggs, beaten

1 egg yolk

grated rind of ½ lemon

½ teasp vanilla essence

2 tbspns golden raisins

2 tbspns finely chopped almonds

1 tbspn finely chopped candied peel

confectioners' sugar for dusting

Preparation time: 1½ hours, including chilling pastry
Cooking time: 55 minutes

Sift the flour and salt into a large bowl and stir in the sugar. Make a well in the center and add the butter, lemon rind and egg yolks. Using the fingertips, gradually mix the ingredients together to form a firm dough. Wrap in waxed paper and chill for 1 hour.

Preheat the oven to 400°F. Use the pastry to line a 8in fluted flan dish, pressing into the dish rather than rolling the pastry out. Bake blind for about 10 minutes. Remove from the oven and reduce the oven temperature to 350°F.

Drain and sieve ricotta cheese if using. Beat all the filling ingredients together, except the confectioners' sugar. Spoon into the pastry case. Bake for about 45 minutes. Leave to become cold, then sprinkle with the sugar.

Apricot Refrigerator Cake

Serves 8

2 cups crushed graham crackers

½ cup unsalted butter, melted

grated rind of 1 orange

Filling:

½ cup fresh orange juice

1 tbspn unflavored gelatin

14oz canned apricots, drained

generous 1 cup cream cheese

¼ cup superfine sugar

grated rind of ½ orange

½ cup milk

½ cup heavy cream, lightly whipped

2 tbspns apricot jelly, melted and sieved

Preparation time: 25 minutes
Chilling time: 5 hours

Mix the crackers, butter and orange rind together. Press the mixture into a 9-10in flan tin with a removeable base. Chill.

Heat the orange juice in a small pan. Sprinkle over the gelatin and stir vigorously until dissolved. Leave to cool. Place 4oz of the apricots in a blender and whizz to a purée.

Beat the cheese, sugar and orange rind together in a bowl. Beat in the milk, orange juice mixture and apricot purée. Fold in the whipped cream. Brush the base of the crumb case with apricot jam and pour in the filling. Chill for 5 hours. Decorate with the remaining apricots.

Pears Belle Helene

Serves 4

4 large ripe pears, peeled, cored and halved	3 tbspns light cream or milk
4 large scoops vanilla ice cream	1 tbspn butter
Sauce:	
4 squares semi-sweet chocolate	

Preparation and cooking time: 10 minutes

For the sauce, melt the chocolate with the cream in a small bowl set over a pan of simmering water. Stir in the butter.

Place a scoop of ice cream into 4 chilled dishes.

Arrange the prepared pears either side of the ice cream, so they touch at the top. Pour over the hot chocolate sauce and serve at once.

Fruit Salad in Pineapple Boats

Serves 6

4oz strawberries, hulled and halved	1 large ripe pineapple
4oz cherries, stoned	1 ripe peach, halved, stoned and sliced
⅔ cup red wine	1 small banana
1 tbspn brandy, kirsch, or fruit liqueur	1 tbspn lemon juice
3 tbspns superfine sugar	⅔ cup heavy cream, whipped
	Garnish: borage or lemon balm leaves

Preparation time: 30 minutes
Macerating time: 8 hours or overnight

Put the strawberries and cherries in a bowl and pour over the wine and brandy. Add 1 tablespoon of the sugar and stir in. Cover with plastic wrap and leave in a covered bowl in the refrigerator overnight.

Cut the pineapple in half lengthways keeping the leaves intact. Scoop out the flesh with a spoon. Discard the core and chop the flesh into cubes. Reserve the shells.

Shortly before serving, mix the strawberries and cherries together with the pineapple and peach. Peel the banana, cut into slices and toss in lemon juice. Add to the fruit. Place the pineapple shells in a serving dish and fill with the fruit. Garnish with borage or lemon balm leaves and serve the whipped cream separately.

Pears in Red Wine

4 large dessert pears	½ cup superfine sugar
1 cup red wine	½ cinnamon stick

Preparation time: 10 minutes
Cooking time: 15-20 minutes

Peel the pears, leaving them whole with the stalk intact. Pour the wine into a large saucepan and add the sugar and cinnamon. Heat gently until the sugar has dissolved then lay the pears in the saucepan. Add enough water to barely cover the pears and gently simmer covered for 15-20 minutes or until the pears are tender.

Remove the pears and place them in a serving dish. Bring the liquid to the boil. Cook for a further 5 minutes to reduce the liquid further then pour it over the pears and allow the dish to cool.

Serve well chilled with whipped cream.

Caramelized Oranges

Serves 6

6 large oranges

1 cup sugar

1½ cups water

1 tbspn orange juice

2 tbspns orange liqueur

Preparation and cooking time: 40 minutes
Chilling time: 3 hours

Pare the rind from two of the oranges and cut into matchstick strips, then remove the pith from these. Cut the rind and pith from the remaining oranges. Cut each orange across into slices, then reassemble into whole orange shapes. Put the strips of rind in a pan, cover with cold water, bring to the boil and drain.

Put the sugar and ⅔ cup of the water in a pan and heat gently to dissolve the sugar. Add the strips of rind and boil over high heat for 10 minutes or until the syrup reaches 300°F on a sugar thermometer, or turns a rich caramel color. Remove the rind, remove the pan from the heat and stir in the remaining water. Return to gentle heat to dissolve the caramel. Stir in the orange juice and liqueur. Spoon over the oranges, decorate with rind and chill for 3 hours before serving.

English Trifle

Serves 6

8oz stale sponge cake	1 vanilla pod
2 tbspns brandy	2 egg yolks
2 tbspns sweet sherry or Marsala	¼ cup superfine sugar
2 ripe pears, peeled, cored and sliced, or 14oz canned pear halves, drained	1¼ cups heavy cream, whipped
Custard:	**Decoration:**
1¼ cups milk	candied cherries
	angelica diamonds

Preparation time: 40 minutes
Chilling time: 1½ hours

Cut the sponge into slices and line the base of a glass dish. Pour over the brandy and sherry. Arrange the pears on top. For the custard, put the milk and vanilla pod in a pan and scald. Cover the pan and set aside to infuse for 15 minutes. Whisk the egg yolks and sugar together in a heatproof bowl until pale and creamy, then gradually stir in the strained milk. Set the bowl over a pan of simmering water and stir until the custard is thick enough to coat the back of a wooden spoon. Pour over the pears and chill until set. Spread over the cream and decorate with cherries and angelica.

Variation: Sprinkle the cream with chopped or flaked almonds instead of the cherries and angelica. Use peaches, nectarines or apricots in place of the pears.

Charlotte Russe

Serves 6-8

16 lady fingers	4 egg yolks
⅔ cup liquid lemon jello, cooled	¼ cup superfine sugar
angelica stalks, cut into leaves	2 tbspns unflavored gelatin
½ candied cherry	4 tbspns hot lemon juice
Custard:	1¼ cups heavy cream, lightly whipped
2 cups milk	
1 vanilla pod	

Preparation time: 45 minutes
Setting time: 3½ hours

Cut off one rounded end of each sponge finger. Pour half the jello into a wetted charlotte mold. When almost set, arrange the sponge fingers, rounded sides down, around the outside of the mold. Arrange the angelica and cherry in a decorative pattern on the jello and leave to set. Pour over the remaining jello and leave to set.

Scald the milk with the vanilla pod and leave to infuse for 15 minutes and strain. Whisk the egg yolks and sugar together in a heatproof bowl until pale, then gradually whisk in the strained milk.

Place the bowl over a pan of simmering water and stir until the custard coats the back of the spoon. Dissolve the gelatin in the hot lemon juice and stir into the custard. Leave to cool. When the custard begins to set, fold in the cream. Spoon into the mold and chill until set. To serve, run the tip of a knife around the edge. Dip the base of the mold in hot water for a few seconds and invert onto a serving plate. Tie a ribbon around the charlotte to decorate.

Summer Pudding

Serves 6

2lb mixed soft fruit (ie blackberries, blackcurrants, raspberries, loganberries or redcurrants)

3 tbspns water

superfine sugar, to taste

6-7 slices day-old white bread, crusts removed

whipped cream (to serve)

Preparation time: 40 minutes
Cooking time: 5 minutes
Chilling time: 8 hours or overnight

Place the fruit in a pan with the water and sugar to taste. Cook over gentle heat until soft – about 5 minutes. Grease a 5 cup pudding basin and line the base and sides with the bread, cutting to fit. Spoon in the fruit and as much juice as it will hold. Cover with the remaining bread and spoon over more juice. Place a plate that fits just inside the rim of the basin on top and hold down with a heavy weight. Chill overnight, then turn out on to a serving plate. Serve with cream.

Hazelnut Meringue Layer

Serves 6

4 egg whites	1 tbspn instant coffee dissolved in 2 teasps boiling water
1 cup superfine sugar	1-2 tbspns brandy or coffee-flavored liqueur
few drops vanilla essence	**Decoration:** whole hazelnuts, whipped cream
1 cup ground hazelnuts	
1¼ cups heavy cream	

Preparation time: 15 minutes
Cooking time: 30 minutes
Cooling time: 45 minutes

Preheat the oven to 375°F. Grease two 7-8in sandwich tins and line the bases with waxed paper, then grease the paper.

Whisk the egg whites until they form stiff peaks. Whisk in half the sugar and the vanilla. Fold in the remaining sugar, then the hazelnuts. Divide the mixture between the tins and spread out evenly. Bake for 30 minutes. Allow to cool in the tin for 15 minutes then turn out onto a wire rack, remove paper and leave to cool completely.

Whip the cream until stiff then fold in the coffee and brandy. Sandwich the meringues with the cream. If liked, decorate the top with more piped whipped cream and a few whole hazelnuts.

Coffee Gâteau

Serves 6-8

2×Genoise sponge cakes (see page 205) made with 2 tbspns instant coffee dissolved in 1 tbspn boiling water and cooled	**Filling**
	1 cup unsalted butter, softened
Decoration:	2 cups confectioners' sugar, sifted
4 squares semi-sweet chocolate	2 tbspns instant coffee dissolved in 1 tbspn boiling water and cooled
1 cup chopped nuts	1¼ cups heavy cream, whipped
chocolate coffee beans	2 tbspns brandy

Preparation time: 30 minutes
Cooking time: 30-40 minutes

To make the chocolate decoration for the cakes, melt the chocolate, then spread thinly onto a cool smooth surface – marble is ideal, but waxed paper on a work surface can be used instead. When cold cut out decorative shapes.

For the filling, cream the butter and sugar together and stir in the coffee. Whip the cream until stiff then fold in the brandy. Split the cakes in half to make 4 layers. Spread one layer with butter cream, top with another layer and spread with cream. Top with the third layer and spread this with buttercream. Top with the last layer. Spread a little cream around the outside of the cake, then roll in the nuts pressing them on firmly. Pipe alternate swirls of buttercream and cream on top of the cake and decorate with the chocolate shapes and chocolate coffee beans.

Chocolate Roulade

Serves 6

flavorless oil for greasing	confectioners' sugar for dusting
⅔ cup superfine sugar	**Filling:**
6 eggs, separated	4 squares semi-sweet chocolate
7 squares semi-sweet chocolate	1¼ cups heavy cream
¼ cup milk	1 tbspn brandy or rum

Preparation time: 25 minutes
Cooking time: 12 minutes

Preheat the oven to 400°F. Oil a 9×12in Swiss-roll tin and line the base with waxed paper. Brush the paper with oil.

Melt the chocolate and milk in a bowl set over a pan of simmering water. Meanwhile whisk the sugar and egg yolks in a bowl until pale and fluffy. Stir the chocolate mixture into the yolk mixture. Whisk the egg whites until stiff and stir a little into the chocolate mixture with a metal spoon. Fold in the remaining egg white. Spoon into the tin, spread out evenly and bake for about 12 minutes. Cover with a damp tea towel and leave in the tin until cold.

For the filling, melt the chocolate and cream together over low heat. Bring to the boil, remove from the heat and allow to cool. Stir the mixture occasionally and when it begins to thicken, whisk until thick. If the mixture doesn't thicken chill in the refrigerator for 5 minutes, then whisk again. Whisk in the brandy.

When the cake is cold, turn it out onto a piece of waxed paper sprinkled with the sugar. Peel away the lining paper carefully. Spread the filling over the cake and roll up.
Note: This type of cake uses no flour and is very moist and delicate, therefore it will crack as you roll it up.

Hazelnut Meringue Layer (left); Chocolate Roulade (right).

Mille Feuille

Serves 6-8

puff pastry made with 4 cups flour (see page 55)	1 cup confectioners' sugar
1¾ cups heavy cream	2-3 tbspns cold water
2 tbspns superfine sugar	few drops red food coloring
1 cup strawberry jelly	

Preparation time: making pastry, then 25 minutes
Cooking time: 10-15 minutes, plus cooling

Preheat the oven to 425°F. Roll out the pastry on a lightly floured surface to a rectangle 15×12in. Cut into three 5×12in rectangles. Slide onto a large baking sheet and prick all over with a fork. Bake for 10-15 minutes or until risen and golden brown. Cool on a wire rack. Carefully split each rectangle to give 6 layers. Discard any uncooked pastry in the middle. Trim the edges to neaten. Leave until cold.

Whip the cream until thick then whip in the sugar. Spread the first layer with cream and place on a plate. Spread the underside of a second layer with jelly and place, jelly side down, on top of the cream. Make layers with remaining pastry, cream and jelly. Sift the confectioners' sugar into a bowl and stir in enough cold water to make a stiff glacé icing. Put a little icing into another bowl and color it red. Spoon into a small icing bag. Spread the white icing over the top of the pastry. Pipe parallel lines of red icing across the width, then draw a skewer in alternating directions lengthways, to create a feathered effect. Allow the icing to set before serving.

Lemon Meringue Pie

Serves 6

shortcrust pastry made with 2 cups flour (see page 55)	grated rind and juice of 2 large lemons
1 cup water	2 tbspns arrowroot mixed to a paste with 3 tbspns water
1¼ cups superfine sugar	4 eggs, separated

Preparation time: 15 minutes
Cooking time: 1 hour

Preheat the oven to 400°F. Roll out the pastry and use to line a 9in fluted flan dish. Bake blind for 15 minutes. Remove from the oven and reduce the temperature to 350°F.

Put the water, ¼ cup of the sugar, the lemon rind and juice in small saucepan. Stir over low heat until the sugar has dissolved. Stir in the arrowroot paste and stir until thickened and clear. Remove from the heat and cool slightly. Stir in the egg yolks and pour the mixture into the pastry. Whisk the egg whites to stiff peaks. Whisk in ¾ cup of the sugar until shiny. Fold in the remaining sugar and spoon the meringue over the filling, making sure it covers the filling completely. Bake for 30 minutes or until browned on top.

Fruit Flan.

Fruit Flan

Serves 6

puff pastry made with 3 cups flour (see page 55)	**Crème patissière**
1 egg yolk, beaten	1¼ cups milk
4 tbspns apricot jelly, warmed and sieved	2 egg yolks
fresh fruit in season, or canned fruit, left whole or sliced or halved if large (ie green and black grapes, peaches, apricots, kiwi fruit, strawberries, nectarines and pineapple)	¼ cup superfine sugar
	4 teasps flour
	4 teasps cornstarch
	few drops vanilla essence

Preparation time: 35 minutes
Cooking time: 25 minutes
Cooling time: 1½ hours

Preheat the oven to 425°F. Roll out the pastry on a lightly floured surface into a rectangle about 12×9in. Transfer to a baking sheet and trim the edges to neaten. With a sharp knife, score a 1½in border all round the sides. Knock up the edges and brush the border with beaten egg yolk. Bake for about 25 minutes or until well risen and golden brown.

Remove from the oven and pull away the pastry inside the border, removing any uncooked pastry in the center, to make a cavity for the fruit. Leave to become cold.

For the crème patissière, place the milk in a pan and heat gently until bubbles appear around the edges. Beat the egg yolks and sugar together until pale, then stir in the flour and cornstarch. Gradually stir in the milk. Return the mixture to the pan and gradually bring to the boil, stirring constantly, until thick and smooth. Leave to cool then stir in the vanilla. Cover with a circle of waxed paper and leave to become completely cold.

Brush the base of the pastry case with a little of the jelly. Spoon in the crème and spread evenly. Arrange the chosen fruit decoratively, in alternating lines, on top of the crème. Brush the fruit with the remaining jelly to glaze.

Crêpes

Makes 8-10 crêpes

1 cup flour

pinch of salt

1 egg

1¼ cups milk

2-3 tbspns vegetable oil for frying

Preparation time: 5 minutes
Chilling time: 30 minutes
Cooking time: 10 minutes

Sift the flour and salt into a bowl. Make a well in the center and add the egg and half the milk. Gradually stir the flour into the liquid and beat with a wooden spoon until smooth. Stir in the remaining milk, cover and allow the batter to stand for 30 minutes.

Heat a little of the oil in an 8in skillet. Put 1-2 tbspns of the batter into the pan and swirl it round to cover the base. Cook for 1 minute, then turn the crêpe over and cook the other side for about 30 seconds. Make the remaining crêpes in the same way, stacking them between waxed paper as they are cooked.

Crêpes suzette: Heat ½ cup each of unsalted butter and sugar in a skillet. Stir in 2 tbspns orange juice, the grated rind of an orange and 2 tbspns orange liqueur. Fold the crêpes in quarters and simmer in this syrup for a few minutes. Warm 2 tbspns orange liqueur, ignite and pour over the crêpes.
Apple and cinnamon: Fill with sweetened apple purée and dust with sifted confectioners' sugar and cinnamon.
Brandy cream and chocolate: Fill with brandy-flavored whipped cream and pour over melted chocolate.

Apple Fritters

Serves 6

1 cup flour

1 egg

⅔ cup milk

1 tbspn vegetable oil

6 crisp dessert apples

lemon juice

2 egg whites, stiffly beaten

vegetable oil for deep-frying

superfine sugar for dusting

Preparation time: 20 minutes
Chilling time: 30 minutes
Cooking time: 30 minutes

Sift the flour into a bowl. Make a well in the center and add the egg, milk and oil. Gradually stir the flour into the liquid and beat with a wooden spoon until smooth. Cover and chill in the refrigerator for 30 minutes.

Peel, core and slice the apples into rings. Sprinkle with lemon juice to prevent browning. Heat the oil in a deep-fat fryer, without the basket, to 350°F or until a cube of bread browns in about 1 minute. Beat the egg whites and fold into the batter. Dip the apple slices in the batter and shake off the excess. Lower into the oil, one at a time, and fry on both sides, turning with 2 slotted spoons (easing the fritter from one spoon to the other) until golden brown. Drain on absorbent kitchen paper and keep warm. Dust with sugar and serve as soon as they are cooked.
Variation: Try canned pineapple rings or quartered bananas instead of apple slices.
Tip: If the batter coating is thin or patchy, dip the fruit in flour before placing in the batter.

Zabaglione

Serves 6

12 egg yolks

⅔ cup superfine sugar

12 tbspns Marsala (or sweet sherry)

Preparation time: 5 minutes
Cooking time: 5 minutes

Put the egg yolks, sugar and Marsala (or sweet sherry) in a bowl set over a pan of simmering water. Whisk vigorously over gentle heat for about 5 minutes or until the mixture is light and fluffy. Spoon into glasses and serve warm.

Hot Lemon Soufflé

Serves 6

2 tbspns unsalted butter

¼ cup all-purpose flour

⅔ cup milk

2 tbspns superfine sugar

4 eggs, separated

4 tbspns heavy cream

grated rind of 1 lemon *plus*
   3 tbspns lemon juice

Preparation time: 15 minutes
Cooking time: 40 minutes

Preheat the oven to 375°F. Grease a 6-7in soufflé dish and put into a roasting tin.

Melt the butter in a pan and stir in the flour to make a roux. Cook over gentle heat for 1 minute. Remove from the heat, stir in the milk and sugar and mix well. Return to the heat and cook, stirring, until the sauce thickens. Take off the heat and cool for 1 minute, then stir in the egg yolks, cream, lemon juice and rind. Stiffly beat the egg whites in a clean dry bowl with a clean balloon whisk, and fold into the mixture quickly but thoroughly. Spoon into the dish – it should not come more than two-thirds of the way up the sides. Run a knife through to get rid of any large air bubbles. Pour in enough boiling water to come halfway up the sides of the roasting tin. Bake for about 25-30 minutes. Serve at once.

Tips: Make sure your equipment is clean and grease-free and work quickly. Take care when opening the oven as the steam from the water could burn.

Baked Alaska

Serves 6

1×8in All-in-one cake (see page 203), chilled	pinch of salt
2½ cups vanilla ice cream	1 cup superfine sugar
4 egg whites	few drops vanilla essence

Preparation time: 5 minutes
Cooking time: 3-4 minutes

Preheat the oven to 450°F. Place the sponge cake on a large ovenproof plate. Put the ice cream on the cake and mold to the shape of the sponge, doming it slightly in the middle. Place in the freezer or icebox.

Beat the egg whites and salt until stiff. Beat in half the sugar and the vanilla. Fold in the remaining sugar.

Working quickly, use the meringue mixture to coat the ice cream and cake completely. Bake for 3-4 minutes or until the meringue is lightly browned. Serve at once.

Treacle Tart

Serves 6

shortcrust pastry made with 1½ cups flour (see page 55)	grated rind and juice of 1 lemon
6 tbspns light corn syrup	6 tbspns fresh brown breadcrumbs

Preparation time: about 25 minutes
Cooking time: 35 minutes

Preheat the oven to 375°F. Roll out the pastry on a lightly floured surface and use to line a 7in pie plate or tin. Prick the base with a fork.

Heat the syrup, lemon rind and juice together gently until runny. Pour half into the pastry case. Sprinkle over 4 spoons of the breadcrumbs and let them soak into the syrup. Pour the remaining syrup and sprinkle over the remaining breadcrumbs. Place the plate or tin on a baking sheet and bake for 30 minutes.

Shoofly Pie

Serves 6-8

1⅓ cups large seedless raisins	shortcrust pastry made with 2 cups flour (see page 55)
½ cup dark rum	1¼ cups flour
½ cup soft brown sugar	⅓ cup unsalted butter

Macerating time: 8 hours or overnight
Preparation time: 20 minutes
Cooking time: 35 minutes

Put the raisins, rum and brown sugar in a dish and mix together. Cover and leave to macerate overnight at room temperature.

Preheat the oven to 400°F. Roll out the pastry and use to line a 9in flan dish. Sift the flour into a bowl and rub in the butter to make a 'crumble' topping.

Spoon the raisin mixture into the flan case and sprinkle over the crumble mixture. Place the dish on a baking sheet and bake for 35 minutes. Serve hot, warm or cold, with cream.

Spiced Rhubarb Tart.

Spiced Rhubarb Tart

Serves 6-8

1lb young rhubarb, chopped into ½in lengths	**Pastry:**
1¼ cups heavy cream	1½ cups flour
½ cup superfine sugar	½ cup ground almonds
1 teasp ground cinnamon	⅓ cup superfine sugar
3 teasps flour	½ cup cold butter, diced
	2 egg yolks

Preparation time: 20 minutes
Chilling time: 1 hour
Cooking time: 30 minutes

First make the pastry. Sift the flour into a bowl and stir in the ground almonds and sugar. Quickly rub in the butter and mix to a dough with the egg yolks. Knead for 2 minutes – preferably on marble to keep the pastry as cool as possible. Wrap in plastic wrap and chill for 30 minutes. Press the pastry into a 10in flan tin. Roll the base with an empty jar to smooth it out. Chill for 30 minutes. Preheat the oven to 425°F.

Arrange the rhubarb in the tin. Beat together the remaining ingredients and carefully pour over the rhubarb. Put the tin on a baking sheet and put in the oven. Immediately reduce the heat to 300°F and bake for 30 minutes. Allow to cool slightly before serving or serve cold with whipped cream.

Fruit Pies

Serves 4-6

shortcrust pastry made with 3 cups flour (see page 55)	1 teasp cornstarch
about 1½lb prepared fruit (see tip below)	1 teasp spices (see below)
sugar to taste	**Glaze:** milk, superfine sugar

Preparation time: preparing fruit, making pastry plus 10 minutes
Cooking time: about 50 minutes

Preheat the oven to 425°F. Roll out the pastry and use about two-thirds to line a 1½ quart deep pie dish. Chill dish and remaining pastry while you prepare the fruit.

Fill the lined dish with the fruit, sprinkle with sugar to taste, cornstarch and spices. Roll out the remaining pastry, dampen the edges and place on top of the dish. Trim, seal and flute the edges. Roll out pastry trimmings and use to decorate. Cut a small vent to allow the steam to escape and brush with milk and sprinkle with sugar. Bake for 15 minutes. Reduce the temperature to 350°F and bake for a further 30-35 minutes or until the pastry is cooked.

Tips: Placing the pie dish on a baking sheet will help transfer the heat and reduce the likelihood of the base pastry going soggy. If you use a metal dish, the baking sheet is not necessary, but will make handling easier.

It is necessary to cut a small vent in the top of the pastry to allow the steam to escape, otherwise the pastry crust will be soggy. Most fruits collapse during cooking, so it is a good idea to use a pie funnel to keep the pastry elevated.

Cornstarch is included to thicken the fruit juices slightly, but it is not essential.

Fillings: Different fruits will need varying amounts of sugar, for instance, cooking apples, rhubarb and gooseberries will need more sugar than blackberries or dessert apples.

Try mixing fruits for different flavors and use spices – cinnamon, cloves, mace, allspice or ginger – to complement. Dried fruits and nuts will also give flavor and texture contrast.

Pecan Pie.

Pumpkin Pie   Serves 8-10

shortcrust pastry made with 2 cups flour
    (see page 55)

1lb fresh cooked pumpkin (see tip below), or canned
    pumpkin purée

1 cup heavy cream

3 eggs

4 tbspns soft brown sugar

3 tbspns light corn syrup

⅛ teasp ground cloves

1 teasp ground cinnamon

½ teasp ground allspice

½ teasp ground ginger

pinch of salt

Preparation time: making pastry then 10 minutes
Cooking time: 55 minutes

Preheat the oven to 400°F. Roll out the pastry and
use to line a 9-10in flan tin. Prick the base with a
fork or line with waxed paper and baking beans.
Bake blind for 15 minutes.

   Mix all the remaining ingredients together and
pour into the case. Reduce the oven temperature
to 375°F and bake for about 40 minutes or until
the filling has set.

Tip: When you buy fresh pumpkin it is worth
using it in this pie. Halve the pumpkin, remove
the seeds and stringy pieces. Bake, skin side up,
on a baking sheet at 325°F for about 1 hour, or
until the flesh is soft enough to scrape out of the
shell.

Pecan Pie   Serves 8-10

shortcrust pastry made with 2 cups flour
    (see page 55)

⅓ cup unsalted butter, softened

1 cup soft dark brown sugar

4 eggs

1 teasp vanilla essence

4 tbspns light corn syrup

1 cup chopped pecans

1½ cups halved pecans

Preparation time: making pastry, then 10
    minutes
Cooking time: 50 minutes

Preheat the oven to 400°F. Roll out the pastry and
use to line a 2in deep 9-10in flan tin. Prick the
base with a fork or line with waxed paper and
baking beans. Bake blind for 15 minutes.

   Cream the butter and sugar together, then beat
in the eggs, one at a time. Beat in the vanilla
essence, syrup and the chopped nuts. Spoon into
the case, and arrange the halved nuts on top in a
decorative pattern. Bake for about 35 minutes or
until the filling has set. Serve warm or cold with
whipped cream or ice cream.

Apple-Raisin Crumble

1½lb cooking apples

2 tbspns lemon juice

3 tbspns superfine sugar

⅓ cup raisins

1 teasp ground cinnamon

½ teasp ground mace

Crumble:

1¼ cups flour

⅓ cup unsalted butter

¼ cup superfine sugar

2 tbspns finely chopped walnuts

Preparation time: 25 minutes
Cooking time: 25-30 minutes

Preheat the oven to 400°F. Grease a large ovenproof dish. Peel, core and thinly slice the apples
and toss in the lemon juice. Put in the dish with
remaining ingredients.

   Sift the flour into a bowl, rub in the butter and
stir in the sugar and walnuts. Spoon the crumble
over the apples and pat down with the back of a
spoon. Bake for 25-30 minutes or until golden
brown. Serve with cream or custard.

BREAD, CAKES & COOKIES

Bread Baking

Flour
It is very important to obtain the right flour for bread making – ordinary all-purpose or self-rising flours will not give satisfactory results so make sure that any flour which you buy is suitable for bread or rolls.

White bread: Always buy *strong* white flour for making white bread; it absorbs water easily and proves well, giving a good volume and a light loaf.

Brown bread: There is quite a choice of flours to use for brown breads and rolls. Wheatmeal has some of the coarser bran and wheatgerm removed by the milling process but it gives a smooth, even-textured brown bread. Wholewheat contains all the bran and wheat germ but it gives a heavier, closer-textured loaf. Granary flour contains malted grains of flaked wheat which add a nutty flavor to the bread. There is also a range of specialist flours such as stone-ground and rye which give very different results and are interesting to experiment with.

Flavorings: Once you have mastered the basic technique of bread making why not try adding flavorings such as herbs or seeds and even ingredients such as cheese, garlic or onion.

Yeasts
Fresh yeast possibly gives the very best results but is increasingly hard to obtain and does not keep in good condition for very long. When using fresh yeast, always blend it with a little of the warm liquid specified in the recipe.

Dried yeast is now much improved and does not need to be activated with water before using. You merely stir it into the flour before the liquid is added. It will keep (unopened) in good condition for up to about 6 months if stored in a cool, dry place.

Homemade Bread.

White Bread and Rolls

Makes 3 1lb/500g loaves or approx 18 rolls

6 cups strong all-purpose white flour	1 sachet (¼oz) blended dried yeast or ½oz fresh yeast
2 teasps salt	2 cups lukewarm water
2 tbspns lard or vegetable shortening	

Preparation time: 20 minutes
Total rising time: approx 1 hour 40 minutes
Cooking time: 30 minutes

Mix the flour and salt in a large bowl and lightly rub in the flour as if you were making pastry. Stir in the dried yeast (if using fresh yeast, mix with a little of the water before adding) and mix to a pliable dough.

Turn the dough onto a lightly floured surface and knead for about 10 minutes until smooth. Place the dough back in the bowl (washed and greased) and wrap it in a large, oiled polythene bag. Leave the bowl in a warm place until the dough has doubled in size (about 1 hour). Turn the dough out onto a lightly floured surface again and knead for about 5 minutes.

Divide the dough into 3 equal pieces, knead each lightly and place in 3 1lb greased loaf tins. Wrap each tin loosely in an oiled polythene bag and leave to prove in a warm place until the dough rises to the top of the tins (about 30 minutes).

Remove the bags and bake in a preheated oven (450°F) until the bread is golden brown. When it is fully cooked the loaf should sound hollow when tapped on the bottom.

Variation: Divide the dough into ⅔ and ⅓. Bake the larger piece in a greased 2lb loaf tin for 40-50 minutes. Roll the remaining dough into 6 rolls and bake these on a greased baking sheet for 20 minutes.

Wholemeal Coburg

Makes 3 loaves

4 cups wholewheat flour	1 sachet (¼oz) blended dried yeast or ½oz fresh yeast
generous 2 cups strong all-purpose white flour	2 cups lukewarm water
2 teasps salt	salted water
2 tbspns shortening	cracked wheat

Preparation time: 20 minutes
Total rising time: approx 1 hour 40 minutes
Cooking time: 30-40 minutes

Mix the flour and salt in a large bowl and lightly rub in the flour as if you were making pastry. Stir in the dried yeast (if using fresh yeast mix with a little of the water before adding) and mix to a pliable dough with a wooden spoon.

Turn the dough onto a lightly floured surface and knead for about 10 minutes until smooth. Place the dough back into the bowl (washed and greased) and wrap it in a large, oiled polythene bag. Leave the bowl in a warm place until the dough has doubled in size (about 1 hour). Turn the dough out onto a lightly floured surface again and knead for about 5 minutes.

Divide the dough into 2 and shape into balls; make a deep cross on the top of each and place them on greased and floured baking sheets. Brush with salted water and sprinkle with cracked wheat. Place the baking sheets in large oiled polythene bags and leave to prove for a further 30-40 minutes.

Remove the polythene bags and bake in a preheated oven (450°F) for 30-40 minutes until golden brown. When it is fully cooked it should sound hollow when tapped on the base. Cool on a wire rack.

Danish Pastries

Makes 12

2 cups all-purpose flour	½ cup, plus 2 tbspns, unsalted butter
1 teasp sugar	**Almond filling:**
pinch of salt	½ cup unsalted butter
2 tbspns shortening	1 cup confectioners' sugar
1 egg, beaten	scant ⅔ cup ground almonds
5 tbspns cold water	few drops vanilla essence
1 sachet (¼oz) blended dried yeast	

Preparation time: 50 minutes (including resting time)
Rising time: 15-20 minutes
Cooking time: 12-15 minutes

Mix the flour, sugar and salt in a large mixing bowl. Rub the shortening into the flour, make a well in the center, stir in the egg, water and yeast and mix to a soft dough. Turn on to a floured board and knead until smooth (about 10 minutes). Place dough on a plate and cover with plastic wrap. Rest in the refrigerator for at least 10 minutes.

Soften the butter into a rectangle about ½in thick. Roll out the dough to approximately 10in square. Spread the butter down the center of the square, fold the sides over the butter in the middle to overlap about ½in and seal the bottom and top.

Roll out the dough to an oblong strip approximately 18in×6in. Fold evenly in 3. Place the dough on the plate, cover and allow to rest for 10 minutes. Repeat the rolling, folding and resting twice more. The dough is now ready to be shaped into any of the styles described below.

To rise: Once you have shaped your pastries, cover them with plastic wrap and allow them to rise in slightly warm place for about 15-20 minutes until they are puffy and have doubled in size. Do not put them in the oven or in a very warm spot to prove or the butter will run.

To bake: Remove the plastic wrap and bake in a preheated oven at 425°F for 12-15 minutes.

To make the almond filling: Beat in all the ingredients together.

To shape Danish pastries: This basic dough is sufficient for the following two styles:
Windmills (makes 6): You will need half the almond filling; a little beaten egg; raspberry jelly.

Roll out half the basic dough to a 8in×12in rectangle. Trim the edges and divide the dough into 6 4in squares. Place on a greased baking tray. Put a little almond paste in the center of each square and brush the paste lightly with beaten egg.

Make 4 cuts in the corners of each square to within ½in of the center making 3 triangle shapes. Fold every other triangle point down to the center and press into the almond paste (it will look like a child's toy windmill). Brush over with beaten egg, allow to rise and bake. When cool, place raspberry jelly in the center of each pastry.
Crescents (makes 6): You will need a little beaten egg; half the almond filling; ¼ cup flaked almonds.

Roll out half the dough thinly into a circle 12in in diameter. Divide the circle in half and cut each half in 3 to make 6 triangular sections. Brush the straight sides of each piece with beaten egg. Place a little of the almond paste in the middle of the curved side. Roll up towards the point and bend into a crescent.

Place the crescents on a greased baking sheet and brush with beaten egg. Scatter with flaked almonds. Allow to rise and bake.

Chelsea Buns.

Iced Tea Ring

4 cups strong white flour, sifted	⅔ cup mixed dried fruit
1 teasp salt	2 tbspns raw sugar
¼ cup butter	pinch of mixed spice
1 sachet (¼oz) blended dried yeast or ½oz fresh yeast	¾ cup confectioners' sugar
	2 tbspns lemon juice
1¼ cups warmed milk	**Decoration:** flaked almonds and candied cherries

Preparation time: 40 minutes
Proving time: 50 minutes-1 hour
Cooking time: 30 minutes

Mix the flour and salt and rub in the butter as if making pastry. Stir in the dried yeast (if using fresh yeast, blend with a little warm milk). Stir the milk into the flour mixture and mix to a soft dough.

Turn on to a lightly floured board and knead until smooth – about 10 minutes. Place the dough in a greased bowl and cover with plastic wrap. Leave in a warm place until the dough has risen and doubled in size (about 50 minutes-1 hour).

Return to the lightly floured board and roll the dough into an oblong 14in×10in. Brush with a little melted butter and sprinkle with the dried fruit, brown sugar and spice. Dampen the edges and, starting from one of the long sides, roll up like a Swiss roll and seal well. Place the dough on a greased baking tray and form it into a circle, sealing the ends together well. With a pair of scissors, make cuts along the outside edge without slicing right through to the inner edge. Cover with plastic wrap and leave in a warm place for 20-30 minutes. Preheat the oven to 400°F.

Bake for about 30 minutes or until golden brown. When cool, mix the confectioners' sugar and lemon juice together and drizzle over the ring. Decorate with cherries and flaked almonds.

Chelsea Buns

4 cups strong white all-purpose flour, sifted
2 teasps salt
¼ cup butter or block margarine
¼ cup superfine sugar
1 sachet (¼oz) blended dried yeast or ½oz fresh yeast
⅞ cup milk, warmed
2 eggs, beaten
Filling:
2 tbspns butter or block margarine
¼ cup superfine sugar
1 teasp ground cinnamon
¾ cup currants or golden raisins, washed and dried

Preparation time: 25 minutes
Rising time: approx 1½ hours total
Cooking time: 25 minutes

Mix the flour and salt together and rub in the margarine. Stir in the sugar and dried yeast (if using fresh yeast, blend with warmed milk). Add the milk and eggs to the flour mixture. Mix well then turn onto a board and knead for about 10 minutes until you have a smooth dough.

Place the dough in a greased bowl and place the bowl in a large oiled plastic bag. Leave in a warm place until the dough has doubled in size (about 1 hour). Roll out the dough to a 14in square and put on the filling. Melt the fat, brush over the dough and sprinkle with the sugar, cinnamon and currants or golden raisins. Roll up the dough like a swiss roll and cut into 16 slices. Arrange the buns, cut sides down, on 2 greased 7in sandwich tins. Cover with oiled plastic and leave in a warm place until doubled in size.

Bake for 25 minutes at 400°F. While still hot, brush with a hot sugar glaze made with 2 tbspns each of sugar, milk and water, heated until the sugar has dissolved, then simmered for about 2 minutes.

Boston Brown Bread

Makes 2 loaves

1 cup rye flour	⅔ cup raisins
1 cup wholewheat flour	2 cups buttermilk
1 cup cornmeal	7 tbspns molasses
1 teasp baking powder	
1 teasp salt	

Preparation time: 30 minutes
Cooking time: 3 hours

Grease two cleaned, empty cans ('family-size' vegetable, soup or fruit cans), about 6×4in. Mix the flours, cornmeal, baking powder, salt and raisins together in a bowl. Heat the buttermilk and molasses together gently in a pan, stirring, until well combined. Gradually stir into the dry ingredients.

Divide the batter between the cans, cover with pleated foil and secure with string. Put the cans in a large pan and pour in enough boiling water to come halfway up the sides of the cans. Cover the pan and steam over low heat for about 3 hours. Remove from cans and eat hot, or cold, spread with butter.

Fruit Loaf

Makes 1 2lb loaf.

2 cups mixed dried fruit
⅔ cup water
⅔ cup soft margarine or butter
4 tbspns sweetened condensed milk
1¼ cups self-rising flour, sifted with a pinch of salt
1 egg, beaten
grated rind of 1 lemon

Preparation time: 15 minutes
Cooking time: 2-2¼ hours

Preheat the oven to 325°F. Grease and line a 2lb loaf tin.

Place the fruit, water, margarine (or butter) and condensed milk in a pan and bring to the boil. Reduce the heat to moderate and cook for 2 minutes, stirring. Turn into a bowl and stir in the flour, egg and lemon rind. Spoon into the prepared tin and bake for 2-2¼ hours. A skewer inserted in the center should come away clean when the cake is cooked. Cool in the tin for 15 minutes, then turn out onto a wire rack to cool completely. Store wrapped in foil in an airtight container for 2 days before eating. Serve sliced and spread with butter.

Banana and Walnut Bread

Makes one 2lb loaf.

2 cups self-rising flour
pinch of salt
½ cup butter, softened
½ cup superfine sugar
½ teasp vanilla essence
2 large eggs
9oz ripe bananas, weighed after peeling, mashed
⅓ cup chopped walnuts
½ cup golden raisins

Preparation time: 25-30 minutes
Cooking time: 50-60 minutes

Preheat the oven to 350°F. Grease a 2lb loaf tin. Sift the flour and salt together. In a separate bowl, cream the butter and sugar together until fluffy and add the vanilla. Beat in the eggs, one at a time, adding a little of the sifted flour after each egg. Fold the remaining flour and then the mashed bananas into the mixture. Fold in the nuts and fruit. Spoon into the prepared tin and bake for 50-60 minutes or until a skewer inserted into the center comes out clean. Cool in the tin for 5 minutes, then turn out on to a wire rack to cool completely.

Cherry Cake.

Cherry Cake

Makes one 7in cake

1 cup self-rising flour	grated rind of 1 lemon
1 cup wholewheat flour	2 eggs
½ teasp baking powder	½ cup ground almonds
pinch of salt	1 cup candied cherries, washed and quartered
⅔ cup block margarine, cubed	5 tbspns milk
scant 1 cup raw sugar	

Preparation time: 25 minutes
Cooking time: about 1 hour 10 minutes

Preheat the oven to 350°F. Grease, line and flour a 7in round cake tin.

Sift the flours, baking powder and salt into a bowl, and stir in the cherries and ground almonds. Tip the bran from the sieve into the bowl and stir in. Cream the margarine and sugar together in another bowl with a wooden spoon. Stir in the lemon rind. Beat in the eggs, one at a time, adding a little flour if the mixture shows signs of curdling. Fold the flour mixture and the milk into the creamed mixture using a metal spoon. Spoon the mixture into the prepared tin and bake for 1 hour 10 minutes or until a skewer inserted in the center comes out clean. Leave the cake in the tin for 5 minutes, then turn out onto a wire rack to cool.

Tip: Many cherry cakes sadly become half cherry cake and half plain cake because the cherries sink to the bottom. The secret is to quarter the cherries, coat them in flour (this helps to make them cling to the cake mixture) and to use part wholewheat flour (heavier flour which can hold the weight of the cherries).

Dundee Cake

Makes one 8in cake

2 cups flour	1⅓ cups currants
1 teasp baking powder	1⅓ cups raisins
½ cup ground almonds	⅓ cup candied cherries, quartered
¾ cup unsalted butter, softened	⅓ cup mixed chopped candied peel
¾ cup superfine sugar	½ cup whole blanched almonds
3 eggs	grated rind of 1 lemon

Preparation time: 20 minutes
Cooking time: 2½-2¾ hours

Preheat the oven to 325°F. Grease and line an 8in round cake tin, then grease the paper.

Sift the flour and baking powder into a bowl and stir in the ground almonds. In a separate bowl, cream the butter and sugar together until light and fluffy, then beat in the eggs, one at a time, adding a little flour with each egg. Once the eggs are well mixed in, fold in the remaining flour. Fold in the currants, raisins, cherries, peel and lemon rind evenly. Spoon into the prepared tin, making a slight hollow in the center. Arrange the whole almonds lightly in circles on top of the cake. Bake for 2½-2¾ hours or until it is firm and springy to the touch. Cool in the tin before turning out. When cold, wrap in foil and keep in an airtight tin for 2 days before eating.

Christmas Cake.

Rich Christmas Cake

2¼ cups all-purpose flour

pinch of salt

1 teasp mixed spice

1 cup butter

⅓ cup dark brown sugar

1 tbspn molasses, slightly warmed

few drops vanilla essence

4 eggs

1½ cups golden raisins

1½ cups currants

1½ cups raisins, chopped

⅓ cup chopped mixed peel

⅔ cup candied cherries, chopped

⅔ cup whole blanched almonds, chopped

grated rind of 1 lemon

1 tbspn lemon juice

2 tbspns brandy or sherry

Preparation time: 1 hour
Cooking time: 3½-4 hours

Preheat the oven to 300°F.

To prepare the tin: Place the tin on a sheet of waxed paper and draw round it with a pencil. Cut just inside the circle to make the base lining. Cut a double strip of waxed paper long enough to line the sides. Make a 1in fold along the length. Snip this fold at intervals all the way along. Use this double-thickness paper to line a greased 8in round or a 7in square cake tin with the snipped edge down flat on the base to anchor it. Insert the circular paper base. Now lightly brush the base and sides with melted butter. Next, wrap a double strip of thick brown paper round the *outside* of the tin and secure with string and/or a paper clip. This will prevent the outside of the cake from overcooking.

Sift the flour with the salt and mixed spice. Cut up the butter and beat well until soft with a wooden spoon or in a food processor. Add the sugar and molasses; beat until light and fluffy.

Add the vanilla and beat in the eggs one by one, adding a little of the flour each time to prevent curdling. Beat thoroughly, then fold in the rest of the ingredients except the flour and make sure that they are well mixed in. Finally fold in the flour lightly but thoroughly. Turn the mixture into the prepared tin; spread evenly and make a slight hollow in the center to counteract the rise in the top. Protect the top with a double thickness of waxed paper. Bake in the center of the oven for about 4 hours.

To check whether the cake is cooked through, insert a skewer into the center – if it comes out clean and there are no hissing or sizzling noises coming from it, then the cake is ready. Allow it to cool in the tin (it will shrink away from the sides slightly) before turning out.

If you wish to store it, make sure that it has cooled completely, wrap it in waxed paper and pack it in an airtight tin or wrap it up well in foil.

To coat and ice the cake
Almond paste: 4 tbspns superfine sugar; ¾ cup confectioners' sugar; 1½ cups ground almonds; 1 small egg, beaten with the strained juice of half a lemon plus ½ teasp vanilla essence and ½ teasp almond essence.

Sieve the sugars into a bowl, add the almonds and mix well. Pour in the egg mixture and mix to a workable paste with a palette knife. If the paste seems too crumbly and dry, add a little more lemon juice; if too wet and sticky add a little more sugar and ground almonds. Knead lightly into a ball but do not over-handle or it will become oily.

To coat the cake: Trim the top of the cake to level it. Dust a piece of waxed paper with confectioners' sugar. Place the ball of paste on it and roll out a circle slightly larger than the cake. Brush one side with beaten egg or sieved jelly and coat the *base* of the cake (this is nice and flat) with the almond paste, trimming the edge level with the sides of the cake. Cover loosely with waxed paper and leave for a week before icing.

Royal icing
4 egg whites; 5¼ cups confectioners' sugar; 1 teasp glycerine; few drops of lemon juice.

Stir the egg whites lightly in a bowl. Gradually add the sugar, beating vigorously with a spoon with each addition. Add the glycerine and lemon juice and continue beating (a food mixer makes light work of this) until the icing is like whipped cream – forming soft peaks. Cover the bowl with a damp cloth and leave for about 1 hour before applying to the cake. You can store it overnight in the refrigerator if you cover it tightly with plastic wrap.

Fatless Sponge

Makes one deep 7in round cake or one Swiss roll

½ cup superfine sugar

3 eggs

¾ cup flour

Preparation time: 20 minutes
Cooking time: 30 minutes

Preheat the oven to 375°F. Grease and line the base of 1 7in sandwich tin or one Swiss roll tin and grease the paper.

Whisk the sugar and eggs together until the mixture is thick and pale and holds the impression of the whisk when lifted. This will take a good 5 minutes by hand. Gently fold in the flour. Spoon the mixture into the tin, level it and bake for 30 minutes, or until firm to the touch. Leave to cool in the tin for 5 minutes, turn out onto a wire rack, peel off the paper and leave to cool completely before filling (see page 205).

Chocolate Swiss roll
Replace ¼ cup flour with cocoa powder and sift into the flour. Make cake mixture as above but bake in 12×9in Swiss roll tin at 425°F for 8-10 minutes. Place a piece of waxed paper on the work surface and turn the cake out onto the pap-

er. Trim the edges and roll up the sponge inside the paper. Cover with a damp tea cloth and allow to cool. When cold carefully unroll, take out the paper and fill with whipped cream. Roll up the cake again and top with chocolate glacé icing (1½ cups confectioners' sugar sifted with ½ cup cocoa powder and mixed with hot water), or sprinkle on confectioners' sugar or chocolate curls.

Walnut Fudge Layer Cake

Makes one 7in cake

2×7in All-in-one cakes (see page 202) adding to the ingredients the following:

1 tbspn cocoa powder

1 tbspn instant coffee dissolved in 2 teasps boiling water

2 tbspns finely chopped walnuts

Filling:

1 cup milk

2 cups sugar

2 squares semi-sweet chocolate

⅔ cup unsalted butter

Decoration: chopped walnuts

Preparation time: 15 minutes plus assembling
Cooking time: 30-40 minutes

Make the cakes, adding the cocoa powder, coffee and chopped walnuts to the cake mixture before baking at 325°F for 30-40 minutes.

Heat the milk, sugar and chocolate in a pan and stir until the sugar dissolves. Boil until the mixture reaches 240°F on a sugar thermometer or until a 'soft ball' is formed when a drop is placed in cold water. Pour into a bowl and allow to cool for 20 minutes. Do not stir. Beat in the butter with the vanilla, until melted. Chill for 10 minutes, then beat again until a spreading consistency is reached. Split the cakes in half and sandwich together with the filling (ie 3 layers of filling).

Spread the remaining mixture over the top and decorate with the chopped walnuts.

All-in-one Sponge

Makes two 7in cakes

¾ cup self-rising flour	¾ cup superfine sugar
1½ teasps baking soda	3 eggs
¾ cup soft margarine	1 teasp vanilla essence

Preparation time: 15 minutes
Cooking time: 30-40 minutes

Preheat the oven to 325°F. Grease and line the bases of two 7in sandwich tins. Grease the paper.

Sift the flour and baking soda into a bowl. Add all the remaining ingredients and beat well, preferably in a food processor, until well combined and smooth. Spoon into tins and level the surfaces. Bake for 30-40 minutes until golden and firm to touch. Leave the cakes in tins for 5 minutes, then turn out onto a wire rack and peel off the paper. When completely cold, fill with jelly or buttercream and decorate.

Cup cakes: Spoon the mixture, flavored with 1 tbspn cocoa powder, into paper cases. Bake for 15-20 minutes. Top with 4 squares semi-sweet chocolate boiled with ⅔ cup heavy cream. Leave until set.

Walnut Fudge Layer Cake.

Victoria Sponge

Makes one 7in sponge

½ cup block margarine or butter

½ cup superfine sugar

2 eggs

1 cup self-rising flour, sifted

Preparation time: 15 minutes
Cooking time: 20-25 minutes

Preheat the oven to 350°F. Grease and line with waxed paper two 7in sponge tins. Cream the fat and sugar with a wooden spoon until the mixture is soft and fluffy. Beat in the eggs one at a time with a little of the flour (to prevent the mixture curdling). Using a metal spoon, carefully fold in the remaining flour until thoroughly mixed but do not beat.

Divide the mixture between the 2 tins. Bake in the center of the oven for about 20-25 minutes until the cakes are well-risen and golden. Leave for a few minutes in the tins before turning out to cool on a wire rack.

When cool, sandwich the 2 cakes together with jelly or cream (or both). Try the following variations:

Chocolate Gateau
Replace ¼ cup of flour with ¼ cup of cocoa powder and continue as above. Fill and coat with chocolate-flavored butter icing (see opposite).
Coffee Gateau
Add 1 teasp coffee essence or dissolved instant coffee to the basic recipe. Fill and coat with coffee-flavored butter cream (see opposite).

Victoria Sponge.

Glacé Icing

Sufficient for the top of a 6-7in cake.

1 cup sieved confectioners' sugar; 1 tbspn hot water; chosen flavoring or coloring. Stir the water into the sugar until smooth. Flavor and color to taste and use immediately.

American Cake Frosting

This meringue-like icing is sufficient for coating the top and sides of an 8-9in cake and can be flavored with chocolate or coffee.

2 cups granulated sugar; ⅔ cup water; 2 egg whites. Pour the sugar and water into a pan over low heat and stir until the sugar dissolves. Boil, without stirring, until a sugar thermometer measures 240°F. If you have no sugar thermometer test a little syrup by dropping it in cold water, when ready it will form a soft ball. While you are waiting for the syrup to reach the correct temperature, whisk the whites until stiff. Take the syrup off the heat and when it stops bubbling pour it slowly on to the whites, whisking as you do so until it holds its shape in stiff peaks. Quickly spread over the cake as it sets very quickly.

Butter Cream or Icing

Sufficient to fill and coat a 7in cake.

½ cup butter; 1 cup confectioners' sugar, sifted; flavorings. Cream the fat, gradually beating in the icing sugar until smooth. Add the flavoring and/or coloring of your choice: a few drops of either vanilla essence or almond essence; grated rind of an orange or lemon plus 1 teasp of the juice; 2 teasps coffee essence or dissolved instant coffee with 1 tbspn chopped walnuts; 1oz chocolate, melted; or 2 teasps cocoa powder plus 2 teasps instant coffee powder mixed with a little hot water (mocha).

Genoise Sponge Cake

Makes one 8in cake.

4 eggs
generous ½ cup superfine sugar
generous 1 cup all-purpose flour, sifted
¼ cup unsalted butter, melted
Dusting: superfine sugar; flour

Preparation time: 25 minutes
Cooking time: 40 minutes

Preheat the oven to 375°F. Grease and line an 8in deep cake tin. Grease the paper and sprinkle the tin with sugar and flour. Shake out any excess.

Place the eggs and sugar in a bowl. Place the bowl over a pan of water which is barely simmering and whisk over low heat until the mixture has doubled in size. Do not allow the mixture to get too warm or it may curdle. Remove the bowl from the heat and keep whisking until pale and thick enough to make a ribbon trail when the whisk is lifted. Gently fold in a third of the flour, then half the butter, another portion of flour, the remaining butter then finally the remaining flour. Quickly pour into the tin and bake for about 40 minutes. Cool slightly, then turn out onto a wire rack to become cold. Use this sponge cake for gâteaux and iced cakes (see page 203).

Biscuit Chocolate Cake

Serves 8-10.

11 squares semi-sweet chocolate
1⅓ cups unsalted butter
3 eggs
⅓ cup superfine sugar
½ cup chopped candied peel
⅔ cup candied cherries, quartered
¾ cup chopped mixed nuts
grated rind of 1 orange
grated rind of 1 lemon
scant 3 cups crushed graham crackers
6-8 tbspns Cointreau or Grand Marnier

Preparation time: 30 minutes
Chilling time: 8 hours or overnight

Grease a 9-10in flan tin with a removable base.

Melt the chocolate with the butter and leave to cool slightly. Whisk the eggs and sugar together until pale. Gradually stir in the melted chocolate, peel, cherries, nuts and citrus rinds. Add the crackers and liqueur. Press into the tin, cover and chill for 8 hours or overnight.

Sachertorte

Makes one 9in cake

6 squares semi-sweet chocolate	6 eggs, separated
1 tbspn water	**Topping:**
¾ cup unsalted butter, softened	4 tbspns apricot jelly, warmed and sieved
¾ cup superfine sugar	8 squares semi-sweet chocolate
1½ cups self-rising flour, sifted	2 tbspns water

Preparation time: 40-45 minutes
Cooking time: 1½ hours

Preheat the oven to 300°F. Line a 9in cake tin with waxed paper and lightly grease the paper.

Melt the chocolate with the water in a heatproof bowl set over a pan of simmering water. Beat in the butter and ⅔ cup of the sugar. Remove from the heat and gradually beat in the egg yolks. Add a little flour if the mixture shows signs of curdling. Whisk the egg whites until stiff, then fold in the remaining sugar. Fold half the egg white into the mixture, then half the flour, then the rest of the egg white and the rest of the flour.

Spoon into the prepared tin and bake for 1½ hours. Leave to cool in the tin for 5 minutes, then carefully turn out onto a wire rack to cool completely.

Brush all over with the apricot jelly. Melt the chocolate with the water in a heatproof bowl set over a pan of simmering water and pour over the cake. Dip a palette knife in hot water and use it to spread the chocolate over the top and sides of the cake. Leave until set before carefully transferring to a plate and serving.

Brompton Cake

⅔ cup all purpose flour	**Frosting:**
⅓ cup cornstarch	1½ cups superfine sugar
¾ cup superfine sugar	2 egg whites
finely grated zest of 1½ lemons	4 tbspns lemon juice
4 large eggs	¼ teasp cream of tartar
⅓ cup unsalted butter, melted	9-10oz selection of crystallized fruits (eg ginger, figs, clementines, pineapple)
	1 tbspn toasted flaked almonds

Preparation time: 40 minutes
Cooking time: 20-25 minutes

Preheat the oven to 350°F. Grease and line three 7in sandwich tins.

Sieve the flour and cornstarch together. Whisk the sugar, lemon zest and eggs in a bowl resting over a bowl of simmering water, until the mixture is light in color and thick. Remove from the pan of hot water and continue whisking for 2-3 minutes. Pour half the tepid butter into the mxture and fold in lightly with a metal spoon. Fold in half the flour then the remaining butter, taking care not to add any sediment from the butter. Lastly add the remaining flour. Divide the mixture between the tins. Bake in the oven for 15-20 minutes until golden then turn out on to a rack to cool.

To make the frosting: Whisk the sugar, egg whites, lemon juice, and cream of tartar for 7-8 minutes in a bowl resting on a pan of simmering water. Remove from the pan and continue whisking until the frosting is thick. Chop the crystallized fruits. Reserve about a third of the frosting, stir the fruits into the remaining two thirds.

To assemble the cake: Place one cake onto a plate, spread half the frosting and fruit mixture over the top and cover with a second cake. Spread the remaining frosting and fruit mixture over the cake and sandwich between the last cake. Swirl the plain frosting over the last cake and scatter over the flaked almonds.

Devil's Food Cake

Makes one 8in cake

3 squares semi-sweet chocolate	1 teasp vanilla essence
1 cup buttermilk	**Fudge frosting:**
⅔ cup soft brown sugar	7 squares semi-sweet chocolate
2 cups all-purpose flour	⅔ cup light cream
pinch of salt	⅔ cup sour cream
1 teasp baking soda	2 tbspns butter, softened
½ cup soft margarine	2 tbspns superfine sugar
½ cup superfine sugar	1 teasp vanilla essence
2 eggs	

**Preparation and decorating time: about 45 minutes
Cooking time: 45-50 minutes**

Preheat the oven to 350°F. Grease and line the bases of two 8in sandwich tins.

Melt the chocolate with the buttermilk and brown sugar in a heatproof bowl set over a pan of simmering water. Sift the flour, salt and soda into a bowl. Cream the margarine and sugar together until light and fluffy, then beat in the eggs one at a time, adding a little flour with each egg. Beat in the vanilla. Fold in the rest of the flour, alternating it with spoonfuls of the chocolate mixture until thoroughly combined. Divide the mixture between the prepared tins and bake for 45-50 minutes. Cool in the tins for 5 minutes, then turn onto wire racks to cool completely.

For the frosting, melt the chocolate in a bowl set over a pan of simmering water. Whisk in the remaining ingredients. Split each cake in half and sandwich together with one-third of the frosting. Spread remaining frosting over the top and sides of the cake.

Brompton Cake.

Barquettes

shortcrust pastry made with 2 cups flour (see page 55)

1 egg white

a selection from apricots, peaches, mangos, seedless grapes, dessert apples, kiwi fruit, strawberries, blackberries, redcurrants, loganberries, raspberries, oranges etc.

3 tbspns jelly, warmed and strained

Preparation time: 40 minutes
Cooking time: 10 minutes

Preheat the oven to 400°F. Roll out the pastry and use to line 12 barquette molds. Prick with a fork, brush the bases with egg white and bake blind for 10 minutes. Cool.

Fill decoratively with a mixture of fruits or one fruit alone, and brush with jelly to glaze.

Cream Horns (left); Profiteroles (center); Barquettes (right).

Profiteroles

Makes about 16

⅓ cup all-purpose flour	4 tbspns unsalted butter
pinch of salt	6 tbspns milk
⅔ cup water	**Filling:**
¼ cup unsalted butter	1⅓ cups heavy cream
2 eggs, beaten	1 tbspn superfine sugar
Chocolate sauce:	few drops vanilla essence
8 squares semi-sweet chocolate	

Preparation time: 15 minutes
Cooking time: 35 minutes

Preheat the oven to 400°F. Grease a large baking sheet and run cold water over it.

Sift the flour and salt on to a piece of waxed paper. Put the water and butter in a pan and bring to the boil. As soon as the mixture boils and the butter has melted remove from the heat and tip all the flour in at once. Beat vigorously with a wooden spoon or an electric whisk until the dough leaves the sides of the pan clean. Beat in the eggs, a little at a time, until the mixture is smooth and glossy.

Pipe or place the spoonfuls of the mixture onto the baking sheet and bake for 30 minutes or until firm, puffed up and golden. Make a slit in the sides and return to the oven for 5 minutes to dry out the insides. Cool on a wire rack.

Melt the chocolate and butter together in a bowl set over a pan of simmering water. Beat until smooth and stir in the milk. Whip the cream until stiff then beat in the sugar and vanilla.

Spoon a little of the filling into each profiterole and pile up on a serving plate. Pour over the chocolate sauce.

Tip: Don't put the cream inside until the last minute, as profiteroles go soggy very quickly.

Cream Horns

Makes 6

12oz puff pastry	angelica stalks, cut into leaves
superfine sugar for dusting	
⅔ cup heavy cream	
1 tbspn superfine sugar	
6 teasps strawberry jelly	
3 candied cherries, halved, or 3 strawberries, halved	

Preparation time: 40 minutes
Cooking time: 10-15 minutes plus cooling

Preheat the oven to 425°F. Roll out the pastry on a lightly floured surface to a rectangle 12×6in. Trim the edges and cut into 6 12×1in strips.

Dampen one long edge of each strip and, starting at the base of a cream horn mold, wind the strip around the mold, making sure the dampened edges overlap. Press the edges gently to seal. Sprinkle with sugar.

Place on a baking sheet, with the end of the strip at the top of the mold underneath. Bake for 10-15 minutes or until puffed up and golden. Leave to cool for a few minutes then carefully remove from the molds. Leave until cold on a wire rack. Whip the cream with the sugar until stiff. Spoon 1 teasp jelly into each cream horn then pipe in the cream. Decorate with cherries or strawberry halves and angelica.

Strawberry Shortcake

Serves 6-8

2 cups all-purpose flour	1¼ cups heavy cream
½ cup confectioners' sugar	1lb strawberries, hulled and sliced
¾ cups unsalted butter, at room temperature	2 tbspns superfine sugar
1 large egg yolk	

Preparation time: 30 minutes
Chilling time: 30 minutes
Cooking time: 12-15 minutes

Lightly grease two large baking sheets. Preheat the oven to 375°F. Sift the flour and confectioners' sugar into a mixing bowl. Cut the butter into the mixture, and rub in. Stir in the egg yolk and 2 tbspns of the cream and mix to a soft dough. Wrap in waxed paper and chill for 30 minutes. Divide the dough in half. Sprinkle lightly with flour, then roll out the dough, actually on the baking sheets. Trim to 9in circles and mark one into 8 wedges. Bake for 12-15 minutes or until golden and crisp. Cool on wire rack.

Whisk the remaining cream until stiff. Fold in the strawberries. Pile onto one of the shortcakes. Cut the other shortcake into 8 equal wedges. Arrange the wedges over the strawberry mixture. Decorate with whole strawberries and piped whipped cream if preferred.
Note: This dough is quite difficult to handle. Chilling is very important and also rolling the dough straight onto the baking sheet helps. If you have a food processor, this will make light work of the operation.

Strawberry Shortcake (above); Carrot Cake (right).

Brownies

Makes 12 squares

4 squares semi-sweet chocolate	1 cup all-purpose flour, sifted
½ cup unsalted butter	pinch salt
3 eggs	½ cup chopped pecans or walnuts
6 tbspns superfine sugar	
1 teasp vanilla essence	

Preparation time: 20-25 minutes
Cooking time: 30 minutes

Preheat the oven to 325°F. Grease a 12×9in cake tin.

Melt the chocolate and butter together in a bowl set over a pan of simmering water. Allow to cool.

Beat the eggs, sugar and vanilla together until pale and creamy. Stir in the melted chocolate.

Fold in the flour, salt and nuts. Pour into the tin and bake for about 30 minutes. Leave to cool in the tin then cut into bars. Cool on a wire rack.

Carrot Cake

Serves 8-10

1 cup all-purpose flour	1½ cups grated carrots
½ cup wholewheat flour	⅓ cup chopped walnuts
2 teasps baking soda	⅔ cup seedless raisins
1 teasp ground cinnamon	**Topping:**
½ teasp grated nutmeg	½ cup cream cheese
½ teasp salt	2 tbspns unsalted butter, softened
1⅓ cups soft brown sugar	½ cup superfine sugar
¾ cup sunflower oil	2 rings of canned pineapple, finely chopped
2 eggs	few drops of vanilla essence

Preparation time: 25 minutes
Cooking time: 1¼ hours plus cooling

Preheat the oven to 350°F. Brush a 7in square cake tin with oil, line the base with waxed paper and brush the paper with oil.

Sift the flours, soda, cinnamon, nutmeg and salt into a bowl. Whisk the sugar and oil together, then beat in the eggs, one at a time. Stir in the flour mixture, then fold in the carrots, nuts and raisins. Turn into the prepared tin, and bake for 1¼ hours. Leave to cool in the tin for 15 minutes, then turn out onto a wire rack to cool completely.

For the topping, beat all the ingredients together until smooth. Spread over the top of the cake.

Tip: Put the chopped pineapple on absorbent kitchen paper to make sure it is as 'dry' as possible, otherwise the juice may curdle the topping.

Chocolate Chip Cookies

Makes 25-30 cookies

1¼ cups flour	⅔ cup soft brown sugar
pinch of salt	1 egg
¼ teasp baking soda	few drops vanilla essence
½ cup plus 1 tbspn butter	⅔ cup chocolate chips

Preparation time: 15 minutes
Cooking time: 15 minutes

Preheat the oven to 375°F. Grease 2 large baking sheets.

Sift the flour, salt and baking soda together. In a separate bowl, cream the butter and sugar together then beat in the egg and vanilla. Stir in the flour and the chocolate chips.

Place teaspoonfuls of the mixture on the baking sheets, well spaced apart and bake for about 15 minutes. Allow the cookies to cool on the sheets.

Gingernuts

Makes about 20

1½ cups self-rising flour	¼ cup sugar
1 teasp baking soda	2 tbspns light corn syrup
2 teasps ground ginger	1 tbspn molasses
⅓ cup unsalted butter	

Preparation time: 20 minutes
Cooking time: 15-20 minutes

Preheat the oven to 400°F. Grease two large baking sheets.

Sift the flour, soda and ginger into a bowl. Rub in the butter and stir in the sugar. Add the syrup and molasses and mix to a firm dough. Pull off pieces of dough and roll into balls. Place them on the baking sheets, well spaced apart and flatten slightly. Bake for 15-20 minutes. Cool for 5 minutes. Transfer to wire racks to finish cooling.

Brandy Snaps

Makes about 12

¼ cup unsalted butter	¼ cup superfine sugar
2 tbspns light corn syrup	½ cup all-purpose flour, sifted
	½ teasp ground ginger

Preparation time: 12 minutes
Cooking time: 10 minutes

Preheat the oven to 350°F. Grease two large baking sheets and the handle of a wooden spoon.

Melt the butter, syrup and sugar in a pan over low heat. Stir in the flour and ginger. Put teaspoons of the mixture onto the baking sheets, well spaced apart. Bake for about 10 minutes.

Leave for 1 minute then, using a greased spatula, lift off the baking sheet and quickly roll around the handle of the spoon and keep in position for a few seconds, until set. Cool on a wire rack. Brandy snaps can be stored in an airtight tin for 4-5 days. Fill with brandy-flavored whipped cream and serve as an elegant dessert.

Tips: Bake one sheet at a time to allow you to roll the snaps while still warm. If they have become too hard, simply put them back into the oven for a few minutes to soften again.

Viennese Rosettes and Fingers

1 cup butter	pinch of salt
½ cup confectioners' sugar, sifted	jelly, sieved
1½ cups all-purpose flour, sifted	confectioners' sugar
½ cup cornstarch	melted chocolate

Preparation time: 45-50 minutes
Standing time: 30 minutes
Cooking time: 20 minutes

Beat the butter and confectioners' sugar in a warmed bowl until very soft. This is very important otherwise the mixture will be too stiff to pipe. Stir in the sifted flours and salt.

Spoon the mixture into a forcing bag fitted with a large star nozzle and pipe as either large rosettes in 16-18 paper baking cases or as 2.5in fingers on greased baking trays.

If possible, leave in a cool place for 30 minutes before baking in a preheated oven at 350°F for about 20 minutes. Remove carefully from the trays while the cakes are still warm and cool on a wire rack.

Sandwich pairs of the finger biscuits together with either jelly or butter cream made with 2 tbspns butter beaten with ½ cup of confectioners' sugar, and a pinch of mixed spice. To finish, dip the ends in melted chocolate and allow to set.

To finish the rosettes, dust with sieved confectioners' sugar and spoon a little spot of jelly in the center of each one.

Left-right, clockwise: Viennese Fingers; Gingernuts; Chocolate Chip Cookies; Viennese Rosettes; Brandy Snaps.

Using Microwave Ovens and Food Processors

Microwave Ovens

One of the main uses for microwave ovens is to be able to produce meals quickly and to speed up the cooking times for a variety of foods. It is important, however, to regard the microwave oven as a supplement to a conventional cooker and not a substitute. There are many foods which benefit from long, slow cooking and the desired textures and flavors of certain dishes cannot be achieved in the microwave, particularly those using the less tender cuts of meat.

Microwave ovens are great energy-savers. In a conventional oven, the electric elements or gas flames heat up the air inside the oven so that food cooks gradually as the heat is conducted through the food from the outside to the inside. This also means that, in order to cook a small cut of meat or small quantity of cakes etc, you have to use up a great deal of energy in preheating the oven cavity and then after you have finished cooking, the remainder of the heat is wasted. With a microwave oven electro-magnetic waves cook the food by passing through it at a very high frequency, causing the molecules of water in the ingredients to vibrate. The friction produced by the vibration provides heat which cooks the food. The waves are reflected off the metal walls of the oven cavity and, aided by a fan, are 'stirred' around so that they bombard the food at great speed from many different directions. There is no slow build-up of heat so the outside and inside of the food are cooked simultaneously and extremely quickly.

Although the waves cannot pass through metal and, therefore, metal containers cannot be used inside the oven, you can use a surprising range of unconventional materials for cooking such as china, glass and even plastic and paper as the waves pass straight through and do not affect their molecular structure.

One disadvantage of older microwave cookers is that cooked foods often do not look appetizingly brown when cooked. Various foods such as steaks or chops can be browned in a browning dish or on a browning griddle in the microwave or simply under a conventional broiler . Large cuts of meat will begin to brown as the air around them heats up during the longer cooking time required.

Uses for the Microwave Oven

Microwave ovens are extremely useful for occasions when members of a family want to eat at different times. Meals can be prepared well in advance and either cooked quickly when needed or cooked and reheated on the plate without drying out or spoiling in any way. Microwave ovens are so simple and safe to use that most of the family can use it to heat up their own snacks and meals from the freezer (provided that they are frozen in non-metallic containers).

Individual hot drinks can be made in seconds and even babies' bottles of milk can be heated directly and safely in the microwave.

The microwave oven can also usefully speed up defrosting times for frozen foods, for example, a 3lb chicken can be fully defrosted in about 45 minutes. Ingredients such as chocolate, butter or gelatin can be either melted or dissolved very speedily and effectively.

Cooking in the Microwave oven

One area where the microwave probably surpasses the conventional cooker is in cooking vegetables, because the flavor, nutritional value and color is preserved far more effectively. It may not always be quicker but the results are

excellent. Fish, too, can be delicious cooked in the microwave – juicy and flavorful and with the added bonus of less odour in the kitchen. Sauces, perhaps surprisingly, are easily cooked in the microwave – the flour and liquid cook together throughout its volume without the problems of the sauce thickening unevenly at the bottom or sides of the pan and thus producing lumps, though it will still need to be stirred during the cooking time.

Tender cuts of meat are also successfully cooked in the microwave oven, though you may prefer to brown them as a finishing touch, unless your microwave browns as it cooks. As with fish, the meat retains its natural juices and flavor.

Another factor in favor of the microwave oven is that there is far less oven cleaning to do. Foods are mostly covered during cooking and there is little splashing of the oven walls. Fats and sugars do not get much chance to 'bake on' and usually all the oven cavity needs is a wipe with a damp cloth after use. You can use the same dishes for cooking and serving – this cuts down on saucepan washing.

Certain factors have to be taken into consideration when cooking in the microwave. The density and content of the food has a bearing on the temperature needed for cooking. For example, meat has a lot of tightly packed fibers and will, therefore, take longer to cook than a cake, which is porous and allows the waves to pass through more easily. The shape of food is also important – a regular-shaped boned cut of meat will cook more evenly than, say a leg of lamb and you may find that you will need to protect the bony end with foil (which can be removed halfway through the time allowed) to slow down the cooking process of this part.

To ensure even cooking, carefully arrange food on plates and dishes; place the thicker ends of meat, fish and vegetables such as broccoli nearer to the outside of the dish. Some microwaves have turntables which help to minimize uneven cooking. If you are cooking two different types of food together such as peas and sliced carrots, make sure that the denser, more fibrous carrots are on the outside while the peas are arranged in the center of the dish.

When following recipes designed for microwave cookery you will notice that there is usually a 'standing time' given in addition to the cooking time. This allows for the residual heat contained in the food, which causes cooking to continue for some minutes after the food has been removed from the oven. You need to take this into consideration when calculating the total length of cooking time needed – always allow less rather than more time if you are unsure.

Food Processors

Food processors have firmly taken their place in the kitchen as welcome assistants to take care of a multitude of culinary tasks, leaving the cook free to deal with the aspects which require more skill and concentration. Previously, machines existed to do the work of mixing, beating, cutting, chopping, slicing, shredding, squeezing, mincing and so on, but you needed several appliances or a number of cumbersome attachments for a standard mixer. A food processor is designed to do all these tasks and more – requiring only a simple change-over of cutting blade or disk.

A processor consists of a base containing a powerful motor which is normally operated by a switch for either continuous action or for a 'pulse' operation. The pulse action only operates when you hold the switch down, the moment you release it, the motor is turned off. This is ideal for working small amounts of food and helps to ensure that it is not over-processed – it will prevent your chopped nuts from being reduced to powder!

The food is placed in a clear, sturdy plastic bowl so you can see what is happening. It can hold hot foods and

liquids and is also tough enough to withstand a dishwasher.

Most machines have a single or double-bladed knife which fits on to the motor shaft at the base of the bowl. A plastic dough knife is also usually supplied, together with a range of slicing and grating disks.

Using a food processor

Food processors are easy to use. The bowl fits on to a central spindle and is locked into position. The blade or disk is rotated on the motor shaft until it drops into position then pressed to lock it. Once the bowl is covered with the lid, the machine is ready for use.

The knife blade This is the cutter which deals with most of the mixing and chopping operations. It will make most sorts of pastry (including choux paste) quickly and easily and whisk together the ingredients for biscuits and cakes, including sponges and fruit cakes, in moments. It beats up batter for pancakes, makes fluffy mousses, ice creams and sorbets, mayonnaise, salad dressings and sauces. The knife blade can also be used for mincing cooked and raw meats and for chopping herbs, vegetables and nuts and puréeing cooked foods for soups.

The dough blade This is used for breadmaking and effortlessly mixes the ingredients and kneads the dough to the right consistency.

The slicing and grating disks These are great time-savers when grating cheese and other hard foods, such as chocolate, and for making salads such as coleslaw from winter vegetables. The slicing disks make a neat job of slicing vegetables such as cucumbers and carrots and, with some models, you can get a slicer which gives an attractive 'ripple edge' to vegetables or one which slices fine julienne strips. To use these, having fitted the disk of your choice, you merely push the food down the feed tube in the lid of the bowl with the pusher supplied (never with the fingers); the amount of pressure which you apply dictates the thinness of the slice.

Having a food processor and using it often will undoubtedly change your methods of cooking. You will find it invaluable when batch cooking ready-meals for the freezer or for processing home-grown produce. It is important, however, when making cakes and pastries with the processor to follow the recipe supplied with the machine as the methods and, in some cases, the ingredients, will vary from standard recipes.

Using the Freezer

The popularization of the domestic freezer has done more to revolutionize cooking and shopping habits than almost any kitchen appliance. Few homes are now without some form of freezer, whether it is simply an ice-box within the refrigerator or a full-scale chest freezer. For almost any household, the advantages are enormous, in time, convenience and cost. Freezers can be used for a number of purposes and people invariably evolve their own patterns of use.

For some large and busy families, the freezer's biggest advantage is for storing frozen cuts of meat, fish, vegetables and commercially-prepared dishes bought cheaply in bulk. Other people prefer to use the freezer for stockpiling home-cooked ready-meals for everyday consumption or for dinner parties. Batch-cooking techniques can be used to prepare large quantities of food for future use.

A common use for freezers, particularly in country areas, is to freeze locally obtained meat, fish, vegetables and fruit in bulk and for storing home-grown fruits, vegetables and herbs. Sometimes a combination of these three patterns suits a family's needs. Often the difficulty is in deciding what is worth freezing – you should always ask yourself whether it justifies the space. Do you really want to freeze a large amount of gooseberry purée just because you have had a bumper crop? Will it all be eaten? Is that special offer on a huge pack of stewing lamb really worthwhile, or is it going to clog up the freezer for months as you work your way through it? Perhaps the family will rebel against variations on navarin of lamb after several weeks!

Types of Freezer
The choice of freezer is quite extensive, ranging from combinations of refrigerator and freezer to small free-standing uprights with a counter top through to large-capacity upright and chest types. The chest freezers probably give the maximum storage space for the minimum cost but they take up a lot of floor area and, because of the hinged lids, nothing can be placed on top of them. These are ideal for locating in a dry outhouse or garage and used for storing bulk foods which you will probably not wish to use up on a daily basis.

Think carefully about the size and try not to buy a freezer which is too small because, once you start to use it regularly, it is amazing how quickly it fills, especially if you wish to freeze bulky items like bread and large cuts of meat. It is unlikely that a freezer in a household of three people or more would ever get really empty but if you do find difficulty in keeping it topped up, pack the items fairly closely together in one drawer or section of the freezer and fill the spaces with scrunched-up newspaper. This helps to prevent the large inrush of warm air when you open the door which will raise the temperature inside the cabinet, causing the motor to work overtime to maintain the correct low temperature. Running the freezer half-full adds to the build up of frost which, in turn, reduces efficiency in temperature control.

Defrosting
From time to time the build-up of ice needs to be removed from the freezing shelves. If it is not too thick this can be done gently with a brush (with nylon bristles) or with a plastic scraper. Do not use a knife or anything sharp to prise off the ice as it may damage the surfaces. If the ice is very thick then you will need to defrost the cabinet fully.

Plan defrosting ahead and try to do it in cool weather when your stocks of food in the freezer are low. Switch off the motor and take out all the food. Store it in another freezer if possible (particularly the vulnerable items like

ice cream) or in the refrigerator. If you run out of space, wrap items such as meat and solid blocks of food in layers of newspaper and then in thick towels or blankets. Defrosting should only take about 2-3 hours and most foods, unless highly perishable, should survive and can be refrozen, provided that they have not fully thawed (see Refreezing).

Having emptied the freezer, scrape away as much frost as possible with a plastic scraper. Place bowls of hot water on the shelves and leave the door wide open. Gradually, the ice will loosen and can be carefully prised off with the scraper. Try to remove as much ice as possible before it melts to make the job less messy. Use newspapers or old towels to line the bottom of the cabinet to soak up the water and lay paper or old towels under the cabinet of an upright freezer to soak up any seepage.

Once you have removed all the ice and mopped up the water, wash the cabinet out with a solution of bicarbonate of soda (about 1 tbspn to 2 pints liters of hot water) and dry thoroughly with a clean cloth. Then switch on the motor and run on 'fast freeze' (q.v.) for about 30 minutes before repacking the frozen food. Continue to run the freezer on 'fast freeze' for 3-4 hours.

Emergency action
If the power supply to the freezer is cut off or the freezer develops a fault, take action immediately and check to see how long the power will be cut off or ring your service depot. If the fault in either power or motor can be rectified within 5-6 hours the food within should be quite safe, provided that you do not open the cabinet. If you keep a large and valuable supply of frozen food it is worth considering some form of insurance against breakdowns and spoilage. These are often available through freezer manufacturers or from freezer centers.

Frozen Food Storage
Most foods have a certain life-span in the freezer and the manufacturers of the freezer usually supply a chart, either printed on the inside of the door of the freezer or in the accompanying handbook, which you can use as a guide. Try not to keep foods much beyond the recommended times given or you will find them lacking in taste and texture and generally disappointing.

Freezer Containers and Packaging
The main objective when packing food for the freezer is to seal it to exclude air and prevent it from drying out. If food is inadequately packed, it may develop 'freezer burn' indicated by grayish, fibrous-looking patches. This is harmless but it does considerably affect the taste and texture of the food, particularly meats and fish.
Freezer bags Freezer-proof plastic bags are available in a range of sizes for use in the freezer. These are made from heavy-duty plastic and have wire ties. When using freezer bags, it is important to exclude as much air as possible from the bag. The easiest and most efficient way of doing this is to suck it out with a straw to help create a vacuum.
Boilable bags Extra-strong plastic bags are available in which the food can be cooked in boiling water, direct from the freezer. These can be sealed by wire ties or heat.
Plastic Containers Rigid plastic containers can be obtained for use in the freezer. These have a longer life than non-freezer-proof plastic containers which become brittle with use at low temperatures. An advantage of using preformed containers is that they make a neat, regular shape and help to make the most of the available space in the freezer. They can be washed and reused many times.

Aluminum foil and foil containers Ordinary foil can be used in double or triple thickness for wrapping food but it is probably more cost-effective to buy the heavier-gauge aluminum foil designed for freezer use. Foil is useful for wrapping irregular-shaped items such as meat cuts but it should be carefully molded to the shape of the food to exclude as much air as possible and overwrapped with a plastic bag to protect the foil from tears.

Foil containers are made in a variety of shapes and sizes and can be used for casseroles, pies, soups, sauces and many other foods. Commercially-prepared ready-meals are often sold in foil containers and these can be scrubbed out with boiling water and reused. Rigid foil containers can be used directly from freezer to conventional oven but if you are intending to freeze and cook dishes in a microwave oven, then food must be removed from the foil container or frozen in plastic, paper, toughened glass or oven- and freezer-proof ceramic dishes.

Other types of container Many heat-proof glass and ceramic containers are also freezer-proof but it is wise to check before exposing them to low temperatures. The disadvantage of using household items such as casseroles and gratin dishes for freezing is that they generally take up more space than plastic or foil containers and it means that these dishes are taken out of circulation for other uses. One way round this is to line the dish with foil before putting in the food, fast-freezing it into a block which can then be lifted out of the dish and double-wrapped for storage. When you wish to serve the dish, simply unwrap it and pop it back into its original container. Alternatively you can fast-freeze the casserole in its own dish and when it is solid, dip the dish in a bowl of very hot water so that you can then unmold the food and double-wrap it for storage.

What to Freeze

The choice of foods to be stored in the freezer very much depends on the needs of the individual families but, in general, do not freeze too much of any one item unless you are sure that it will be popular. Always select the best-quality foods for freezing and ensure that fruit and vegetables are as fresh as possible. The following suggestions may form useful guide-lines:
* Favorite whole seasonal vegetables such as asparagus, broccoli, garden peas, beans of various sorts, new potatoes, Jerusalem artichokes, baby carrots, corn, leeks, sugar peas and young zucchini. Tomatoes can be frozen whole but their firm texture breaks down so they are best frozen as a purée.
* Whole fruits such as strawberries (though these tend to go mushy if fairly ripe when frozen), raspberries, blueberries, blackberries, cranberries, gooseberries, loganberries, mulberries and currants.
* Purées of fruits such as apples, pears, plums, rhubarb and the berry fruits are very useful standbys as quick desserts or for pie fillings. Slices or halves of fruit such as peaches apricots, oranges and lemons can be frozen in sugar syrup.
* Fresh herbs such as chives, parsley, mint, thyme, marjoram, tarragon and chervil can be successfully frozen.
* Fresh meats, poultry, game and fish mostly freeze successfully.

Foods which are unsuitable for freezing

Do not freeze vegetables with a high water content such as lettuce, watercress, cucumber, celery (although this is fine for use in soups or stews) or radishes. Whole large onions do not freeze particularly well, nor do squashes. Avocado pears and bananas do not freeze well whole but can be mashed or puréed to form part of a made-up dish. Hard-boiled eggs become rubbery when frozen, though fresh eggs will freeze out of their shells (the shells burst at low temperatures). Mayonnaise should not be frozen as it separates on thawing, as does custard. Milk and light cream tends to separate but heavy cream freezes quite

successfully. Cheeses often deteriorate in texture during freezing, becoming more crumbly, but this may still be fine for cooking. Cream, cottage and curd cheeses should not be frozen.

Fast Freezing

Most freezers have a control or switch which will reduce the cabinet temperature to about 18°F for initial freezing. This lowering of temperature is important for both freezing foods quickly and effectively and to counteract the rise in temperature in the cabinet due to the introduction of fresh foods. It is essential to run the freezer on 'fast freeze' for the recommended period of time (check your freezer manual) if you are freezing fairly large quantities of food at once, otherwise the rise in cabinet temperature may cause partial thawing in the existing frozen foods.

Small quantities of foods or individual items can be placed directly into the freezing section or shelf of the freezer without lowering the temperature appreciably. For safety and best results always consult your freezer manual.

Freezing Vegetables

Vegetables for storage in the freezer should be washed, carefully picked over, then blanched and chilled before freezing. Blanching is a process of heating the vegetables, usually in boiling water, to kill off any bacteria and stop enzyme action which could cause deterioration to the food during storage.

Blanch about 1lb of vegetables at a time. Place them in a fine wire-mesh blanching basket and plunge into fast-boiling water. Once the water has returned to the boil, the vegetables should remain in it for between about 1 to 8 minutes depending on the vegetable being blanched; your freezer manual will give you the exact times. Once the blanching is complete, remove the basket from the water and immerse it in a large bowl of iced water to chill rapidly. Once the vegetables are cold, pat them dry with kitchen paper. You can then weigh out suitable quantities and pack them into freezer bags or plastic containers, according to preference.

Label the containers or bags clearly with the name of the vegetable, the weight and date packed. Note that the cooking time for blanched, frozen vegetables will be slightly less than for fresh vegetables. Fast freeze according to the freezer manufacturer's recommendations.

Freezing Fruit

Berries such as currants, raspberries or strawberries can be open or flash-frozen. Spread the fruit out on a tray, well separated, and fast-freeze until hard. The frozen berries can then be weighed, poured into freezer bags or cartons, labelled and returned to the freezer.

Fruits other than berries are successfully frozen in sugar syrup. The strength of the syrup depends on personal preferences and the sweetness of the fruits being frozen. In general, a proportion of 1 cup of white sugar to 2½ cups of water will make an acceptable syrup for reasonably sweet fruit. Dissolve the sugar in the water, bring to the boil and strain. Leave the syrup to become quite cold and chill in the refrigerator. Prepare the fruit by peeling, stoning or coring and slicing; do not leave it standing around or it will discolor – put the fruit straight into a container then cover with syrup. Always remember to leave at least ½ inch space at the top of the container to allow for expansion during freezing.

Freezing fresh meat, poultry, game and fish

Foods such as these (apart from highly-salted meats), usually freeze very well but they must be well packed and fast-frozen at the lowest temperature setting to get the best results. Different cuts of meat and types of poultry and game have differing storage times so it is wise to check these (marked on the door of your freezer or in the

handbook) and make a note in your freezer log book (or on your calendar) of when they should be used up. It is very disappointing to carefully freeze and store special items like a brace of game birds only to find them dry and tasteless due to deterioration in the freezer. Items should be double-wrapped for protection against freezer burn. Where possible, bone meat and poultry to save space. When buying meat in bulk for the freezer, make sure that you will have enough room for it and that you can make good use of it all, and above all, that it is good enough to merit freezing.

Freezing Ready-cooked Foods
The freezer really proves its worth when it comes to freezing ready-meals. A wide range of dishes can be frozen successfully – the key thing to remember is to cool the foods quickly and freeze as soon as possible. It is always a relief to have a stand-by casserole or pie for those occasions when a quick meal is called for.

Most types of casserole and stew freeze successfully, provided that they are not too well-cooked beforehand, otherwise the texture of the meat and vegetables may break down. Avoid freezing potatoes in stews as they disintegrate and garlic and herbs can taste rather musty after a while.

Stews can be frozen in block form in plastic containers, cut into bricks with a serrated freezer knife in individual or double portions and then frozen in plastic bags. For best results do not store stews for more than about 2 months.

Unbaked pastry freezes well so sweet and savory pies are good items to store, together with all kinds of quiches and tarts with uncooked fillings.

Cooked meat loaves, pâtés and terrines all freeze well, provided that they are well wrapped and sealed. These types of food, however, should not be stored for longer than about 1 month.

Puréed soups freeze well but those containing milk, cream or eggs often separate during freezing. These ingredients should be added on reheating. Do not forget to allow ½in headspace for expansion in the container.

Vegetable and fruit purées are useful additions to the freezer store cupboard and can be used to flavor cooked dishes and as bases for sauces and soups. Sauces themselves freeze well unless they contain eggs or cream; it is always useful to have tubs of tomato sauce or Bolognese sauce for quick meals with pasta. Cooked pasta will freeze but is rather a waste of space unless it is in the form of a ready-meal such as lasagne. Do not freeze pasta or rice in soups or stews as it tends to go mushy. Dishes containing rice do not freeze very well but left-over cooked rice will freeze fairly well provided that it is dry and not too well-cooked.

Refreezing Frozen Food
It is not generally recommended to refreeze food which has been previously frozen and then fully thawed, especially cooked foods meats or fish, as there is a risk to health. If however, the foods have just begun to thaw due to a breakdown, power failure or defrosting procedure, normally they can be safely refrozen provided that they still contain a high proportion of ice crystals and are hard to the touch. Bread and cakes can be refrozen safely but the texture and flavor may suffer. If you have any doubts about thawed or partially-thawed food then *do not refreeze it*. When buying meat or fish always ask whether it is fresh and let the store-keeper know that you intend to freeze it. It is, however, quite safe to cook raw thawed food and refreeze after cooking as a ready-meal (ie frozen stewing beef can be cooked and refrozen as a casserole).

Roasting Meat

Roasting in dry heat in an oven is probably the most popular and successful way of cooking large, prime cuts of meat and poultry. There are a number of different ways of roasting meat and most cooks evolve their own methods depending on how well done the family prefer their meat or what type of oven is being used. The following chart provides a guideline for roasting various types of meat.

For tender cuts a quick roasting method can be used whereby meat is cooked at a high temperature and rapidly forms a brown outer crust which seals in the flavor and juices. Less tender cuts are better suited to a slower cooking method which causes less shrinkage of the fibers and produces a tender result. The roasting method given for beef combines the two techniques by giving a quick burst of high heat to seal the outside and a slower heat to give a juicy, succulent roast. The other types of meat given such as pork and lamb are cooked for longer periods in a cooler oven to ensure that they are not underdone.

Small cuts of meat can be seized or sealed by browning in a hot pan or under a hot grill (broiler) before roasting. Check during the cooking time to see if the joint requires basting or turning and test with a skewer for the degree of doneness – juices will run pink if underdone. If you are cooking several dishes together in the oven you may need to allow extra cooking time and if you wish to cook Yorkshire pudding with beef, remember that you will need to turn the oven up quite high towards the end of the cooking time.

Oven temperature and cooking times

	Rare	Medium	Well done
BEEF			
Rib roasts/sirloin etc. weighing 5lb and upwards	425°F for 15 minutes, then 350°F for 15 minutes per 1lb	425°F for 20 minutes then 350°F for 20 minutes per 1lb	425°F for 25 minutes then 25 minutes per 1lb
Boned rib roasts or sirloin, rump roast, rolled round roasts or topside of 3-4lb	425°F for 20 minutes then 350°F for 20 minutes per 1lb	425°F for 25 minutes then 350°F for 25 minutes per 1lb	425°F for 30 minutes then 350°F for 30 minutes per 1lb
Whole beef tenderloin; chateaubriand	425°F for 10 minutes then 10 minutes per 1lb	425°F for 15 minutes then 15 minutes per 1lb	
VEAL			
Veal on the bone: leg, shoulder or loin		375°F for 30 minutes per lb plus 30 minutes	
Veal off the bone: boned rolled shoulder; stuffed breast etc.		375°F for 35 minutes per 1lb plus 35 minutes	
LAMB			
Lamb on the bone: leg, shoulder loin or rib roast		375°F for 25 minutes per 1lb plus 25 minutes	375°F for 30 minutes per 1lb plus 30 minutes
Lamb off the bone: boned rolled shoulder, boned leg or stuffed breast		375°F for 30 minutes per 1lb plus 30 minutes	375°F for 35 minutes per 1lb plus 35 minutes
PORK			
Pork on the bone: leg, shoulder, loin		375°F for 30 minutes per 1lb plus 30 minutes	
Pork off the bone: leg, rolled, stuffed shoulder butt, spare ribs etc			400°F for 35 minutes per 1lb plus 35 minutes
GAMMON			
Gammon, Virginia hams, picnic hams etc.			375°F for 20 minutes per 1lb plus 20 minutes

Index

ACKNOWLEDGMENTS
The author and publisher
would like to thank the
British Egg Information
Bureau, Coralie Dorman,
Magimix, the Potato
Marketing Board, Prestige
Cookware and the Scottish
Salmon Association for
their help and
contributions to this book
and the following people

and organizations for
supplying pictures and
recipes (page numbers
refer to pictures):
British Chicken
    Information page 90.
Buxted Poultry Ltd pages
    93, 96, 172.
Carmel Produce pages 104,
    135.
Colman's of Norwich page
    152.

Danish Bacon pages 61, 70/
    1, 89, 156-7.
Danish Dairy Board page
    196 (recipe only).
Dornay Foods (Uncle Ben
    Rice) page 171.
Eden Vale page 159.
John West Foods pages 56,
    153.
Meat Promotion Executive
    pages 87, 158.
Mushroom Growers

Association page 154.
New Zealand Lamb
    Information Bureau
    pages 68-9, 84, 85.
Pasta Information Centre
    pages 28, 162, 165.
Rank Hovis McDougall
    Foods Ltd page 196.
Sea Fish Industry
    Authority pages 41, 44,
    45, 49, 50, 52, 53, 59, 112.